Making the MIRV:
A Study of Defense
Decision Making

Making the MIRV: A Study of Defense Decision Making

Ted Greenwood
Political Science Department,
Massachusetts Institute of Technology
and
Program for Science and International Affairs,
Harvard University

Published for the Program for Science and
International Affairs, Harvard University

Ballinger Publishing Company • **Cambridge, Mass.**
A Subsidiary of J.B. Lippincott Company

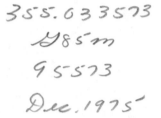

355.633573
Y85m
95573
Dec.1975

 This book is printed on recycled paper.

International Standard Book Number: 0-88410-033-2

Library of Congress Catalog Card Number: 75-11635

Printed in the United States of America

Library of Congress Cataloging in Publication Data

Greenwood, Ted, 1944-
    Making the MIRV.

    A revision of the author's thesis, entitled Qualitative improvements in offensive strategic arms, the case of MIRV, submitted to Massachusetts Institute of Technology, 1973.
    Bibliography: p.
    1. Multiple independently targetable reentry vehicles. 2. Strategy. 3. United States—Military policy. I. Title.
UG1312.M2G73 1975   355.03'35'73   75-11635
ISBN 0-88410-033-2

For Dru

Contents

Preface   ix

A Note on the Use of Interview Material   xi

Introduction   xiii

**Chapter 1
Overview**   1

Technology   2
History   3

**Chapter 2
Innovation**   13

The Organizational Environment   15
Conception and Proposal   27
Building the Consensus   37
Something for Everyone   49

**Chapter 3
Bureaucracy, Strategy, and Politics**   51

Strategy as Bureaucratic Argument   52
Strategy as Ideology   57

Strategy as Policy Determinant   65
The Politics of MIRV   73
The Woven Fabric   79

**Chapter 4
Intelligence Information and Uncertainty**   83

Strategic Intelligence and Its Limitations   84
Intelligence Information for Advocacy   90
Hedging Against Uncertainty   96
The Action-Reaction Cycle   104

**Chapter 5
Controversy**   107

Prelude   107
To Test or Not to Test   123
MIRV and SALT   129
Too Little Too Late   138

**Chapter 6
Propositions and Implications**   141

Propositions   144
Implications   151

Appendixes   157

Appendix A: Early Consideration of Multiple Warheads   159
Appendix B: The Technical Precursors of the MIRV Bus   167
Appendix C: Intelligence Information Concerning Soviet ABM Programs   171
Appendix D: Glossary of Acronyms and Technical Terms   179

Notes   185

Bibliography   219

Index   233

About the Author   238

Preface

This book is a substantial revision of a Ph.D. dissertation entitled *Qualitative Improvements in Offensive Strategic Arms: The Case of MIRV* that was submitted to and accepted by the Political Science Department at the Massachusetts Institute of Technology in August 1973. The revisions involved the addition of some factual information, the correction of some minor errors, and, most importantly, the extension and sharpening of the analysis. The general outline of the historical material and the major conclusions remain unchanged.

Without implicating others in this study's inadequacies and errors, of omission as well as commission, for which I take full responsibility, I wish to acknowledge the valuable assistance of many individuals. The research would have been impossible without the generous help and cooperation of over a hundred persons who were interviewed or who provided information in other ways. In all cases they searched their memories to reconstruct both history and the motivations of important participants in that history. In some cases they went beyond that and assisted their memories with documents or the help of their colleagues. Although they must remain nameless, I am deeply grateful to them all. Valuable criticism was received from Eugene B. Skolnikoff, William W. Kaufmann, and particularly George W. Rathjens, who served as my thesis committee, and from Paul Doty, Patrick Friel, Richard L. Kugler, Michael L. Nacht, Jack P. Ruina, Harvey M. Sapolsky, Herbert P. Scoville, and John Yochelson, each of whom read part or all of the manuscript in one of its many drafts.

I also wish to gratefully acknowledge the assistance of the Canadian Department of National Defence for scholarship support (awarded through the Association of Universities and Colleges of Canada) while the research was being conducted, of the Fund for Peace for support of the research itself, and of the Program for Science and International Affairs, Harvard University, for support while revisions were being made.

For typing assistance I am indebted to Gayle Hightower, Lynn Jubelirer, Dru Jaffe, and especially Sara Haines. For his help in verifying and correcting the references, I am indebted to Ed Timmins.

Particular thanks are due to my wife who has been typist, editor, proofreader, critic, and prodder, and who through frustration and satisfaction has provided constant and long-suffering encouragement.

A Note on the Use of Interview Material

From the very beginning of this study the author realized that published materials such as newspaper reports, industry publications and journals, government documents, congressional hearings, and scholarly books or articles would be necessary but insufficient sources of data. The reasons for the inadequacy are twofold. First, the subject matter bears on information held secret for reasons of national security. Second, information about the decision-making processes of the United States government is not reliably and systematically documented in the public record except by scholars who set themselves that task. Since the author had no access to classified documents the option of examining the full written record of the decision-making processes was not available. A methodology had to be employed therefore that would both generate sufficient data and not require classified materials.

The methodology chosen was one used previously by other scholars faced with the same problem. It involved telephone conversations, exchanges of letters, and extensive personal interviews with individuals who had participated in the events and decisions investigated. In all significant information was received from over a hundred individuals,[a] who personally or through an organizational

[a]From within the executive branch of the government present or past officials were contacted from the following offices and agencies: in the Department of Defense, the Office of the Secretary, including very senior officials, special assistants and advisors to the Secretary, the Office of the Assistant Secretary (Systems Analysis), the Office of the Assistant Secretary (International Security Affairs), the Office of the Director of Defense Research and Engineering, and the Defense Science Board; in the Navy, the Special Projects Office (now the Strategic Systems Project Office), the Office of Offensive and Defensive Strategic Systems and the civilian Secretariat; in the Air Force, the Ballistic Systems Division (now the Space and Missiles Systems Organization), the Air Staff, including senior officers, the civilian Secretariat, the Air Force Scientific Advisory Board, and the Ballistic Systems Division Advisory Group; the State Department; the Arms Control and Disarmament Agency; the Bureau of the Budget (now the Office of Management and Budget); the President's Science Advisory Committee; and the White House national security staff. From outside the executive branch of the government individuals were contacted who were or had been members of: the Atomic Energy Commission's weapons laboratories, JASON, several companies that act as consultants to the Department of Defense or the services, several industrial contractors who participated in the MIRV programs, legislative staffs, and the non-government arms control community.

affiliation had some familiarity with the MIRV programs. Contacts ranged from brief letters or telephone calls focusing on a particular point to receiving answers to detailed questions submitted by letter and lengthy (and in a few cases several) interviews.

In all of these contacts the author himself made no attempt to avoid classified or sensitive material. Each individual was permitted to set his own boundaries for what should or should not be said. In order to encourage frank and open conversation the author assured each interviewee that any written product of the research would avoid attribution of any sort. Although on many occasions security restrictions did restrict the range of subjects interviewees would discuss, the author is fully persuaded that the degree of forthrightness of many individuals was a direct result of the assurances of anonymity and that without such assurances this study would have been less successful.

The employment of this research methodology imposes on the author a responsibility to his sources that conflicts with his responsibility to his readers. In order to assure the promised anonymity the reader cannot be told the source for many of the statements he will read. While this is regrettable it is also unavoidable. The reader must simply assume that statements addressing matters that are not common knowledge and that are not footnoted are based on information conveyed in interviews. Similarly, when a cited reference does not provide a sufficient basis for footnoted statements, the reader must assume that the reference was supplemented by interview data.

While relying heavily on interview material, certain ground rules were followed. The attempt was made to use interview material as a source of factual information only when information could be verified from public sources, when it was corroborated by several individuals, when it was fully consistent with related, more reliable information, or when the interviewee's memory was either judged to be obviously accurate or was aided by reference to documents. In many cases, of course, interviewees misremembered events and particularly the sequence of events. In the face of contradictory or inconsistent information the author has exercised judgment, based on all available evidence. For data about attitudes, opinions, and reasons for particular actions less rigor has been demanded. This is not only because public sources are rarely available to verify such information, but also because the interviewees often were able to remember such things much better than particular dates, names, and written statements. Nonetheless, efforts were always made to verify information with more than one individual. Occasionally, however, one person's statement about the position of his particular organization has been accepted as reliable without corroboration. The author is very conscious of the need to have evidence for statements of fact and for attributions of attitudes and opinions. Full documentation of his interviews, telephone conversations, and letters is maintained in his files, and inquiries concerning his sources from serious scholars will be given careful consideration.

Introduction

The programs of the United States Navy and Air Force to develop and deploy multiple independently-targetable reentry vehicles (MIRVs[a]) on their strategic missiles both are and are not examples of successful arms control. In that these programs did not simply move ahead propelled by their own bureaucratic momentum but were actively encouraged, fostered, and supported by senior decisionmakers, they provide an example of fairly successful control, in the sense of management of technological innovation. In that the systems have been deployed and that efforts to prevent deployment were unsuccessful, they provide an example of unsuccessful control, in the sense of limitation of qualitative improvements. In order to explain these seemingly contradictory statements this study will identify and explain the interweaving of the many competing and reinforcing strands of the decision-making process through which the MIRV concept became reality.

For those interested in the history and course of the strategic arms competition and strategic arms control, the military importance of MIRV would in itself provide sufficient motivation for this study. Indeed MIRV is probably the single most important technical innovation in the field of offensive strategic forces since the ballistic missile. Initially each ballistic missile carried only one warhead and one reentry vehicle. A reentry vehicle is a container that protects and carries the warhead during the long journey from launch point, out of the earth's atmosphere, and back into it again. It also includes the detonation device that causes the warhead to explode at its designated target. By early 1975 the Soviet Union had tested three different missile systems that can carry more than one reentry vehicle and begun to deploy one of these. The United States had already deployed two such missile systems, one that carries three reentry vehi-

---

[a]The term MIRV has now become such a familiar acronym that it is widely used as if it were a legitimate English word. It may be declined as a noun and conjugated as a verb.

cles and one that can carry up to fourteen, each aimed at a different target. These are MIRVs; their advent has had far-reaching implications.

The deployment of MIRV increased severalfold the number of separately-targetable warheads in the strategic forces and thereby greatly enhanced the destructiveness, the penetration capability, and the overall reliability of these forces. The primary purpose of MIRVed missiles and other nuclear forces is to deter attacks by potential adversaries. In that role they are threatening, but benign. If ever used in warfare, however, each MIRV could obliterate a small city; one MIRVed missile could annihilate a sprawling metropolis and almost all of its inhabitants. In the traditional military contest for primacy between offensive and defensive weapons, MIRV gave a decisive advantage to the offense. Its existence contributed in a major way to the willingness of the United States and the Soviet Union to agree by formal treaty in June 1972 to refrain from deploying significant missile defense systems. MIRV also helped determine the nature of the interim agreement on offensive forces reached at the same time. Subsequently, the presence of MIRVs in the strategic balance has been both an incentive and an inhibiting factor in the ongoing effort to achieve a lasting agreement limiting offensive strategic weapons.

There are other reasons as well for studying the MIRV programs. Over the years they have required the expenditure of $12.1 billion of public funds, $4.8 billion for the Navy Poseidon missile, submarine conversions and support ships, and $7.3 billion for the Air Force Minuteman III missile and associated improvements of their launching silos.[b] But Poseidon and Minuteman III are just two of a long list of past, present, and future programs intended to improve the quality and increase the effectiveness of the offensive nuclear forces. As shown in Table I-1 expenditures for development and procurement of these forces, although a small fraction of the defense budget, have in recent years consumed a generally increasing amount of resources whether measured in current dollars, as a percentage of total expenditures for strategic forces or as a percentage of the total defense budget. To see that these expenditures are controlled and managed wisely is an important issue of public policy.

The impetus for new weapons programs comes from a variety of sources. Sometimes old systems simply wear out or degrade in reliability so much that they must be replaced. Rarely is it suggested that old equipment be replaced by simply reopening old production lines or that deployment should be phased so that a single production line could supply replacements indefinitely. Although the former possibility can be expensive,[c] the latter would significantly

---

[b]These are Department of Defense costs only and do not include an additional $2-3 billion for nuclear warheads paid out of the Atomic Energy Commission (now Energy Research and Development Administration) budget.

[c]Reopening production lines once they have been shut down is both expensive and time consuming. The Air Force has estimated that once the Minuteman III production lines were shut down $320 million and three to four years would be required to reopen it.[1]

reduce the unit price of new hardware. The use of ten- or fifteen-year-old technology for new weapons is apparently unthinkable. Sometimes changes in technology, in the strategic environment (especially resulting from perceived Soviet activities), or in notions about the purpose of strategic nuclear forces seem to demand new, more advanced weapons. In addition, the incentive structures of the military and civilian organizations that design, develop, build, contract for or oversee new weapons developments provide an impetus for new systems. The result of these various pressures has become predictable because of its frequent repetition. A lengthy and costly development program is initiated to incorporate the latest technical advances into new hardware. The eventual replacement is almost always more expensive, and sometimes much more expensive, than the old system, even taking account of inflation. For example, recent estimates put the average cost of each Trident submarine-launched ballistic missile, excluding the cost of warheads and the submarine platform, at $12.1 million compared to $5.42 million for the average cost of a Poseidon missile excluding warhead costs and submarine conversion.[2] A new B-1 strategic bomber will cost much more than a B-52 produced today and the price continues to rise.[3] Anyone who wishes to limit, to expand or simply to manage rationally these weapons development programs must first understand the nature of the development process.

This study of MIRV illuminates that process for one important case. It shows the process of technical innovation within its broad historical and institutional context. The development programs for the Poseidon and Minuteman III, the strategic missiles that carry the first generation MIRVs, are examined, as are the several competitive warhead systems that were one by one abandoned. The relationship of MIRV to fluctuations in strategic thinking, and to perceptions about Soviet weapons programs is analyzed. The organizational environment and the changes in domestic politics that affected the MIRV programs are explored. It is the complex interplay of technological opportunity, bureaucratic politics, strategic and policy preferences of senior decisionmakers and great uncertainty about Soviet activities that fostered the development of MIRV. Although one or another of these factors may have dominated at one particular time or for one particular actor, each made an important contribution to the course of the programs.

MIRV is a particularly interesting and, in many ways, a unique example of a strategic weapon innovation. Because of the attractiveness of MIRVs for accomplishing a wide variety of military missions, because of the relative lack of serious technical problems in the development programs and because the systems satisfied many of the strategic and political objectives of the services, the Secretaries of Defense and the successive administrations they served, MIRV was a system that encountered almost no opposition until very late in its development cycle. The political uncertainties that plague so many weapons programs, and the continuous fights over their purpose, characteristics, and cost, were virtually absent in the MIRV case. There were reorientations of

Table I-1.   Expenditures for Development and Procurement of American Offensive Strategic Forces (In Millions of Current Dollars)

	1971[1] (Actual)	1972[2] (Actual)	1973[3] (Actual)	1974[4] (Actual)	1975[4] (Planned)	1976[4] (Proposed)	Trans.[4] Period (Proposed)
Minuteman III development and procurement, silo upgrading and other related programs	695	938	816	720	728	780	105
Advanced ICBM technology, including MX	–	–	8	4	37	41	15
Poseidon submarine conversion, missile development, procurement, and associated efforts	952	718	698	323	183	91	7
Trident submarine and missile development and procurement	44	105	794	1433	2030	2142	622
Advanced Ballistic Reentry Systems and technology development	100	96	93	90	112	101	29
B-52D modification	–	15	46	38	95	43	–
B-1 development	75	370	445	449	445	749	196
Short Range Attack Missile	281	245	203	133	2	3	2
Strategic Cruise Missile Bomber launched and submarine launched versions	–	–	53	13	98	153	55
Advanced Strategic Tanker	–	–	–	–	2	5	1

Total expenditures for development and procurement for offensive strategic forces	2147	2487	3156	3203	3732	4108	1032
Total expenditures for strategic forces	7671	7486	7253	6835	7394	7721	2100
Offensive development and procurement as percentage of total strategic forces	28.0%	33.2%	43.5%	46.8%	50.4%	53.2%	49.1%
Total Defense Budget (Total Obligational Authority)	75,101	77,731	80,452	84,992	88,993	104,684	24,642
Offensive development and procurement as percentage of total defense budget	2.9%	3.2%	3.9%	3.8%	4.2%	3.9%	4.2%

Notes:

[1] Secretary of Defense Melvin R. Laird, *National Security Strategy of Realistic Deterrence: Annual Defense Department Report FY 1973* (Washington: Government Printing Office, 1972), pp. 68 and 189.

[2] Secretary of Defense Elliot L. Richardson, *Annual Defense Department Report FY 1974* (Washington: Government Printing Office, 1973), pp. 55 and 118.

[3] Secretary of Defense James R. Schlesinger, *Annual Defense Department Report FY 1975* (Washington: Government Printing Office, 1974), pp. 53, 54, and 235.

[4] Secretary of Defense James R. Schlesinger, *Annual Defense Department Report FY 1976 and FY 197T* (Washington: Government Printing Office, 1975), pp. II-22, 23, and D-1.

the Minuteman MIRV and arguments over what the mix of different warheads would be, but these were relatively minor. Opponents of the program were few, ineffective, and could be ignored. Only as testing and deployment were about to begin were reservations expressed at a level that was politically meaningful. Nonetheless, the richness of the issues raised by the MIRV programs, the time span over which the MIRV was developed, and the environmental changes that took place during the development, testing, and deployment of the systems permit the identification of the critical variables controlling not only this but also other weapons innovations. An analysis of these variables in the MIRV case suggests a number of propositions that may be applicable to other cases and that have important policy implications.

Chapter One

Overview

The fundamental characteristic of MIRVed missiles is their ability to deliver accurately each of several warheads along separate trajectories. This independent targeting capability can be used in several ways to enhance the capability of a missile against a single target. Potential destructiveness can be optimized by precise distribution of the MIRVs with respect to a large target. A missile defense system can be effectively exhausted or penetrated by carefully phasing the arrival time of the MIRVs, either from one or from several missiles. MIRVs can also be used to attack different targets as long as these are all within range of the system's ability to produce separation of the warheads, that is, within its footprint. The maximum separation of reentry vehicles for deployed MIRVs is measured in hundreds of miles: about 300-400 miles in down-range separation and about half that in cross-range separation for Poseidon at a distance of 1800-2000 nautical miles and more in down-range, but less in cross-range for Minuteman III at intercontinental distances. In order to achieve a desired pattern, however, less than maximum separation would be achieved and the footprint would therefore be less.

A missile with these capabilities is quite attractive from a military point of view. One of Minuteman III's 170 to 200 kiloton warheads,[a] or even one of Poseidon's 40-50 kiloton warheads, is large enough to destroy most high-priority targets. Dividing a missile's total throw weight into separate warheads that can be delivered to different targets greatly improves the destructiveness of each missile and of the whole force. Overall expected destructiveness of a force can also be enhanced by cross-targeting, that is, by aiming one reentry vehicle from each of several missiles at important targets. By delivering a large number of warheads separated in space or in time, a MIRV

---

[a] A kiloton is the amount of explosive power contained in a thousand tons of TNT. The bombs dropped on Hiroshima and Nagasaki were in the fifteen to twenty kiloton range.

system is more reliable than decoys and more effective than multiple, unguided warheads in overcoming missile defense systems. Since the Poseidon force that would survive a massive Soviet first strike and even a relatively small number of surviving Minuteman IIIs could visit overwhelming destruction on Soviet society, the deployment of MIRVs also helps preserve the credibility of the American deterrent despite the perception that land-based missiles are becoming increasingly vulnerable. Moreover, the MIRV systems and the improvements in accuracy that come with them substantially enhance the capability for destruction of the Soviet fixed, land-based missile force and other hardened military targets and provide an excellent weapon for precision attacks against targets that might appear attractive in a war fought below the level of an all-out nuclear exchange. Finally, although each MIRVed missile is very expensive, the greater usefulness of each means that MIRV is a cost-effective weapon system.

There follows a brief description of MIRV technology and operations and a capsule history of the development programs. These sections will prepare the reader for the more general and less technical analysis of subsequent chapters.

TECHNOLOGY

Although the MIRV systems could have been designed with a separate guidance system and propulsion package on each reentry vehicle, the reentry vehicles, as actually deployed on the Poseidon and Minuteman III, do not themselves carry either one. Instead, a maneuvering final stage of the missile, called a Post Boost Control System (PBCS) or bus, carries both the reentry bodies and the missile's guidance and control system. This bus has the ability to change velocity, orientation, and trajectory. The missile booster provides most of the thrust, dropping away once the bus has been placed on a trajectory close to that programmed for the first of the reentry bodies. The rocket motor on the bus then ignites, the trajectory is corrected and the first reentry vehicle is carefully dropped off. In the Minuteman III the main engine of the bus uses liquid fuel and can shut down while the reentry vehicle is disengaged. Small vernier rockets are used for precise positioning, changing orientation, and moving the bus away from the free-falling reentry vehicle.[1] Since the solid fuel engine on the Poseidon bus cannot be shut down and restarted, a complex system of valves and nozzles is used to adjust the movements. This process of altering the velocity of the bus and dropping off a reentry vehicle is repeated as many times as there are reentry vehicles, up to three for Minuteman III, and up to fourteen for Poseidon. Of course the bus can also carry penetration aids in place of some reentry vehicles. Penetration aids, or penaids, are things that can be released from a ballistic missile in order to confuse or otherwise neutralize an opponent's anti-ballistic missile system and thereby improve the ability of the missile's reentry vehicles to penetrate to their intended targets. Decoys, intended to attract the fire of defensive missiles and thereby exhaust the defense system, and chaff, small metal wires that are placed in the path of on-coming missiles and reflect radar signals, are examples of penaids.

Developing the technology for MIRV was a difficult and expensive task.[b] The bus, the guidance system, the reentry vehicles, the mechanism that holds and releases them and the nuclear warheads account for about half the cost of each MIRVed missile produced. The warheads represent major advances in electronics miniaturization and improvements in yield-to-weight ratio.[c] The reentry vehicles operate at higher than previously experienced levels of aerodynamic stress, use a variety of advanced materials, and rely on special fusing devices. The guidance and control system not only has to have enough computer memory to store target information and to solve the guidance equations for each vehicle, but also has to prevent damaging oscillations as the dropping of successive vehicles suddenly alters the system's mass distribution. To achieve the required accuracy, precise and reliable vernier rockets and inertial components (gyroscopes and accelerometers) are required. The entire package must be made small enough and light enough to meet the severe volume and weight constraints of the missile's overall design. These requirements provided a challenge to the technical community, but a manageable one, and the sort that can stimulate the interest and excitement of an engineer. Even during the early development phase, few members of the technical community doubted that it could be done. Although unanticipated technical problems were encountered, all were overcome.

HISTORY

The years following the launch of Sputnik I on October 4, 1957, were a period of tremendous activity and growth within the military-industrial community in the United States. The rapid and parallel development of two intercontinental ballistic missiles (ICBMs) and three intermediate range ballistic missiles (IRBMs) was followed closely by a third ICBM and advanced versions of Polaris. The civilian and military space programs were also burgeoning, driven by a large-scale reconnaissance satellite program, competition with the Soviet Union for leadership in manned space capability, and eventually by the commitment to land a man on the moon in the 1960s. A variety of technically advanced, space-based missile defense systems were also conceived in this period, none of which survived much beyond the design stage. One result of all these programs was the

---

[b]For a more detailed discusssion of the technical origins of the MIRV bus, see Appendix B.

[c]Yield-to-weight ratio is the quotient of the explosive power of a nuclear device divided by its weight. In order to deliver several weapons, stay within the weight constraints of the missile, and not sacrifice too much in lowering yield, improvement of the yield-to-weight ratio was critical for MIRV.

rapid advance of technology in many areas related to strategic missiles, including inertial guidance, rocket propellants, vernier rocket motors, and nuclear weapons. By the early 1960s the technical community was considering the feasibility of a maneuvering bus for accurate delivery of multiple warheads.

The idea of using unguided multiple warheads on strategic missiles predated this concept of a maneuvering bus by several years.[d] As early as 1958 multiple warheads had been thought of as one technique for penetrating an anti-ballistic missile (ABM) system. Thereafter this theme played an important role as deployment money for the Nike-Zeus ABM system was sought and refused from year to year. Moreover, by 1961 concern began to mount within the defense community that the Soviets might eventually deploy a large-scale ABM. Multiples were actively considered, therefore, not only as an argument against deploying Zeus, but also as a means of neutralizing any such Soviet deployment.

The first multiple warhead missile to be developed in the United States was the Polaris A-3. This missile, the third in the Polaris series, carried three vehicles of about 200 kilotons each.[2] After the A-3's booster burned out, the three reentry vehicles were separated by mechanical means into a triangular pattern centered at the target. Since this separation was not adjustable, the pattern or footprint on target was a function of the flight distance. The system was designed so that from maximum range the separation would not be greater than the extent of a city, but from minimum range all three reentry vehicles could not be destroyed by one Zeus-type interceptor. The resultant separation was on the order of one mile between reentry vehicles.[3] The A-3 was authorized in September 1960, first tested on August 7, 1962, and became operational in September 1964.[4]

In 1960-61 the Ballistic Systems Division (BSD) of the Air Force Systems Command was studying a series of new reentry vehicles: the Mark 12, 13, and 14, for use in a multiple mode on Minuteman, Titan II, and Atlas/Titan I respectively. Several mechanisms were considered for releasing these multiple warheads: an explosive charge, spring loading, small rockets placed on each reentry vehicle, or a spinning platform that would release reentry vehicles one at a time. The Mark 13 and 14 were never authorized, but the Mark 12 was.

BSD issued a request for proposals for the Mark 12 in late 1962. Actually, designs for two new reentry vehicles were sought simultaneously: a Mark 12 light and a Mark 12 heavy. Both were intended for use on an improved version of Minuteman, later called Minuteman II, scheduled for deployment in Wing 6,[5] the final Minuteman wing to be deployed. The Mark 12 heavy was the design preferred by most of the Air Force since it could carry a single large warhead of about two megatons. The light would carry individual warheads of about 200 kilotons and would be used in a multiple mode. Both were to

[d]For a more detailed discussion of the early consideration of multiple warheads see Appendix A.

utilize new low-radar-cross-section techniques,[e] advanced ablative materials, and were to have high ballistic coefficients for rapid, accurate reentry and ease of decoying.[f] Not long after it began, this initial industry competition was interrupted and reoriented by the Office of Defense Research and Engineering (DDR&E).[6] This was because DDR&E did not think a new large reentry vehicle was needed and was dissatisfied with the technical analysis on which BSD had based its design. The reentry vehicle was redesigned, including specifications for a higher radar cross-section and the size question was temporarily settled by a compromise in which DDR&E promised to authorize the heavy vehicle at a later date, depending on the availability of funds.

A second request for proposals was issued by BSD in July 1963 for a revised version of only the Mark 12 light. A two-part contract was issued to General Electric in October. The first part was to research, design, and flight test the reentry vehicle. In fact, since the uncertainties concerning the optimum configuration of the reentry vehicles were still quite large, General Electric also did much of the conceptual design work. A weight constraint of 350 pounds per reentry vehicle, which had been calculated in DDR&E to allow the projected missile to carry three reentry vehicles to full range, was almost the only definite specification. The requirements for high ballistic coefficient and very rapid reentry, and for hardening to withstand a nuclear environment[g] led to several difficult technical problems which contributed to the long delay before the vehicle was finally tested. The second part was a nine-month study of a deployment mechanism for a multiple warhead configuration, and for penetration aids such as decoys, chaff, and electromagnetic countermeasures. The studies were to include an examination of the feasibility and desirability of using various combinations of these penaids and reentry vehicles.[7]

By the time this contract had been issued to General Electric the bus concept was extant in the technical community. It had been conceived and suggested to the military in the 1962-63 time period, but, because of time

---

[e]General Electric Company had been particularly active in developing these advanced reentry techniques in the years immediately prior to the Mark 12 competition. In the spring of 1961 it was awarded the contract for Nike-Zeus target vehicles, the requirements for which led the company to examine many of the technical problems they would meet later with the Mark 12.

[f]The ballistic coefficient, β, is defined by $\beta = \dfrac{W}{C_D A}$, where W is the weight of the reentry vehicle, C_D is its drag coefficient, and A is the representative area used in calculating the drag coefficient. The higher the value of β the faster and the less accuracy-degrading is the reentry through the atmosphere.

[g]In order to reduce the vulnerability of reentry vehicles to ABM defense they are made resistant to the nuclear effects on which ABM interceptors rely for their effectiveness. The various measures that are taken to accomplish this are together known as hardening.

constraints resulting from the desire to use the Mark 12 on the Minuteman II and the technical uncertainties involved, the authorized design did not yet include independent guidance capability. The Navy also had a new strategic missile, the Polaris B-3, in exploratory development by 1963. However, the design of this missile, for which the Special Projects Office unsuccessfully sought funding for FY 1965, did not yet include MIRV either.

The year of decision for MIRV was 1964. During the summer, a review of the Minuteman II scheduling and the delays in the Mark 12 program led to the decision to deploy the missile with the old Mark 11 vehicle. This freed the Mark 12 development from rigid time constraints and permitted its reorientation. During the FY 1966 budget review in the fall of 1964,[h] the decision was made to proceed with development of a Mark 12 MIRV system for Minuteman II and with a larger version of the B-3, later renamed Poseidon C-3, which would also carry MIRVs. At the same time, a revised version of the Mark 12 heavy, renamed the Mark 17, was also funded for design and was intended as an option for both Minuteman II and Poseidon.

In about October 1964, the General Electric Mark 12 program was reoriented to include a deployment mechanism for a MIRV system. The following January, North American Rockwell Autonetics Division, the Minuteman guidance contractor, was authorized to develop specifications, select subcontractors, and prepare plans for the full-scale development of a Minuteman II Post Boost Control System, or MIRV bus. Bell Aerospace received a subcontract for the propulsion system in June and the following month Autonetics received a design and development contract for the Post Boost Control System.[8]

In November 1964 the Special Projects Office was instructed to include both MIRV and accuracy improvements in the design for its new missile.[9] This is reflected in President Johnson's January 18, 1965 message to Congress announcing the Poseidon development program. He said the missile would have "double the payload of the . . . Polaris A-3. The increased accuracy and flexibility of the Poseidon will permit its use effectively against a broader range of possible targets and give added insurance of penetration of enemy defenses." He also announced the development of "remarkable new payloads," including "guidance and reentry vehicle designs to increase manyfold the effectiveness against various kinds of targets."[10] The FY 1966 budget contained a request for $35 million to initiate development of the missile.[11] Despite this small figure, which reflects the rather tentative nature of the missile's design at this stage, the 1964 decision was widely interpreted within the Navy as a full commitment to the missile.

Many questions about both new missiles remained unresolved in

[h]The government's Fiscal Year (FY) begins on the July 1 of the preceding calendar year. FY 1966 began July 1, 1965. As is usual, the FY 1966 budget was presented to Congress in the early part of 1965 and was under preparation by late 1964.

early 1965. In the Navy these included particularly the pace at which the development program would proceed. Special Projects' analysis had shown that the cheapest way to deploy the Poseidon would be very fast. However, the rest of the Navy did not want the heavy concentration of funds that such a crash program would entail. Furthermore, there were real uncertainties about "the ultimate shelf life of the present Polaris missiles and the time when a potential aggressor might deploy an ABM system."[12] As a result, the pace of the program was left undecided. There was as yet no schedule for the retrofitting of the submarines.

Concerning the Poseidon MIRV itself, no decision had been made either about the use of decoys or about a choice of reentry system. DDR&E expected to use both the Mark 17[i] and the Mark 12 on Poseidon. The planners in the Office of the Chief of Naval Operations were interested primarily in the Mark 17. Special Projects favored a much smaller vehicle that would carry a warhead in the 50 kiloton range that the scientists at the Atomic Energy Commission's Livermore Laboratory had said they could design and build. During 1965, the Mark 12 option was dropped and replaced by the smaller reentry vehicle, called the Mark 3.

The major issue still undecided about the Minuteman MIRV in early 1965 was the precise design of the missile that would carry it. The authorized program called for the Mark 12 MIRV and the Mark 17 to be retrofitted onto the Minuteman II booster.[14] But there were problems with this approach. Although the Mark 12 had originally been designed so that a Minuteman II could carry three of them to full range, it was soon recognized that weight increases would reduce the missile's range and that an undesirable hammerhead design[j] would be required.[15] One of the Minuteman engine contractors had been trying for years to sell the Air Force a wider and more powerful stage that would have eliminated both these problems. Although the utilization of this new stage had long been recommended, the development program as approved for FY 1966 did not include it.[16] Instead, probably to compensate for the weight increases, only two Mark 12 reentry vehicles were planned. Through 1965 the advantages of a more powerful third stage became increasingly evident. These included, besides the ability to carry three reentry vehicles and the elimination of the hammerhead design, room for more penaids and more propellant for the bus.

During 1965, Poseidon's design was specified by contractor committees charged with determining the interface characteristics of the missile and retrofitted submarine. In August Autonetics was awarded a contract to study

---

[i]The intention to deploy the Mark 17 on Poseidon for counterforce missions is suggested by the following passage in the FY 1966 Posture Statement: "Alternately [Poseidon] could be used to attack a hardened point target with greater accuracy and a heavier warhead."[13]

[j]A hammerhead design is one in which the base of the missile's front end is wider than the third stage. Although there do seem to be legitimate aerodynamic reasons for avoiding such a design, aesthetic considerations seem to have been at least as important.

improvements in the Ship's Inertial Navigation System (SINS) to adapt it to Poseidon requirements.[17] The final reports on the contractors' project definition studies were submitted to Special Projects in October. Hercules Powder Company was chosen to manage the propulsion development in the only aspect of the program that was opened for competitive bidding. Thiokol Chemical Corporation was chosen to assist with the first stage.[18] After a review in Special Projects the package was handed to DDR&E for authorization. Since the decision to proceed had already been made, DDR&E's review was quite rapid. Go-ahead for engineering development was given in December 1965.[19]

The decision to deploy the MIRVed missiles was officially made during 1965 as part of the FY 1967 budget and five-year force plan. At the same time the Poseidon development program was accelerated to advance the date of expected deployment by about a year.[20] A schedule for retrofitting the first submarines had been established by early 1966, but the decision on how many submarines to retrofit was delayed.[21]

The initial procurement of Minuteman III was funded in FY 1967,[22] but still no decision had been made concerning the replacement of the Minuteman II third stage with a larger one. Autonetics continued to work on a MIRV bus for the Minuteman II configuration until April 1966. Hardware was produced but never flown. By March 1966, however, when the Minuteman III was officially authorized for development, the new third stage was included in the design.[23] The number of Mark 12s per missile was thereafter increased to three, and the hammerhead design was eliminated. In August, Autonetics began to redesign the Post Boost Control System to take account of the larger throw-weight of the missile. The size of the MIRV footprint was increased by more than doubling the amount of propellant carried by the bus. That same month, Aerojet-General lost out to Thiokol.[24]

Although the ability to carry the Mark 12 MIRV was the primary purpose of this new version of the Minuteman missile, other improvements were made at the same time. These included, besides the new third stage, improved resistance to nuclear effects, improved penetration aids, more flexible targeting options, an improved guidance system, better accuracy, and improved ground equipment including increased silo hardness. The Mark 12 reentry vehicle developed serious and unanticipated problems during its test program in 1966.[25] A coupling of the spinning motion to small pitch variations caused by atmospheric nonuniformities led to nonuniform ablation and side-slipping. The discovery and implementation of remedial measures required almost two years and considerable added expense.

After the go-ahead for the Poseidon development program was issued at the end of 1965, the work proceeded rapidly through 1966 and 1967. On December 12, 1966, the first Poseidon test vehicle was launched from a land-based launcher at the San Francisco Naval Shipyard.[26] Five days later, production of the missiles was approved. After an extended planning period and design competition, AVCO Corporation received a development contract for the Mark 17 in April 1966.[27] Flight testing of the Mark 3 reentry vehicle, using the Athena test rocket, began in 1967. During this period the decision was made to rely on identical reentry vehicles rather than decoys to penetrate possible Soviet defenses.

The FY 1968 Posture Statement belatedly announced the addition of the new Minuteman third stage and also proposed to increase the number of Minuteman IIIs programmed for the forces from 350 to 450.[28] The possibility was left open for further increases later. At the same time authorization was requested to "commit the Poseidon missile to production and deployment"[29] and funds were sought "to procure long leadtime components as well as tooling and test equipment to permit Poseidon missile production start-up in Fiscal Year 1969."[30] The decision had been made by this time to convert thirty-one submarines, the maximum possible number, to carry the Poseidon.[31] The first three conversions were authorized and funded in FY 1968, but the Navy diverted the funds for one of these to meet "urgent Southeast Asia military requirements."[32]

Also in FY 1968, funding was initiated for a stellar inertial guidance system for Poseidon.[33] Stellar inertial guidance had first been investigated in the early 1960s, in connection with the ill-fated mobile medium range ballistic missile (MMRBM) and the Skybolt airlaunched ballistic missile as a technique for providing accurate inertial coordinates to the guidance system. In the case of the MMRBM, hardware was actually built and tested.[34] When the MMRBM was cancelled in 1964, the stellar inertial guidance program was retained as the Stellar Aquisition Feasibility Flight (STAFF) program. Several flight tests were conducted using Polaris A-1 missiles which demonstrated the feasibility of the concept.[35] About 1967 the contractor, Kearfott Division of Singer-General Precision, developed a new concept that could greatly improve the accuracy of Poseidon. It was this new concept that was funded in FY 1968. The program was cut back, however, during an expenditure reduction drive soon after. The date of the initial operational capability was slipped about a year.[36]

The Mark 17 reentry vehicle survived only as long as its costs were low.[37] It was cancelled in January 1968 without ever having advanced beyond early development.

The FY 1969 Posture Statement announced a further increase in the proportion of Minuteman IIIs to be introduced into the force.[38] The programmed number was now 550.[39] Since delays had been experienced in the development program, the phase-out of the remaining Minuteman I missiles was slowed "to compensate for the slip in the Minuteman III program."[40] Funds were requested that year for the conversion of six submarines to Poseidon and for advanced procurement for nine more.[41] However, congressional concern that the conversion would proceed too rapidly before sufficient reliability testing had been conducted held the authorization to two conversions.[42]

Technology for a Poseidon penaid package was also to be developed in the Advanced Ballistic Reentry Systems program, although no immediate plan existed to use penaids.[43]

Production contracts for both Minuteman III and Poseidon were issued in 1968. In March, Lockheed Missiles and Space Company received a $456.1 million contract for development and production of Poseidon.[44] In June, Autonetics received a production contract for the first 76 Post Boost Control Systems. On July 10, General Electric received a $33.9 million production contract for 68 Mark 12s.[45] On August 16, the first full-scale flight tests of both Poseidon and Minuteman III were conducted from Cape Kennedy. Both were successful. Thereafter tests proceeded at a rate of one every two or three months, increasing to about one a month in 1969.

Six more Poseidon conversions were requested in FY 1970 of which four were authorized.[46] The first ship entered the yard for conversion on February 3, 1969.[47] As originally submitted by the Johnson Administration, the FY 1970 budget cut the number of reentry vehicles to be deployed on the Poseidon missile to an average of ten each[48] and further stretched out the stellar inertial guidance development.[49] The Nixon Administration decided to stretch out the Minuteman III deployment even further in order to reduce the overlap between development and production but restored full funding to the stellar inertial guidance program for Poseidon.[50] Later, however, this program was cancelled altogether.

The development tests for Poseidon were completed in June 1970[51] and for Minuteman III the following month. The first group of ten Minuteman III missiles became operational in June 1970,[k,52] having slipped about a year from the original target date.[53] The first patrol of a Poseidon submarine began March 31, 1971.[54] The Fiscal Year 1974 budget concluded the funding for the Minuteman IIIs,[55] but the Congress delayed the appropriation for the last three Poseidon conversions until FY 1975.[56] In order to keep open the Minuteman III production line and thereby to maintain the option of deploying additional missiles and in order to provide hardware for the on-going test program, 61 Minuteman IIIs were procured in FY 1975 and 50 in FY 1976.[57] The programmed number of 550 Minuteman IIIs was expected to be fully deployed before the end of FY 1975.[58] As Minuteman III is being deployed, the missile silos are being modified to improve their ability to survive a nuclear attack, to make the ground equipment compatible with the new missile, and to reduce the time required to re-target both individual missiles and the entire force.

The FY 1975 appropriations included funds for the conversion of the last three Poseidon submarines and the last submarine tender.[59] Subsequent appropriations went to counteract the effects of inflation, for outfitting and

---

[k]It is not unusual that the initial operational capability of the Minuteman III should have been achieved before the completion of development testing. The same had been true of other Air Force missile systems in the past.

post-delivery costs, support of the Poseidon missiles and the Poseidon modification program.[60] The latter program is intended to correct missile deficiencies that were encountered during the operational test program. Unlike demonstration and shakedown tests that use missiles that have not been carried on patrol and serviced by operating personnel, the operational tests use randomly selected missiles from a returning submarine and exhibit reliability degradations resulting from aging and maintenance handling. Aside from a weakness in the nose tip of the Mark III reentry vehicle most of the failures encountered were thought to be attributable to "random deficiencies in small piece-parts such as transistors, electrical connections, fuses, etc., and in the preparation of operational missiles for flight tests."[61] The final Poseidon conversion is scheduled for completion in April 1977.[62]

Already follow-on programs and modification to Minuteman III and Poseidon are well under way.[63] A new higher yield warhead and improved arming and fusing systems are being developed for retrofit into the Mark 12 reentry vehicle. Refinements are also being made in the Minuteman III guidance system. A program is underway to test the Minuteman III with a new MIRV configuration, carrying a larger number of smaller reentry vehicles. Beyond this, design and basing studies are in progress for an altogether new and much larger ICBM that could be developed as a follow-on to the Minuteman III. A new terminally-guided, maneuvering reentry vehicle is being developed for use on this missile. In addition, a new ballistic missile submarine called Trident and new longer range missiles called Trident I are being procured. Initial operational capability of this system is expected in FY 1979 and the Trident I missile is expected to be retrofitted into ten Poseidon submarines. Studies are also in progress for a longer, more accurate submarine-launched ballistic missile called Trident II that could eventually be retrofitted into the Trident submarine.

Chapter Two

Innovation

Since World War II the military services of the United States have become dependent on continuing technological innovation to an unprecedented degree. This is particularly true in the field of strategic nuclear forces where the nation's ultimate security has been entrusted to highly sophisticated and very expensive nuclear weapons systems. As technology improves and global political relationships change, successive generations of these systems are developed and deployed. Development times are usually quite long—typically five to ten years depending on the type of weapon—and the useful lifetime before a major retrofit program is begun or the weapon is simply replaced is often only about the same.[a] Long before the deployment of a particular system is complete, its successor is being considered. Frequently a series of improvements is introduced during production, resulting in several versions of the same weapon system.

This process of continual replacement is to some extent self-perpetuating. Large organizations have been created that owe their continued existence solely to their ability to invent or design new weapons and sell them to political decisionmakers. These organizations include not only the development commands of the services but also some of the largest of the nation's corporations who together employ millions of workers and represent a powerful political force. These companies have tended to compete with each other on a technical rather than a financial basis, primarily because the most salable commodity that they can offer their military customers is advances in technology. At least until

---

[a]It is not true that the useful lifetime of strategic weapons is always short. The Titan IIs, fully deployed by 1964, are still in the force structure more than a decade later. B-52 bombers and Polaris submarines have had comparable longevity. This does not, however, contradict the basic point. The B-52s were deployed in several different versions, they have been continually improved even after deployment and the avionics and weapons they carry have been improved several times. The missiles carried by the Polaris submarines have been replaced at least once and in some instances more often. Although the Titan IIs have been largely unaltered, the Minuteman force has gone through several upgradings.

recent years, when the rapidly rising costs of new hardware have stimulated reappraisals, there was almost no disagreement that new weapon systems should incorporate the latest advances that technology would permit. In part this commitment to high technology has been the result of the traditions and institutional arrangements that have developed in the last thirty years. In part it is a response to the observed or anticipated parallel activities by potential adversaries. To the military, therefore, unlike most technically-oriented organizations, the important question is not *whether* to introduce technical innovations but *how to choose* from a wide assortment of possibilities, what the costs will be, and how fast to proceed.

The existence of specialized technical organizations within the Air Force and the Navy charged with the development of strategic missiles eliminated in the case of MIRV a frequent inhibitor of technical innovation, the need to provide a base for the innovation by creating new institutional structures or by significantly altering existing ones. Originally created to perform a particular task and, in the case of the Special Projects Office, expected to disappear with the completion of that task, the missile development organizations of the services grew into strong bureaucratic advocates of new missiles and new technology. Some relatively minor changes in the internal structure of the development organizations and some alteration of their task structures would have to accompany any major new program. But the benefits flowing from initiation of a new project far outweighed such minor dislocations. Without a continuous stream of new challenges the missile development organizations could not long remain viable or perhaps even survive. In the Office of the Secretary of Defense as well, the basic organizational structure dealing with strategic forces remained unchanged through the 1960s despite the introduction of several generations of new weapon systems. The existence of the Office of the Director of Defense Research and Engineering, created in 1958, and the division of responsibility between it and the Office of Systems Analysis provided an environment very receptive to technical innovation.

Operating within such a context, this study cannot focus on the questions usually asked about innovation, namely, why technical innovation is so difficult and how organizations change to accommodate it. In the case of MIRV, innovation was not very difficult and no significant organizational changes were necessary. It was not an organizational or structural innovation, but a purely technical one within organizations whose purpose was the exploitation of technology. The innovation was fully consistent with existing organizational and policy objectives. Indeed the most striking aspect of the MIRV innovation is the relative lack of opposition and the ease with which it occurred. The task of this chapter therefore will be to describe the innovation process and account for some interesting differences between the Air Force and Navy cases.

MIRV was clearly a technology whose time had come. It was firmly grounded in the technical developments of the 1950s and was primarily an extrapolation of concepts of the same period. It is therefore not surprising that MIRV was "invented" almost simultaneously in several places within the technical community. It was rapidly accepted within both the military and civilian sides of the Defense Department, with only a brief and scattered resistance. All concerned increasingly saw MIRV as a solution to their own particular problems. The consensus in favor of proceeding solidified rapidly. By 1965 it was fully formed.

THE ORGANIZATIONAL ENVIRONMENT

Despite the elaborate apparatus within the United States government for making decisions affecting national security and military policy, a rather limited number of individuals and organizations influenced the MIRV development decisions. This is partly a result of the personalities in the Kennedy and Johnson administrations and the management techniques they employed and partly because of the relatively noncontroversial nature of the MIRV program during this period.[b] Had there been major internal divisions within the services or between the services and the Secretary of Defense concerning MIRV, the subject would certainly have been fully aired before several congressional committees, just as were the TFX program, the manned bomber and the limitation on the number of Minutemen. Lacking such disagreements, the Congress had no incentive to focus its attention specifically on MIRV. Moreover, the strong tendency in both houses of Congress to prefer more rather than less expenditure for strategic programs created a climate in which the MIRV development programs could proceed smoothly with the overwhelming and perhaps uncritical support of Congress. Indeed, since MIRV was presented to Congress as a program that permitted holding the line in other strategic programs, and since many legislators were far from convinced that other development programs should be limited, they were not about to be critical of those, including MIRV, which the Secretary strongly supported.

Within the executive branch, the President, the Department of Defense, the Department of State, the Arms Control and Disarmament Agency (ACDA), the Bureau of the Budget, and the President's Special Assistants for National Security Affairs and for Science and Technology all had a potential interest in the MIRV programs. In fact, however, few of these actually did exert any significant influence on the MIRV development decisions. Although there were discussions about MIRV within both ACDA and State, neither one played a role in the actual decisions. They both lacked the mandate to become involved in such weapons procurement issues and although a few ACDA officials tried to

[b]The secrecy of the MIRV program may also have played some part in limiting the participation in these decisions, but as will be discussed in Chapter 5, this seems to have been quite minor.

exert some influence they were not successful. Moreover, the two presidents that Secretary of Defense Robert McNamara served, and their national security advisors as well, seem to have had sufficient confidence in him to let him run the Defense Department with considerable autonomy.[c] During the Kennedy Administration very close working relationships existed between McNamara, National Security Advisor McGeorge Bundy, and Science Advisor Jerome Wiesner and their respective staffs. Carl Kaysen, who was Bundy's deputy from April 1961 to July 1963, followed strategic forces questions especially closely.[2] Nevertheless, these officials tended to deal predominantly with major or controversial issues, into which categories MIRV did not fit during its development. President Johnson, because of the distractions first of consolidating his position, then in campaigning for his own election and finally in the growing involvement in Vietnam, relied ever more heavily on McNamara to make weapons procurement choices. The rather different nature of the relationship between President Johnson and his science advisor[d] and the failure to replace Kaysen with someone to cover the same range of issues led to a minimal involvement in strategic weapons decisions during the Johnson Administration of the Special Assistants for Science and Technology and for National Security Affairs and their staffs. Moreover, since both presidents let McNamara act essentially as his own budget director, the Bureau of the Budget was not really involved either.

It is on the Department of Defense itself, specifically the Office of the Secretary, the Air Force, and the Navy, as well as their supporting contractors and advisory committees, that attention must focus in order to understand the process of innovation for MIRV. These, and these alone, were the significant organizations. Their structure and procedures provided the institutional environment in which the MIRV innovation took place. Figure 2-1 provides a schematic diagram of the organizational relationships within the Department of Defense that are discussed below.

Even within the services only a small number of the many sub-organizations are relevant to a discussion of innovation for strategic missiles. In the Air Force these include the Systems Command and especially the Ballistic Systems Division as the weapons developers;[e] the Strategic Air Command (SAC) as the users; and the Air Staff and the civilian secretariat as the decision-making structures within the Air Force. The preferences and points of view of SAC were strongly felt at all levels within the Air Force. Relations between it and the development commands were so close that SAC personnel were assigned to the

---

[c]McGeorge Bundy, President Kennedy's National Security Advisor, has said, "I don't recall that [the MIRV] development was seriously a matter of trouble or concern outside the Pentagon under Mr. McNamara's leadership. Those of us outside the Pentagon had, and I personally had, the highest respect for and confidence in Mr. McNamara's abilities."[1]

[d]See Chapter 5.

[e]In 1967 BSD was merged with the Space Systems Division into the Space and Missile Systems Organization.

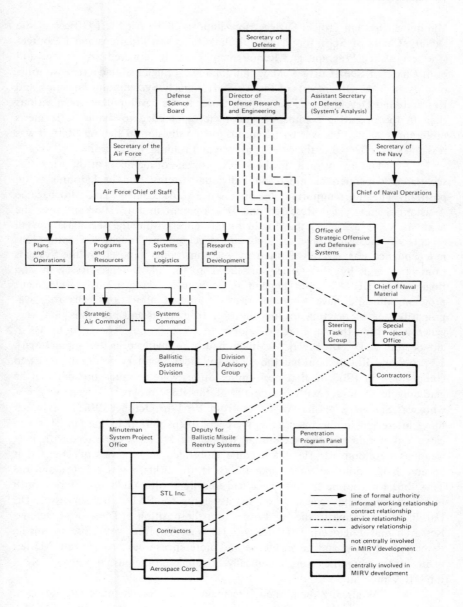

Figure 2-1. Schematic Diagram of Organizational Relationships in MIRV Development

Minuteman System Project Office. More important the Air Staff Offices of the Deputy Chiefs of Staff for Plans and Operations and Programs and Resources (formerly called Programs and Requirements) closely reflected SAC's views and both Chiefs of Staff Curtis LeMay and John McConnell had had extensive tours of duty in SAC. Other parts of the Air Staff, namely Systems and Logistics, and Research and Development, were much closer to the development organizations than to the operating commands, and therefore tended to share the former's preferences. While this was by no means a deep division in the Air Staff, it was real and was reflected in the career patterns and training of personnel.

The involvement in the MIRV program of members of the Air Force secretariat depended as much on individual interest and background as on position. The most important member was Dr. Alexander Flax, who became Assistant Secretary for Research and Development in July 1963 and over the next six years exercised the dominant influence within the secretariat on all aspects of the Air Force research and development budget. Of course, his independence was severely limited by the constraints imposed by the Systems Command and by the Office of the Director of Defense Research and Engineering (DDR&E), but he had to be brought along in any development program and did have some leverage on budget allocations. His role was primarily one of reacting to and choosing from ideas and programs that were generated within the Air Force development organizations. The previous Assistant Secretary, Dr. Brockway McMillan, had been involved in the original Mark 12 proposals of 1962, but had moved up to Under Secretary before the renewed competition in 1963. In that position his duties were so much broader that he gradually lost contact with the details of the R&D program. Eugene Zuckert, who was Secretary of the Air Force from 1961 to October 1965, was much more interested in the management aspects of his job, including his efforts to carve out a role for the secretariat within the McNamara Pentagon, than in weapons development. He did become embroiled in weapons questions that became major political issues, like the B-70, the airlift/sealift debates, and the TFX, but for routine matters he relied heavily on his under secretaries, both technical men, and especially on his assistants for R&D.[3] His successor, Dr. Harold Brown, came to the Air Force from the position of Director of Defense Research and Engineering (DDR&D).[f] He was therefore very close to missile development issues and his influence and preferences were strongly felt. Neither of his under secretaries were technically oriented and they did not play a role in the MIRV program.

As already mentioned, the main thrust for technical innovation in the Air Force has come from within the Air Force Systems Command (AFSC). For strategic missile programs in the 1960s this meant specifically the Ballistic

---

[f]The acronym "DDR&E" is used both for the Director of Defense Research and Engineering and for his office. The reader will be able to tell which is intended from the context.

Systems Division (BSD) at Norton Air Force Base in San Bernardino, California, and after 1967 its successor, Space and Missile Systems Organization in El Segundo, California. Within BSD a Minuteman System Project Office had direct responsibility for the Minuteman program. Reentry vehicle development proceeded under several institutional arrangements until 1963 when a Deputy for Ballistic Missile Reentry Systems was established and given control of both the Advanced Ballistic Reentry Systems (ABRES) program, in which new reentry techniques and experimental vehicles were tested, and the Operational System Development Division, that defined and developed operational reentry vehicles. This entire organizational structure existed primarily to exploit new technology. In the area of ballistic missiles it had, by the early 1960s, successfully developed and turned over to the Strategic Air Command the Thor, the Atlas, and the Titan I missiles and was deeply engaged in the Titan II, the Minuteman I, and the design of advanced reentry systems. Thought was also being given to the Titan III, to be developed for the Space Systems Division, and to follow-ons to the first generation Minuteman.

The prestige, the budget, and the power of BSD within the AFSC and the Air Force depended on its continually generating and selling new missile systems and components. As long as the Minuteman force kept expanding, advanced versions could be sought for those missiles yet to be deployed, as was done in the case of Minuteman II. However, as the likelihood of an imposed ceiling on the force increased, BSD began to seek other ways to introduce improvements. Merely providing support for existing systems and replacing old missiles with identical models would not have been sufficient for the organization to maintain itself. Replacement missiles could be bought from the manufacturer and deployed with little reliance on BSD and the technical community on which it depended. The personnel at BSD were engineers, always looking for new technology and new designs to improve their product. Their morale and job satisfaction depended on continual innovation. Unless a case could be made for replacing existing missiles with new versions, a missile ceiling might eventually put BSD out of business.

BSD was strongly aided and encouraged in this predisposition by its close contacts with the aerospace contractors and technical community that grew up with it in southern California. Foremost among these were the Space Technology Laboratories, Inc. (STL), and Aerospace Corporation. In the fall of 1954 Ramo-Wooldridge Corporation organized the Guided Missile Research Division to provide general systems engineering and technical direction support to the Air Force ballistic missile program. In 1957 this division was renamed Space Technology Laboratories. On October 3, 1958 Ramo-Wooldridge merged with Thompson Products Company to form Thompson-Ramo-Wooldridge or TRW. STL became a wholly owned subsidiary but independent operating division of TRW.[4] In 1960, because of a controversy over the role of TRW as both manufacturer and system manager for Air Force programs, Aerospace

Corporation was formed as a nonprofit organization to take over some of STL's duties. This new corporation was staffed almost entirely with personnel from other aerospace contractors, the majority transferring directly from STL.[5] Although STL kept responsibility for the Minuteman booster, later including the MIRV bus, all new and operational front ends and payloads including the Mark 12 reentry system were assigned to Aerospace. In November 1967, however, responsibility for the Mark 12 was transferred from Aerospace to STL. The contacts between BSD and both STL and Aerospace were very close, since BSD relied on them heavily for technical support. Being intermediaries between BSD and its industrial contractors, STL and Aerospace frequently served as advocates of new technology and new systems.

Direct contacts with the missile contractors were also very extensive. Unlike other large Air Force development programs, the Minuteman program did not have a prime contractor to integrate the efforts of the subcontractors. Rather, the Minuteman System Project Office "functions as the integrating agency for a number of associate contractors."[6] Since the contracts were issued directly by BSD, close ties developed between it and its many sub-system contractors. Personnel from BSD as well as STL and Aerospace were in residence at many of the contractors' facilities and the contractors had representatives in San Bernardino. Although there were cases when industry was unaware of new thinking in BSD, communications were usually direct, rapid, and informal. New technical opportunities and new mission requirements were widely discussed within the community. The contractors, of course, shared the orientation of BSD, STL, and Aerospace that new systems should employ the most advanced concepts possible. Although company profits came mostly from production rather than development, contracts were won or extended primarily on the basis of a contractor's ability to provide advanced components. Moreover, the contractors' personnel that had working contacts with STL, Aerospace, and BSD were engineers, sharing the enthusiasm for new gadgets and seeking new development programs to challenge their creativity.

Most new projects would begin within BSD at the level of the system project offices as a result of the interplay between their personnel and their industrial contacts. Sometimes a formal proposal would be put together and a briefing given at AFSC headquarters. Other times a presentation would be made based only on a preliminary concept. Ideas would bounce back and forth for a while until a firm proposal was generated and a contracting team was on board. It would then be presented to the Air Staff for approval and the issuing of formal requirements. Such requirements were necessary before any large funding could be requested. The request would then be forwarded to the Secretary of the Air Force and DDR&E for approval.

Although the preceding is a description of the formal decision channels within the Air Force, it omits the very important informal channels.[g]

---

[g]In large part these informal channels were the result of the streamlined reporting and authorization procedures introduced in 1955 after a management study by the Gillette Committee.[7]

On occasion BSD would bypass AFSC headquarters and go directly to the Air Staff with a proposal. If an alliance could be built with the Air Staff from the beginning, approval in AFSC was easier to obtain. Even more useful were the direct contacts at the working level between personnel in BSD and those in DDR&E. Since the technical competence in BSD was much higher than at AFSC headquarters or on the Air Staff, DDR&E tended to work directly with BSD. Briefings were regularly made to DDR&E and personnel from that office visited BSD frequently. Through these indirect channels BSD commonly reported its own preferences to DDR&E, even when these did not correspond to an official Air Force position. Since DDR&E had effective authority over the development budget of the services, agreements worked out between it and BSD were very difficult to overrule. The ABRES program was reported to be particularly difficult to control from within the Air Force. As a favorite of the scientific establishment, with a close working relationship with DDR&E and enjoying considerable financial independence, the Deputy of Ballistic Missile Reentry Systems hardly felt called upon to justify his activities within normal Air Force channels.

An important channel for information and support for BSD was the Division Advisory Group (DAG), formed in the summer of 1961. This was a committee of scientists and technical people from industry and academia. Successive commanders of BSD relied on their DAG for both technical and nontechnical advice. The interest in maintaining contact with the DAG members was so strong that when the Office of the Secretary of Defense cut the authorized numbers of members from nine to five at the beginning of 1963, General W. Austin Davis, commander of BSD, exercised the option to keep other members as consultants. During his tenure, ending in July 1964, the DAG held monthly meetings in which BSD would brief the members on recent developments and then seek their help on a variety of issues. There were also extensive informal contacts. In the period 1962-1964, members of the BSDAG included the following: Dr. Charles S. Draper, inertial guidance expert, founder and director of Instrumentation Laboratory, Massachusetts Institute of Technology; Dr. Antonio Ferri, rocket propulsion expert from Brooklyn Polytechnic Institute; Dr. John S. Foster, Jr., Director of Lawrence Radiation Laboratory at Livermore and later DDR&E; Professor David T. Griggs and Dr. William G. McMillan, nuclear weapons experts from the University of California, Los Angeles; Dr. Albert Latter and Dr. Richard Latter from the Physics Department at RAND Corporation; and Dr. Edward Teller, also of Lawrence Radiation Laboratory at Livermore.[8]

Although these scientists brought important technical expertise to BSD and helped it keep in touch with new developments in their various fields, they also provided, through their personal contacts, channels of communication with higher levels of the Air Force and with DDR&E. Several DAG members, including Ferri, Foster, Griggs, Albert Latter, and McMillan, were members of the Air Force Scientific Advisory Board or its panels in the early 1960s.[9] McMillan and Griggs were also members of the Defense Science Board from

1963 and 1964 respectively. They were well placed therefore to provide support and assistance to BSD as it tried to build support for new development programs.

From the early summer of 1961 the penetration aid program of BSD had its own advisory committee, the Penetration Program Panel,[10] under the chairmanship of Lester Lees, an aeronautical engineer from California Institute of Technology. When the office of the Deputy for Ballistic Missile Reentry Systems was established in 1963 this committee became advisory to the Deputy. Members of this committee included Albert Latter and William Graham of the RAND Corporation; two representatives of Aerospace Corporation; one representative from each of Lincoln Laboratory, where responsibility for gathering and analyzing data for ABRES from the Kwajalein test site was vested; Sandia Corporation, a defense contractor working closely with the nuclear weapons laboratories; and Lawrence Livermore Laboratory, one of the nuclear weapons laboratories. The latter representative was Carl Haussmann, who played a significant role in the Poseidon warhead decision. During the period of its existence this committee facilitated communication between several of the individuals and organizations instrumental in launching the MIRV program. It seems to have been rather influential within the Air Force technical community.

Even more significant than their membership on these various committees were the close personal relationships that Foster, Albert Latter, Richard Latter, Carl Haussmann, and others of the weapons community enjoyed with DDR&E, Dr. Harold Brown, who himself had been Director of Livermore until 1961. Brown kept in close touch with this community while in the Pentagon, thereby creating an informal communications link between the Ballistic Systems Division and DDR&E totally outside the normal bureaucratic channels.

Although the U.S. Navy is in many ways a more diverse and decentralized organization than the Air Force, an even smaller number of individuals and suborganizations were really involved in decisions about Poseidon. Most of the Navy was concerned exclusively with missions and weapon systems unrelated to the strategic nuclear forces. Except for major budgetary issues, including the decision to develop a follow-on missile to the A-3, the surface admirals who controlled the Navy were not very interested in the activities of the Polaris developers.

Until 1964 there was no organization within the Office of the Chief of Naval Operations with responsibility for studies and planning for the Polaris fleet, and even after one was created, it was not very influential. When Secretary of the Navy Paul H. Nitze wanted to provide a major Navy input for a strategic forces study conducted by DDR&E in 1964, he created an ad hoc group which came to be known as the Great Circle Group, within the Long Range Objectives Group.[11] Rear Admiral George Miller, director of the Long Range Objectives Group oversaw its operations. It took until February 1967 before the Great

Circle Group was given independent status, again on Secretary Nitze's initiative, as the Office of Strategic Offensive and Defensive Systems. Admiral Miller was the first director. However, since Admiral Miller's group neither controlled the Navy's budget for strategic systems nor had close contacts with the decision-makers in the Office of the Secretary of Defense, its influence on the Poseidon program was minor. On July 1, 1971 the office was renamed the Strategic Offensive and Defensive Division (OP-62) and put under the command of Rear Admiral James B. Osborn.

Within the Navy secretariat only Secretary Nitze played any significant role in the Poseidon development. He had a strong interest in strategic matters and a personal commitment to strengthening the Polaris system. At the critical juncture, he was instrumental in overcoming the resistance of the surface Navy to the Poseidon development. But on the details of the missile's characteristics, including the MIRV, he played no role, except perhaps an informal one resulting from his close relationship with Secretary McNamara. Although the Assistant Secretaries of the Navy for Research and Development reviewed and approved the annual development budget for Polaris, they were not really involved in the decisions that led to that budget.

The real center of decision-making for the Polaris system and the Poseidon missile was in DDR&E and in the development organization, the Special Projects Office (SP). They shared a technical orientation and expertise as well as budgetary authority. On minor matters, if obstacles were encountered within the Navy, particularly from Admiral Miller, SP could work directly with DDR&E to ensure resolution of the issue to their mutual satisfaction. So close were the relations between SP and DDR&E that one former SP officer said that the Poseidon program was run out of the latter's office on the third floor of the Pentagon. Generalizing from Vincent Davis's study on innovation in the Navy, it seems likely that the close ties between SP and DDR&E were resented by much of the rest of the Navy in which there exists a tradition for "dealing with all problems on an 'in house' basis" rather than seeking outside support.[12] That such resentment was indeed felt became clear during interviews with some of the Navy personnel outside of SP.

When SP was established in 1955, it was purposely provided independent status, separate from the existing technical bureaus in the Navy.[13] Through the period of the 1950s, SP secured a reputation for efficiency and successful management resulting in great organizational autonomy within the Navy and the Department of Defense.[14] The Office was afforded exceptional freedom by the Navy secretariat. Even DDR&E did not monitor SP programs as closely as they did Air Force missile developments. Nonetheless, this autonomy, which may have been essential for the successful development and deployment of the Polaris system, also left SP isolated within the Navy. Since the Polaris Program's official sponsorship within the operational Navy changed frequently in the early years, SP did not have a firm base of support within the Navy structure.[15]

Despite the decentralized nature of the organization chart, SP's decision-making power was more tightly controlled by the organization's management than in BSD. The relatively smaller size of SP, its single-minded devotion to one system, and the skillful ways in which the Director and Technical Director manipulated and encouraged competition between the Office's branches and contractors enabled them to maintain strict control over both personnel and technical developments.[16] SP had a non-uniformed Chief Scientist, but when the second incumbent became diverted to the Deep Submergence Systems Project in 1964, the position was allowed to atrophy. Independence like that exercised by the Deputy for Ballistic Missile Reentry Systems in BSD would not have been tolerated. SP also had greater technical competence than BSD and its personnel tended to remain for long periods of time.

The lack of a single system contractor and intermediary organizations, like STL and Aerospace in the Air Force, resulted in even closer contacts with industrial contractors. Although Lockheed Missiles and Space Company was designated the missile system manager, important subsystems, such as guidance and fire control, were contracted directly from branches of SP. As the program's technical manager, SP could exercise very close control over all aspects of the system's development. As Sapolsky has written:

> It was largely the Special Projects Office's design values (or those of the naval, governmental, and private organizations whose support it thought was needed to keep the program politically viable) that were maximized and not those of an outside technical organization.[17]

Contacts between SP and the outside scientific and technical community were much less developed than was the case with BSD. Naval laboratories were used rarely and only when necessary in the development program.[18] Similarly, SP avoided close associations with the outside scientific community. While recognizing that support from such scientists was essential to its organizational independence, and taking appropriate action to guarantee such support, "there was a conscious effort to exclude them from [operational] involvement since the scientists would weaken hierarchical authority."[19] Even the Polaris Steering Task Group (STG), unlike the BSDAG, had as members only individuals closely connected with the development program, namely the senior technical and operational leaders of the major contractors. All committees of the STG except the Systems Appraisal Committee were chaired by a uniformed SP technical branch head. The one exception was chaired by the SP Chief Scientist, but became inoperative in 1964. The STG helped to strengthen SP's managerial control of the overall program by providing it with a route for communication and decision-making that short-circuited the cumbersome bureaucratic channels. It was not, however, a conduit by which new technical ideas reached SP. These were transmitted by more direct channels at the working level.

In the McNamara Pentagon decision-making authority was highly concentrated in the Office of the Secretary of Defense (OSD). Civilian officials were given a mandate by the Secretary to involve themselves in activities that had previously been the responsibility and exclusive province of the services. This mandate was exercised with respect to both force structure and research and development.[20]

To help the Secretary exercise his responsibilities in the area of force requirements and weapons systems, he established the Office of Systems Analysis (SA) within the Office of the Assistant Secretary of Defense (Comptroller). (In 1965 SA became independent of the Comptroller's Office and its director was raised to the level of Assistant Secretary.) SA was responsible for writing McNamara's major management documents, the Draft Presidential Memoranda and the Five Year Defense Plans. It thereby played a central role in determining the force structure and in the major hardware procurement decision. However, SA played a rather minor role in research and development of systems not yet authorized for deployment. In the early stages of a development program, DDR&E had budgetary authority and direct contact with the services. Although SA frequently received briefings on new developments, and tried to stay aware of DDR&E initiatives, the Office was not fully involved until a deployment decision and therefore a commitment for major funding had to be made. In the case of MIRV, SA did not actively consider the program until 1965, by which time a consensus had already been reached within both services favoring MIRV development and a strong alliance had been built between the services and DDR&E.

The lack of involvement of SA in the early development decisions about MIRV should not be interpreted as a lack of involvement of the Secretary himself. He was certainly aware of MIRV technology by 1964 and he approved all the early contracts relevant to the development program. So detailed was McNamara's immersion in defense contracting in the pre-Vietnam years, that all force structure budgetary decisions involving more than about $5 million went across either his desk or his deputy's.

Since 1958 the Director of Defense Research and Engineering (DDR&E) has been the third-ranking civilian in the Office of the Secretary of Defense. He is the Secretary's advisor with respect to weapons development and at the same time has line authority over the research, development, test and evaluation (RDT&E) budget for all but operational systems. Since the incumbents from 1958 to 1973 had moved to this position directly from the directorship of the Livermore Laboratory, they have taken a direct personal interest in strategic systems and especially in nuclear warheads. Particularly Dr. Harold Brown, who was Director when the MIRV development was initiated, kept in close contact with Livermore physicists and other scientists from the weapons community. As already mentioned, these contacts established an informal communications link between the Air Force and the DDR&E since many of these same scientists were members of the BSDAG and the SAB nuclear panel.

Beginning in 1962 a Deputy Director for Strategic and Defensive Systems, later called Strategic and Space Systems, oversaw strategic weapons development. Below the Deputy was an Assistant Director (Strategic Weapons) in charge of the offensive weapons programs. Almost all of the incumbents in both positions have been engineers from major aerospace contractors who entered DDR&E for several years and then returned to industry. This practice of bringing industry personnel into DDR&E was a conscious policy of both the first DDR&E, Dr. Herbert York, and his successor, Dr. Harold Brown.[21] It helped maintain close contact and a continuous flow of information between industry and DDR&E. It was possible for an individual leaving DDR&E to bring to a company the knowledge of future needs as DDR&E perceived them.[h] More important, since DDR&E frequently experienced difficulties in obtaining information from the services and since the staff who dealt with strategic systems was always small, the communications links with industry increased DDR&E's ability to manage the programs. In particular it made easier DDR&E's efforts to restrain the services when their organizational interests caused them to advocate weapons of dubious technical feasibility. Under Herbert York, DDR&E gained the reputation of a restraining force and was the object of much Air Force recrimination as a result. But DDR&E came increasingly to share industry's basic philosophy that technical improvements should continually be made to strategic systems. Under Harold Brown DDR&E became more of an advocate of new technology than it had been under York. From 1965 to 1973, when John Foster was DDR&E, the Office strongly advocated pursuing all available technical avenues. As Morton Halperin has said,

> Foster took it for granted that technology should be pushed as hard as possible, although he recognized the need to choose from the wide variety of different possible new technologies. He also believed that when technology reached the state where it was militarily effective, it should be deployed.[22]

The linkages between DDR&E and the military services were very strong. The Director himself worked closely, especially for budget reviews, with both the service Assistant Secretaries for R&D and the military officers charged with overall responsibility for R&D. However, as has already been suggested, DDR&E's close working relationship with SP and BSD tended to relegate these Assistant Secretaries to interested observers rather than active participants when

---

[h]Such a transfer of information partially explains, for example, why company-funded research on a maneuvering bus began at North American Aviation shortly after Marvin Stern transferred from the position of deputy DDR&E (Weapons Systems) to NAA where he was in charge of their R&D budget.

the discussion turned to strategic missiles. Another channel of communication between DDR&E and the services was provided by the military assistants working with the Deputy Director (Strategic and Defensive Systems). While the role of these officers varied, they tended to act as the services' representatives within DDR&E. The Navy officer was someone who had served with SP; the Air Force officer sometimes came from BSD and sometimes from the technical side of the Air Staff.

The foregoing has indicated that an examination of the MIRV innovation can focus almost exclusively on the Secretary of Defense, DDR&E, SP, BSD, the Air Staff, and the supporting contractors of both services. This establishes the boundaries for the discussion that follows.

CONCEPTION AND PROPOSAL

Of the many possible ways of separating the innovation process into distinct phases the one used by James Q. Wilson seems to be most appropriate for an organizational (as opposed to an economic or purely technical) analysis. He distinguishes between conception (or invention), proposal, and adoption of an innovation.[23] For a technical innovation, the conception phase must involve matching a technology to a desired outcome, a military mission in the case of a weapons innovation. Awareness of a new technology without linking it to a particular mission is no more the conception of a technical innovation than is understanding the importance of a particular mission without linking it to a capability for its realization. The proposal phase involves suggesting the innovation to whomever in the organization (be it an individual, a committee, a component of a formal hierarchical structure or an informal coalition) with the power and resources to authorize the innovation. In the MIRV case that means the Secretary of Defense, acting through DDR&E, and whatever part of each service that was relevant for decisions on such matters. The adoption phase may be a rapid and simple decision by an authorizing agent or, more usually, may last for some extended period of time and include the process of advocacy and consensus-building. The precise nature of this phase depends in large measure on the organization's structure and determines the ease with which the innovation is eventually adopted.

From the point of view of its mission MIRV is an evolutionary advance over multiple warhead systems conceived and designed in the late 1950s and early 1960s.[i] Although each reentry vehicle could not be separately targeted with these early systems, the addition of such a capability was a rather obvious extension of earlier designs and earlier mission concepts. The missile could then act like an unmanned aircraft, dropping bombs on several different targets, or could use its added flexibility to penetrate opposing missile defense systems. Technically as well MIRV required only evolutionary advances in subsystems

---

[i]These early multiple warhead systems are described in Appendix A.

and components available or foreseen in the early 1960s.[j] But neither the availability of the technology nor the awareness of the mission requirements alone can be considered the source of the MIRV innovation. Only by associating one with the other could MIRV be invented.

This point is frequently missed by authors who assume that MIRV was nothing but an inevitable result of the inexorable march of new technology or an obvious solution to the problems of penetration.[k] Those who in the early 1960s were considering a test of reentry vehicle vulnerability to nuclear effects by using a bus to accurately position a reentry vehicle in proximity to a live nuclear device cannot be considered inventors of MIRV. They were dealing with the same technology but for a different purpose. Those like Albert Wohlstetter and Henry Rowen who were aware of the military advantages of a MIRV system,[l] but who, although generally aware of the technical problems and feasibility, did not actively seek to match the mission concept to technical realization, cannot be considered inventors either.

By 1963 the need for both improved penetration capability and more warheads was widely felt in the technical community dealing with strategic missiles. By then, too, technical advances in a variety of areas made the idea of a maneuvering bus seem readily feasible to many people in that community. Because of the extensive mobility of individuals and the rapid diffusion of information and ideas within the technical community each specialist was aware of developments and needs in related areas. The penetration people who were busy designing decoys and deployment mechanisms for a multiple warhead and decoy system knew the prognostications about guidance and warhead size, and the weapons and guidance people understood the problems faced by the decoy designers. All shared the common objective of improving American strategic missiles and were adept at arguing for their favorite programs in terms of current intelligence estimates.

MIRV was invented almost simultaneously by several individuals and groups within the technical community. In the course of interviewing for this study, five quasi-independent inventors of MIRV were discovered: Ernst Krause of Aerospace Corporation and Glenn Kent, Air Force Military Assistant to the Deputy Director (Strategic and Defensive Systems) of DDR&E, working together; engineers of Autonetics Division of North American Aviation, the guidance contractor for Minuteman; Allen Dean of STL; Richard and Albert

[j]The early technical precursors of MIRV are described in Appendix B.

[k]Herbert York, for example, traces in some detail the technical strands and mission requirements that led to MIRV but does not provide any insight into the process of innovation in either its personal or organizational dimensions.[24]

[l]At the American Academy of Arts and Sciences Summer Study on Arms Control in May 1960 Wohlstetter and Rowen both argued that mutual deterrence based on a small number of ICBMs might not be as stable as other participants claimed because of the possibility of multiple independently targetable warheads. Neither were subsequently involved with efforts either to design or to gain acceptance for such a capability.[25]

Latter of the physics department of RAND Corporation; and engineers at Lockheed Space and Missile Company, the system contractor for the Polaris missile. The precise degree of independence is difficult to determine. Since the technical community involved in such activities is quite circumscribed and has excellent modes of communication, there may have been some undiscovered and even unrealized cross-fertilization.

Although technical organizations of the services have as strong an institutional and financial incentive to seek technical innovations as do outside contractors, in fact, in the area of strategic missiles the service organizations have usually relied on the greater resources of their supporting contractors and consultants to generate new ideas. In the case of MIRV the five identified inventors were all external to the service development organizations.

Krause and Kent first considered the concept of a maneuvering bus in 1962 as a mechanism to deploy decoys in a convincing manner. Aerospace engineers and DDR&E had become aware that if an unguided and unstabilized platform deployed both live reentry vehicles and decoys, the trajectories of the decoys would be so distinguishable from those of the reentry vehicles that the defense could simply ignore the decoys. To solve this problem, a process known as spy-proofing, both reentry vehicles and decoys would have to be accurately positioned on specified trajectories. A guided and maneuvering platform was envisioned for this purpose. Because reentry bodies from the same missile could be employed to exhaust a missile defense system so long as their arrival times were sufficiently separated that a different interceptor had to be used to attack each one, a platform with that purpose had only to maneuver within the plane of the trajectory. Such a device could also then provide the added benefit of being able to move the reentry packages far enough from the heavier burned-out third stage that the large radar cross-section of the latter would not assist the defense in locating and tracking the reentry packages.

The transition to a platform that could also maneuver out of the plane of the trajectory and that could therefore be used not just to deploy decoys but also to deliver multiple warheads was a small additional step, both conceptually and technically, but one with a high payoff. It was taken almost immediately. The combination of in-plane and out-of-plane maneuvering would permit optimum coverage of a large target and be an even better countermeasure against ballistic missile defense. Such a system would be much less vulnerable than the Polaris A-3, the spacial separation of whose warheads was so constrained by the requirement that they all impact within the area of a city that one exo-atmospheric interceptor with a large warhead could destroy all three. Actually, since interceptors were more difficult to harden against nuclear effects than reentry vehicles, given sufficient precision, a group of reentry vehicles could be positioned close enough that an exploding interceptor would destroy other interceptors, but not more than one reentry vehicle. If great enough cross-range and down-range maneuvering capability were available, the system could also be used to attack multiple targets tens or even hundreds of miles distant from each other. That would be a true MIRV bus.

Through the influence of Kent and Krause others in DDR&E and Aerospace also became convinced that MIRV was the direction to move with Minuteman. Some BSD personnel must have been informed about this possibility as well. But the concept was still new and neither fully formulated nor well thought through. The expectation of eventually developing MIRV does not seem to have contributed to DDR&E's decision to interrupt the industry competition for the Mark 12 reentry vehicle in 1962. The inadequacies perceived to exist in the Air Force designs were reason enough in themselves.[26] Although more advanced technically, the large version was not sufficiently dissimilar from the Mark 11, recently authorized for Minuteman II, and it could not be carried in a multiple mode. DDR&E wanted a reentry vehicle small enough that the then-programmed missile could carry three of them, or two plus decoys, to full range.

During this same time period, and apparently independent of the Aerospace-DDR&E considerations, Autonetics and Rocketdyne Division of North American Aviation conceived a bus as a product improvement for the Minuteman system. In early 1963, company-funded feasibility studies were initiated to examine placing a hypergolic propulsion system on the guidance wafer, in order to trim out third stage thrust termination uncertainties and to deliver decoys with precision. Aeronutronic Division of Philco-Ford, one of the firms intending to bid in response to the previously-cancelled request for proposals for the Mark 12 reentry vehicle, expected that the revised request would include specifications for a deployment mechanism as well as the reentry vehicle. In order to strengthen its position on that part of the competition Aeronutronic collaborated with Autonetics and Rocketdyne, beginning about April 1963. The concept that emerged from this collaboration provided for in-line deployment of multiple reentry vehicles, with a growth potential for a MIRV with relatively small footprint.[27]

When the second request for proposals was issued for the Mark 12, specifications for a deployment mechanism were not included. Aeronutronic presented a responsive proposal, excluding the bus concept developed with Autonetics. Although Aeronutronic considered submitting an unsolicited proposal for the bus, the idea was dropped when it was announced in October that General Electric had won the Mark 12 contract. Autonetics, on the other hand, did submit an unsolicited proposal for such a bus in August 1963. Industry sources claim that this proposal stimulated BSD to seriously consider such a capability.

The October 1963 contract to General Electric included, besides the development of the Mark 12 reentry vehicle itself, studies of its use with decoys and various deployment mechanisms. As General Electric's studies went forward that fall a similar effort was initiated at STL. Allen Dean looked at a variety of ideas that had been generated, including those from General Electric and

Autonetics, and concluded that, with some minor alterations in the current Autonetics guidance package, both the guidance and propulsion systems could be put into the same unit that carried the reentry vehicles, resulting in a true maneuvering platform. In February 1964 BSD convened the Mark 12 Task Group, consisting of TRW, BSD, and Aerospace personnel to examine these issues. At the first meeting of the Group, Dean presented his proposal. After a series of discussions the Group concluded that "penaid deployment accuracies, and spy proofing would require a bus (called Post Boost Control System PBCS)."[28] Its deliberations and report served to launch the MIRV concept within BSD.

Totally different considerations led Drs. Richard and Albert Latter of the Physics Department at the RAND Corporation to consider the use of multiple independently targetable warheads. They were not seeking potential improvements to American missiles, but were concerned about possible future threats from the Soviet Union. In an October 1962 RAND memorandum, Richard Latter discussed the military implications of the Soviets' achieving some sort of accurate multiple warhead capability. The technical concept contained in this paper was not a maneuvering bus, but the possibility of replacing single reentry vehicles "with a cluster of small, one-stage missiles with self-contained propulsion and guidance."[29] This idea was later called Precision Ballistics or P-Ball. Latter's paper caused a considerable fuss within RAND over the feasibility of the P-Ball concept. The memo was temporarily withdrawn, but regenerated under the title "Some Arguments for AICBM," RAND Corporation Memorandum 3517 PR, August 1963.[30] In the meantime, a May 1963 paper by Richard Latter that discussed areas of concern with respect to the Limited Test Ban Treaty also considered the possibility that the Soviets might split up the large throw-weight of their missiles into a number of smaller reentry vehicles and direct them at separate Minuteman silos. These papers were said not to have received wide attention outside of RAND and not to have been taken seriously. However, they did provide a background for the more influential attempt of Dr. Albert Latter to sell the idea of a true maneuvering bus soon after.

In August 1963 Secretary McNamara and DDR&E Brown both testified before the Senate Foreign Relations Committee concerning the Limited Test Ban Treaty. Both stated that despite remaining uncertainties about the vulnerability of the hardened Minuteman silos to nuclear explosions, the number and dispersal of the silos would assure their survivability.[m] Albert Latter, an op-

---

[m]Secretary McNamara stated in part: "the most pessimistic view of these uncertainties [about U.S. vulnerability, Soviet accuracy and others] suggests a vulnerability ratio for our hardened, dispersed Minuteman sites of less than two sites killed on the average by a single very large-yield Soviet missile. It is clear that the Soviets do not have anything like the number of missiles necessary to knock out our Minuteman force, nor do they appear to have any present plans to acquire such a capacity. If they were to undertake the construction and deployment of a large number of very high-yield missiles, we would probably have knowledge of this and would have ample time to expand our Minuteman force, or to disperse it more widely."[31]

ponent of the Limited Test Ban Treaty, was very concerned that this testimony did not reflect the feasibility of an accurate multiple warhead system. He was, of course, familiar with Richard Latter's paper discussing the potential vulnerability of the Minuteman force if the Soviets used modular payloads and individual guidance, as well as the papers on the P-Ball concept. However, his own conception at this time was a bus vehicle rather than P-Ball. Since he apparently came to this concept independently, Albert Latter too should be called an inventor of MIRV. In fact, he is widely, but incorrectly, thought of as *the* inventor, probably because he was particularly active in advocating the idea. Dr. Latter checked the feasibility of such a bus with engineers at Autonetics and found that they had been thinking along similar lines and did not foresee any real difficulties. He then communicated with DDR&E Harold Brown trying to persuade him that the Soviets could deploy MIRV and that the vulnerability of Minuteman was potentially greater than the testimony had suggested. Although Brown was already aware of the potential for MIRV, Latter's mentioning it to him probably strengthened his interest in it.

More important was Latter's opportunity to suggest MIRV to the commander of BSD several months later. Evidently BSD was unhappy with the preliminary results of Project Forecast with respect to missile developments.[n] This was true despite briefings provided to Forecast which included, among other advanced concepts, multiple warheads and MIRV.[33] BSD Commander General W. Austin Davis, therefore, requested and received permission from General Bernard A. Schriever, Commander of Air Force Systems Command, to conduct a separate study, called Project 75.[o] When General Davis asked his Division Advisory Group for suggestions of things to include in Project 75, Albert Latter, who was vice chairman of the DAG, suggested MIRV. At this point his major concern was still whether the Soviets could build such a system and threaten the Minuteman force. Whether Davis, himself, had heard of the MIRV concept already is not quite clear, but it seems likely. Latter's suggestion, however, was not the only input to Project 75 that included MIRV. Heavy reliance was placed on Aerospace personnel[35] and they were also interested in including the MIRV concept. Moreover, BSD solicited ideas from industry for Project 75 and Autonetics provided, among other things, their thoughts on precision deployment of multiple objects. Like Autonetics and Aerospace, BSD was interested in MIRV primarily as a potential improvement to the Minuteman

---

[n]"Forecast was initiated in 1963 by the Secretary of the Air Force and the Air Force Chief of Staff; General Bernard A. Schriever, Commander of the Air Force Systems Command, was assigned overall project responsibility. The effort in the words of General Schriever, met the Air Force requirement 'to identify the technological opportunities during the next ten to fifteen years and relate them to national security objectives'."[32]

[o]"Project 75 specifically examined ballistic missile capability of the Air Force over the next decade. The effort detailed the capabilities of the currently programmed ICBM force, the short- and long-term improvements that can be made to extend the useful life of current missile systems, various advanced missile system concepts, and the technological advances which can be achieved."[34]

force, not as a possible Soviet threat. The study "supported the feasibility of MIRV, and called it an attractive concept for the current and future ICBM development. [It] recommended that ABRES be augmented and include [a] study of MIRV designs for Titan II and Minuteman."[36] Project 75 marks the full commitment of BSD to MIRV and its initial attempt to propose its adoption.

In May 1964 the Payload Task Group, a follow-on to the earlier Mark 12 Task Group and comprised almost entirely of the same individuals, was convened by BSD. Operating through the summer of 1964 it dealt with the Mark 12, the Mark 17, and a smaller competitor, the Mark 18. It recommended that the Mark 12 be used in a MIRV configuration[37] and provided the concrete technical basis for subsequent BSD advocacy of such a system. Thereafter BSD's efforts were directed to selling the program to the rest of the Air Force and to securing funding from DDR&E. Initially it was hoped that MIRV would be ready for inclusion in the missiles to be deployed in the sixth and final Minuteman wing.

The fifth invention of MIRV, at Lockheed Missiles and Space Company, was made somewhat later and totally independent of these Air Force personnel and contractors. Lockheed engineers were trying to design a reentry system for Polaris missiles that could not be easily destroyed by an exo-atmospheric X-ray warhead. Like the Air Force contractors, they found a solution in a series of objects spaced in time aimed at a single target. In order to deploy reentry vehicles and decoys in that fashion and to take account of the large variability in missile range associated with a mobile platform, they determined that the guidance equations would have to be solved for each object and that a maneuvering bus would be required. These thoughts were made known to the Special Projects Office in 1963, but unlike its counterpart in the Air Force, SP did not readily adopt and support the new concept. Studies had been in progress on the B-3, a follow-on missile to the A-3, almost since the A-3 was authorized.[38] MIRV could have become the design configuration for the front end of this missile, but in fact it did not. When SP proposed a new missile development to DDR&E in the fall of 1963, two front end options were envisioned, neither of them a bus. The first was similar to the A-3, with three reentry vehicles each carrying a 600 kiloton warhead.[P] The other was a reversion to the design of earlier missiles with one large warhead.

Unlike BSD, who already had a design and a commitment for funding from OSD for their next missile, the Minuteman II, and could therefore concentrate on details, such as the nature of the front end, SP was more concerned with other matters. The major technical issue of 1963 was how large the missile should be. Overdesign of the shock mitigation system to protect the

---

[P]Despite the belief of some naval officers who later became part of the Great Circle Group within the Long Range Planning Group that the B-3 was designed to have a single warhead, SP seems to have been considering multiples from the beginning.

Polaris missiles in their launch tubes permitted a major increase in the diameter and therefore in the range/payload characteristics of the new missile. SP came in with a design for a 66-inch diameter missile in 1963. Both Brown and McNamara, however, felt that if a major investment were going to be made in a new submarine-launched missile, an even larger missile should be designed. The design was therefore sent back to SP, with authorization in November 1963[39] to begin concept definition of "the largest Polaris missiles that could be launched from the submarines under procurement."[40] Although one objective for this new missile was increased range compared with the Polaris A-3 (and therefore decreased vulnerability of the submarines while within firing distance of their targets), Rear Admiral I.J. Galantin, Director of SP, was reported to say in November 1963, "The range is not as valuable to the submarine system as it is to a fixed system, so it's the payload and how we slice it [that matters]. And we haven't settled upon where we'll put that extra capability."[41] Within DDR&E, the interest was not nearly so much with the increased range that the larger missile could provide as with its increased payload.

The key political issue confronting SP in 1963 and 1964 was the opposition of the rest of the uniformed Navy. The rapid development and continuing deployment of 41 Polaris submarines and three generations of missiles had been widely perceived as a large drain on the Navy's budget and manpower for years. Since Polaris did not contribute to any of the Navy's traditional missions, many officers strongly resented the apparent cuts in their favorite programs for its sake.[q] With the end of the submarine construction and A-3 procurement in sight, everyone hoped and expected that there would be a respite for several years. When the B-3 was proposed by SP, therefore, the rest of the uniformed Navy, not surprisingly, was not very receptive. The Navy secretariat was also not enthusiastic, although they were not really opposed.

While SP was aware of the MIRV idea in 1963, it was too concerned with other more pressing problems to give it great attention. Moreover, SP has always tended to be technically conservative and to run a low-risk program. Unlike the development organizations in the Air Force that were renowned for their infatuation with fancy and expensive hardware, SP has preferred to stress the ability to deliver a reliable system at cost and on time. These two organizational factors, preoccupation and technical conservatism, prevented SP from becoming an early advocate of MIRV.

DDR&E, on the other hand, was clearly thinking along such lines for the new missile, as demonstrated by the order issued before the end of 1963 to make the Mark 12 reentry vehicle compatible with Polaris.[43] As it turned out, this requirement for inter-service commonality played an important role in

---

[q]Although the McNamara budget-makers claimed that Polaris was not taken out of the Navy's hide, and that all other Navy programs were judged on their own merit, independent of either Polaris or budget totals, almost no one in the Navy seems to have believed this.[42]

convincing SP that it should adopt MIRV. From the outset SP opposed commonality because the Mark 12 was not optimized for the needs of a submarine-launched missile and because it threatened to remove an important part of the missile from the direct control of SP.[r] The result was an unrelenting search by SP for a substitute. Their own particular version of MIRV eventually served that purpose.

MIRV was originally conceived by the technical and industrial community that supports the service missile organizations and was suggested to these organizations and to DDR&E by this community. Because it was not viewed as a new weapon system, but only as an improvement of one that was already authorized or being planned, it was able to advance quite far in conceptual design without receiving explicit authorization from either the services or DDR&E. Unlike a new bomber or a new missile system which requires substantial funding and the Secretary's authorization before it advances very far, MIRV moved through its early stages purely on the initiative of the technical community.

From all appearances this would seem to be a common phenomenon for qualitative improvements to strategic systems in the 1960s. Most aerospace industries were prosperous; money was not hard to find either from their military clients or internally to carry a new idea through its preliminary development. As one Air Force officer who ran a several-million-dollar office at BSD in the early 1960s reported, project directors had considerable freedom in how they spent their money and for every dollar they gave out they could expect a matching dollar of industry's own funds. Examples of industry initiative are easy to provide from the history of MIRV. The Thiokol Chemical Corporation was said to have advanced designs of a new Minuteman third stage as early as 1963. Autonetics and the Instrumentation Laboratory were reported to be continually suggesting to DDR&E and the services improved components for the Minuteman and Polaris guidance systems. Their development of advanced components was encouraged and funded by the Air Force. General Electric continually pushed against the state of the art in reentry vehicles and in doing so worked very closely with Aerospace and the ABRES program. Engineers at Singer-General Precision, Kearfott Division, invented and then sold to DDR&E a greatly improved stellar inertial guidance concept for use on Poseidon.

One could argue that the technical and industrial community is rather self-serving when they invent, propose, and initiate the development of unsolicited new systems in the hope of receiving funds to pursue them. On the other hand, these activities provide an excellent means for alerting the services and OSD to new technical opportunities. Certainly through most of the 1960s there was a broad consensus of opinion in the United States that such a

---

[r]The Air Force and General Electric were also opposed to commonality because it made the development program of the Mark 12 more difficult and more expensive.

mechanism was desirable and perhaps necessary to guarantee the adequacy of American strategic forces in the face of Soviet advances. An early, and still appropriate, statement reflecting this role of the military R&D scientist was made by Amron Katz in November 1948:

> By the time the armed services know they want something, it is needed at once. Research can never be really a short-term process; and the only way to have the products of research *ready and on time*, is to keep an eye to the future, follow carefully the long-range military plans, and do vigorous research on the fundamentals that are likely to be needed in connection with the kinds of devices that appear to be likely necessaries to the long-range military plan.[44] (emphasis in original)

In this view the research scientist must anticipate future military needs and prepare the groundwork so that the need can be satisfied when recognized. Only more recently has the other side of this process been recognized, namely that in doing this the technical community can generate a requirement and sell a weapon that might otherwise have been needed only later, or not at all.

The likelihood that industry will generate and propose new ideas to the service technical organizations certainly depends in part on the availability of funds and therefore on the structure of contracts and the degree of control exerted by budget offices on the contracting agents. But it also depends on the organizational environment within which these activities take place. Much greater organizational complexity and diversity of both task structure and incentive system existed within the Air Force technical community consisting of BSD and its supporting contractors than within the comparable Navy technical community centered around SP. BSD relied more heavily on outside consultants, had a looser and less centralized management structure, was less concerned with efficiency and pursued more projects simultaneously than SP. These organizational characteristics of the Air Force technical community are among those that have been identified by Wilson,[45] Hage and Aiken,[46] and others as being conducive to a high rate of conceiving and proposing innovations.

It is not surprising therefore to find that of the five identified inventors of MIRV four were associated with the Air Force community and only one with the Navy. The rapid acceptance of MIRV by BSD and its subsequent proposal to include MIRV in the Minuteman II and the failure of SP to recommend the same for its B-3 can be partially understood on the basis of the same structural characteristics. Perhaps as important however was the technical conservatism of the management of SP and the technical optimism that characterized BSD and the fact that SP was struggling to win acceptance of its new missile while BSD had already been assured funding for Minuteman II. SP, and through it the Navy, only accepted MIRV after the technology was more advanced, the existence of its new missile was assured and pressure was brought to bear from outside. Nonetheless, for strategic weapons systems, as much as for any technology, the organizational structure of the technical community out of which innovation must emerge is an important determinant of the rate at which innovations will be conceived and proposed.

BUILDING THE CONSENSUS

Adoption of the MIRV idea for use in Air Force and Navy strategic missiles did not happen immediately after the initial proposals were made. A period of consensus building was required before SP's reluctance to adopt MIRV and much of the Air Force's opposition could be overcome. For the Navy, since almost no one outside of SP was very interested in such details as the front end of the new missile, consensus-building really meant reaching agreement between SP and DDR&E. This is to be contrasted with the Navy's very great interest in and opposition to the missile itself that resulted from anticipated adverse effects on the Navy's budget. Within the Air Force the consensus building for MIRV was more complex. The Strategic Air Command and the Air Staff were very interested in what payload their missiles carried and did not favor a Mark 12 MIRV. Although DDR&E had the authority to impose its will on the Air Force as far as weapons programs were concerned and BSD, the executing agent, would have fully supported a ruling in favor of MIRV, in practice the rest of the Air Force had to be brought along or bought off. Through 1964 and 1965 improvement in MIRV-related technology, changes in the political and strategic environment and DDR&E's willingness to fund a larger warhead gradually weakened the opposition of the Strategic Air Command and the operational part of the Air Staff. Eventually they too became strong supporters.

   Air Force resistance to MIRV is difficult to document precisely. No public evidence could be found at all, and information conveyed in interviews was somewhat contradictory. One advisor to the Secretary of Defense suggested that there was no opposition to MIRV from responsible people in the Air Force. This is contradicted by one high level officer and one member of the Air Force secretariat, both of whom felt that MIRV had been forced on the Air Force by DDR&E and Systems Analysis. There is little doubt that such important individuals as Chiefs of Staff LeMay and McConnell, and Assistant Secretary McMillan opposed MIRV in its early stages. The Strategic Air Command and those parts of the Air Staff closest to it in orientation also resisted for some time. The more technical sections of the Air Staff, while skeptical at first about the accuracy projections for MIRV, appear in general to have favored the program more strongly and earlier than their operational counterparts.

   There were four major grounds for opposition to MIRV within the Air Force. The most important was probably the preference of many Air Force officers, particularly in the Strategic Air Command, but including

Generals LeMay and McConnell, for large rather than small warheads.[5] In part this preference derived from a rather general feeling resulting from the formative training of many senior Air Force officers in the strategic bombing campaigns of World War II and reinforced by the massive retaliation strategy of the 1950s that bigger was better. In part it reflected a desire to have weapons able to destroy Soviet land-based missiles even after they were hardened. In part, too, it was a reaction to the Soviet tests of very large weapons in the early 1960s. Warhead size had been a contentious issue during the initiation of the Mark 12 program in 1962 and remained so for years. DDR&E agreed in 1963 to fund the Mark 17 at a later date largely in order to reduce Air Force opposition to the small Mark 12.[48] Still, many Air Force officers and civilians resented the fact that the small Mark 12 had been funded preferentially to a larger warhead. Since the MIRV system would use the Mark 12, it was opposed, or at least resisted, by those in the Air Force who preferred large warheads.

Closely connected to the matter of weapon size was delivery accuracy. Given the Air Force commitment to counterforce strategy by the early 1960s, including but not limited to the destruction of hard targets, the use of small warheads would be acceptable only if very precise accuracy could be achieved. The bomber generals, including the top leadership in the Air Force, generally distrusted all claims made about missiles. They and other non-technical officers were reluctant to rely on a complicated gadget to guarantee target kill. Technically-oriented personnel with more faith in the capability of inertial guidance systems were willing to accept the existence of a yield/accuracy trade-off and were not opposed to small yields in principle. However, there was initial skepticism about the optimistic projections of accuracy improvements that came from the technical community and were accepted by BSD. Until they were convinced that these projections were likely to be met, even many technical Air Staff officers were reluctant to support MIRV.

There was also a feeling within the Air Staff that supporting MIRV would have hurt the Air Force's case for a very large Minuteman force. The Air Force was arguing in this period that its target list could not be covered by only 1,000, 1,200 or even 1,300 Minuteman missiles and that many more were needed. A rapid acceptance of MIRV, and the resultant increase in available warheads would have weakened the case for more missiles. This was indeed an important argument for MIRV within OSD and the view which prevailed. Only as the Air Force became fully convinced during 1964 that its case for more Minute-

---

[5]General LeMay stated his interest in large weapons very clearly in 1964:

The Air Force has always been interested in higher yield weapons in the early days because of the economy of fissionable materials. You could get more megatonnage out of the big explosions than you could the smaller ones. It was more costly to build the smaller ones.

Lately we have been interested in higher yield weapons (deleted). I think that we can probably get by with what we can do in the high yield field now, although I personally would like to go up to one hundred megatons or more, or have the capability of getting there rapidly.[47]

men was hopeless did it turn to MIRV as the only available option for increasing the number of warheads.

The last cause for opposition to MIRV was the pervasive problem of resource allocation between Air Force missiles and aircraft. Those who thought that spending for strategic missiles was taking money that should be spent on aircraft were naturally apprehensive about a new technical development in the missile field that would again take scarce research and development sources and then require major expenditures for deployment of another new missile.

The concerns about accuracy and cost were reflected in the discussion that lasted well into 1965 about the relative merits of MIRV, with a maneuvering bus dropping off reentry bodies, and P-Ball, which included a separate guidance and propulsion system on each reentry vehicle. The argument for separate guidance was that greater accuracy and reliability would be achievable. Its problem, however, would be greater cost. P-Ball also did not help deliver decoys. As the intrinsic accuracy of MIRV guidance began to look better through 1964 and into 1965, the extra cost of P-Ball gradually caused it to be dropped as a serious option.

Since MIRV had been accepted very rapidly within BSD, there was neither the time nor the necessity for the emergence of individual advocates within the technical community. Just the opposite was true at the policy level within the Air Force. Stimulated by the rather considerable resistance there, an advocate emerged[49] who was able to confront the arguments against MIRV directly. This advocate was Glenn Kent, who left DDR&E in July 1965 to become Deputy Director of Development Plans in the Office of the Deputy Chief of Staff, Research and Development. Kent's arguments were twofold. First, in a target-rich environment and with a force that was seen ever-more-clearly as being limited to about 1,000 missiles, the Air Force would be better off with multiple warheads. This was especially true since most targets were soft and could be easily killed by the Mark 12, even without requiring accuracies that seemed difficult to achieve. This formulation of the counterforce mission became a major argument for a mixed force of Mark 12 MIRVs and Mark 17s. Second, Kent pointed out that for systems with equivalent accuracy, the silo kill probability lost by moving to smaller warheads would largely be regained by the increase in numbers.[t] This latter argument was

---

[t]This argument is based on the fact that the probability of kill of a hardened silo can be expressed approximately by

$$P_k = 1 - \exp - (c\frac{NY^{2/3}[F(Y)]}{CEP^2 H^2}),$$

where N is the number of weapons aimed at the target, Y is the weapon yield, $F(Y)$ is a function that expresses the sensitivity of silos to the longer overpressure pulse of larger weapons, CEP is the circular error probable (the distance from the target within which one warhead has a 50% chance of landing), H is the target hardness, and c is a constant determined by the units employed. For fixed CEP the important factor is $NY^{2/3}F(Y)$. Decreasing the size of warheads, therefore, can be partially compensated by increasing the number of available warheads. Because $F(Y)$ can become important for large yields, however, the degree of compensation depends importantly on the yield range being considered.

largely not accepted by operationally-oriented officers. Some were said to argue that the accuracy of the two systems could never be the same, if only because of the greater effects of winds on the lighter warheads. (Actually this effect is probably very small.) Others pointed out that the greater effectiveness of large warheads due to their greater sustained over-pressure pulse was very important and should not be traded for increased numbers of smaller weapons dependent for their effectiveness on uncertain accuracy improvements.

Besides the growing awareness in 1964 that the size of the Minuteman force would really be held at 1,000, several other changes in the environment began to tip the scales in favor of MIRV. Primary among these was the renewed deployment of missile defense installations observed in the Soviet Union. Since MIRV was understood to be the best available means of penetrating a Soviet ABM system, this intelligence information strengthened the position of the MIRV advocates. Particularly within OSD in 1964, the major arguments for MIRV shifted from force economy and coverage of a large target list to ABM penetration. These considerations gained increasing weight within the Air Force as well.

Also in 1964 a design for an even smaller warhead was introduced into the defense community by the weapons scientists. Early that year Livermore Laboratory announced that a very small, high yield-to-weight warhead could be built. Thereafter the weapons community took advantage of all available opportunities to emphasize its feasibility and suggest its adoption. One important opportunity was in a report of the Scientific Advisory Board Nuclear Panel dated June 1964 called "Review of Advances in Design of Multiple Warhead Possibilities."[50] This report was written by Albert Latter, then chairman of the panel. It strongly recommended that both the Minuteman and the anticipated Polaris B-3 be equipped with MIRV employing the small warhead. It was taken to Deputy Chief of Staff for R&D General James Ferguson and then to Harold Brown.[51] Viewed as an attempt to sell the small warhead, this effort was a failure. Brown apparently had no intention of authorizing another major warhead and reentry vehicle development. The small warhead, which came to be called the Mark 100 and later evolved into the Air Force Mark 18, was recommended by the TRW/BSD/Aerospace Payload Task Group,[52] and was also taken as a baseline component for MIRV systems by the Pen-X study.[u] It thereby achieved legitimacy through the support of the technical community. Most of the Air Force, particularly the Strategic Air Command, thought the

[u]Pen-X was a major study conducted over a seven-month period by the Institute for Defense Analysis. It involved representatives of the entire defense community, over 150 people in all, at one time or another. The final report, August 1965, "concluded that small multiples (called Mark 100) were highest confidence, offense conservative, approach to defeating terminal defenses [and] advocated small multiple development for Minuteman and Polaris/Poseidon."[53] This study also helped establish the problem of penetration as the central strategic issue of the mid-1960s. It was said to have received the attention of McNamara, Brown, and other defense decisionmakers.

Mark 100 was, as one defense official expressed their view, the "world's worst idea." But since the Mark 12 was larger and more acceptable than the Mark 100, the increased prominence of the latter may have cast the Mark 12 as a compromise and thereby increased its acceptability for the Air Force. A series of other studies and reports concerning MIRV during 1964 helped to bolster the program within the Air Force. None of these was very important in itself but they were each a part of the gathering momentum pushing the community toward consensus. The previously mentioned SAB nuclear panel report raised the possibility of MIRV at a higher level in the Air Force and it reached DDR&E as well.[v] The SAB Guidance and Control Panel also discussed MIRV in two reports during 1964, "Feasibility of Multiple Independent Re-entry Vehicle Concept," September 1964 and "Multiple Independent Re-Entry Vehicles," December 1964.[54] No doubt these reports suggested the feasibility of MIRV guidance and they probably had some impact on the continuing debate on that subject within the Air Force. Project Blue Dart, an Air Force study dated August 1964, also urged development of MIRV for Minuteman.[55] During this same period the background work associated with Pen-X provided a major source of technical design studies of MIRV systems.[56]

The interested contractors were by no means inactive during 1964. Early in the year Autonetics became acquainted with General Electric's studies of a deployment mechanism for the Mark 12. By June it was under subcontract to General Electric to provide engineering data on the Autonetics/Rocketdyne bus concept. The next month Autonetics was placed on contract directly with BSD to study the Post Boost Control System in depth. A final report from this work was endorsed by the Payload Task Group. Also in July STL received a contract to study guidance requirements for a MIRV system.[57] General Electric was evidently unaware that support within the Air Force technical community had swung sharply away from decoys and toward MIRV until the summer of 1964 when the company went before the ABRES Reentry Committee to discuss the results of its nine-month study of penetration aids and deployment mechanisms. The committee was strongly opposed to decoys and favored the use of multiple warheads. By this time General Electric was recognizing the problems implicit in the requirement to deploy reentry vehicles and decoys in a spy-proof manner from an unstabilized platform. Their suggested solution was to place a second guidance and control system on the deployment platform. On hearing about General Electric's problem and proposed solution, Aerospace engineers

[v]There seems to be considerable disagreement over the importance to be attributed to this report. Several members of the panel and others in the weapons community credit it with jarring the Air Force and DDR&E into action on MIRV. They seem to be unaware that DDR&E and BSD were already committed to the MIRV concept and were gradually moving in that direction. Senior Air Force and DDR&E officials denied that this report was of any particular importance in the decision to initiate development of MIRV.

suggested placing the missile's own guidance and control system on the front end and adding a propulsion system, thus producing a true Post Boost Control System.

Also during the summer of 1964 a Pentagon study team went to Norton Air Force Base to review the status of the Minuteman II program. At this point the Mark 12 reentry system, with mutliple reentry vehicles and penetration aids was still programmed for deployment in Wing 6 with the first Minuteman II missiles. However the Mark 12 program was experiencing delays and probably would not be ready in time for Wing 6 deployment. As a result of the report filed by this study group, the decision was made to deploy the Mark 11A on Wing 6 instead of the Mark 12. This freed the Mark 12 program from the severe time pressures of the Minuteman II program and permitted its reorientation to MIRV.

By budget time in 1964 BSD was quite impatient to begin development of MIRV. With the reduction in opposition from the rest of the Air Force, and the momentum of the ongoing industry studies, BSD felt ready to seek funding. A major effort was undertaken to sell the program to the Strategic Air Command and DDR&E.[58] Within OSD circumstances were propitious. Increased concern about Soviet ABM development and the apparent need to compensate the Air Force for the cutback in programmed Minutemen made MIRV appear very attractive. At the same time pressure was growing on DDR&E to fund the Mark 17, as promised the previous year. This is reflected in a review of the warhead by BSD and a study by Glenn Kent, dated January 1965, advocating a mixed force of Mark 12s and Mark 17s.[59]

The decision was made by DDR&E and Secretary McNamara to fund in FY 1966 the Mark 12 MIRV for retrofit onto Minuteman II. The General Electric contract for the Mark 12 reentry vehicle was reoriented to include a MIRV deployment mechanism and in July 1965 Autonetics received a design and development contract for the Post Boost Control System.[60] Both to placate the Air Force and to provide a counterforce capability for the Poseidon missile, the Mark 17 was also provided initial funding, although at a much lower level. Although the resistance of the Strategic Air Command and its allies, including the Air Force Chief of Staff, to small warheads had not disappeared by the end of 1964, it had greatly weakened. They were willing to go along since DDR&E's promise to fund the Mark 17 was evidently being fulfilled. So long as the Air Force did not strongly object to the MIRV development, the decision of the Secretary, supported by DDR&E and BSD, was final.

Air Force reservations faded even more during 1965, partially as a result of General LeMay's retirement. More important, however, was the growing realization that with the size of the Minuteman force officially frozen at 1000 silos, and with the refusal of OSD to fund a new manned bomber despite the draw-down in the operational force, MIRV was the only way to get more warheads into the force. In fact without MIRV the number of warheads programmed for future forces would have decreased. Two other essential elements were the steady improvement in accuracy projections for a Mark 12 MIRV, and the gradual acceptance within the Air Force that accuracy improvement could indeed compensate to some degree for reductions in yield. The Mark 17 development also continued to move ahead and the goal of a mixed force of Mark 12s and Mark 17s seemed assured. The growing importance of penetration capability as the Soviets appeared to be moving toward a large-scale ABM deployment also played a role, although a less important one, in the Air Force's acceptance of MIRV. It has even been suggested that the Navy's adoption of MIRV for Poseidon in 1964 helped to weaken the residual resistance within the Air Force. By mid-1965, when the decision was made to fund procurement of MIRV, the Air Force was solidly behind it, and by 1968 when the Mark 17 was cancelled, there was apparently no concern that Minuteman's counterforce capability would be significantly jeopardized.

In order to illustrate the growing commitment to the bus concept within the Air Force technical community and DDR&E during this period, it is interesting to note that another bus, called the Sequential Payload Delivery System, was authorized at about the same time.[61] This was for use in ABRES to shoot various reentry packages to the Kwajalein test site as part of the Re-entry Measurements Program Phase B (RMP-B).[62] Aeronutronic won the contract in late 1965[63] by underbidding the competitors, General Electric and AVCO, in what has been called an unsuccessful attempt to buy into the MIRV market.

For the Navy MIRV program the issues were quite different. The new missile itself, not the front end, remained the primary focus of attention for all concerned. Since development of hardware for the front end had a shorter lead time than either the propulsion system or the guidance and navigational changes,[64] some of the decisions concerning it, such as what warheads would be carried, could be deferred. Nonetheless 1964 was also the year of decision for Poseidon MIRV.

The major effort in Special Projects during that year was directed to designing a 74-inch missile and obtaining the authorization for full-scale development. The latter task involved overcoming the still-strong resistance in the Navy to another major commitment of development and procurement funds to the strategic mission. To SP such a commitment was crucial to its continued existence as a separate entity.[65] Even the year's delay resulting from OSD's direction to redesign the missile caused organizational problems. In order to maintain the momentum of ongoing programs, SP broke its own guidelines as a single-mission organization and accepted responsibility for the Deep Submergence Systems Project (DSSP) in June 1964. Sapolsky reports that

> ... since the technologies involved in deep ocean research were somewhat related to the technologies involved in the FBM [fleet ballistic missile] system and since some Special Projects Office

contractors and part of its technical staff were interested in exploring the opportunities such research presented, DSSP provided both a means to keep the FBM team together until Poseidon was approved and a possible follow-on to strategic missile work.[66]

In February 1966, by which time Poseidon was in full development, the DSSP was severed from SP.

In OSD two developments during 1964 led to a willingness to proceed with the new missile by the end of the year. The first was growing evidence that the Soviets intended to begin a major deployment of ballistic missile defense. The other was a desire to increase the counterforce capability of the Polaris fleet. During the preparation of the FY 1966 budget in the fall of 1964, McNamara decided to fund full-scale development of the 74-inch missile, renamed Poseidon or C-3. This was announced by President Johnson in his message to Congress of January 18, 1965.[67] Although this decision had the full support of SP, the rest of the Navy still feared that its other programs would suffer. Despite OSD's assurances that these programs would be judged on their own merits and would not be affected, and probably because of the growing distrust of the McNamara "whiz kids" within the services, the Navy fears had not been allayed. Even Secretary Nitze was not fully convinced that other Navy programs would not be cut to fund Poseidon. He felt, nonetheless, that Poseidon should go ahead. In a series of informal meetings with CNO Admiral McDonald, he managed to break the logjam within the Navy so that the program could move forward.

The decision to include MIRV in the new missile proceeded in parallel to the decision to begin full-scale development, but was much less controversial. The first step was probably a study of penetration techniques conducted by Glenn Kent in early 1964 in response to a request from Secretary McNamara to DDR&E Harold Brown to consider possible American responses to Soviet ABM activity. Among other things this study supported the judgment that the Polaris submarine tubes should be filled completely and recommended modular payload with MIRV capability for the larger missile. These recommendations went to McNamara and came back with his authorization to proceed with such a missile. Within DDR&E the possibility of using MIRV on Poseidon won rapid acceptance, just as the similar suggestion for Minuteman had earlier.

The advantages of MIRV as a means of penetrating Soviet ABM systems was clear to SP. Criticism of the A-3 design had been mounting as the realization grew that it provided insufficient separation to survive an attack by a single large exo-atmospheric interceptor. The use of MIRVs would avoid the same problem with the B-3.[w] MIRV provided two other benefits to SP. The

---

[w]The option of using mechanical separation and enlarging the footprint was not available because of the problem of variable range and because of the limited extent of most targets.

weapons community was disappointed that the Air Force had not solidly supported the small warhead and sought another customer. Two members of the Polaris Steering Task Group, Carl Haussmann, Livermore's spokesman in military applications at the time, and Lloyd Wilson, who as chief engineer of the Polaris program at Lockheed had already been considering a maneuvering bus, made a joint presentation to SP. They observed that guidance and rocket technology were adequate to support a MIRV for the B-3 and recommended the small warhead as the weapon to be used. Admiral Smith and others in SP saw the Livermore weapon as a means of avoiding the Air Force Mark 12 and recognized that for a weapon that small, independent guidance would be necessary. Furthermore SP wanted to accomodate the interest within OSD and the Great Circle Group for improving the accuracy and therefore counterforce capability of the new missile. The only way to achieve the desired accuracy with a multiple warhead system was to use MIRV.

There were several evident advantages, then, in using individually-targetable reentry vehicles rather than the kind of mechanically separated multiples carried by the A-3. These included improved counterforce capability for the missile, the help it could provide to SP in avoiding the use of the Air Force's Mark 12 reentry vehicle and, most importantly, improved penetration of possible Soviet defenses. The decision to place MIRV on the Poseidon was officially conveyed in a directive to SP in November 1964. The same directive instructed the development of an improved-accuracy guidance system.[68]

Despite this decision to include MIRV capability on Poseidon, the question of which reentry vehicle or vehicles would be used was far from settled. OSD still expected to use the Air Force Mark 12 and agreed with some Navy planners that a Mark 17 option should be available to provide greater counterforce capability.[x] Special Projects, on the other hand, was seeking a way to use the Mark 3 instead of the Air Force Mark 12 and did not favor the Mark 17. During 1965, the advantages for penetration of deploying larger numbers of the smaller warhead became decisive. The Pen-X study, for example, had recommended the small warhead for Poseidon as well as Minuteman. The Mark 12 was dropped and replaced by the Mark 3. Nevertheless, the Mark 17 remained an option for Poseidon until 1968.

MIRV was adopted very quickly in the Navy and without opposition. The transition was so rapid that the Navy's Damage Limiting Study, sometimes called Great Circle 1, dated August 1964, did not mention MIRV. A Center for Naval Analyses study dated November 1964 did include it, but only as a hurried addition just as the study was being completed. Once Admiral Smith, Director of SP, DDR&E Harold Brown and Captain Robert Wertheim, the naval military assistant dealing with strategic weapons in DDR&E, were

---

[x]The Mark 17 option is referred to by Mr. McNamara in his FY 1966 Posture Statement. He says, "Alternatively, [Poseidon] could be used to attack a hardened point target with greater accuracy and a heavy warhead."[69]

convinced of MIRV's utility, the issue was essentially settled. Unlike the decision to fund the missile itself, the question was not important to the rest of the Navy (except the Great Circle Group who had little influence but were also in agreement). Most officers in the Navy and part of the secretariat considered the Polaris force and the mission of fighting an all-out nuclear war as an appendage, perhaps an unwelcome one, to their central mission of maintaining strong and combat-ready general purpose forces. They opposed large-scale funding for Poseidon as a threat to their central mission. Once the combined effort of DDR&E, SP and the Secretary of the Navy had overcome this resistance, the rest of the Navy was not concerned about such details as the design for the missile's front end. While the Office of the Chief of Naval Operations, the Assistant Secretary for R&D and possibly one or more of the Navy Bureaus had to sign off on such a decision, their agreement was almost pro forma.

This may be contrasted with the initial opposition to MIRV in the Air Force. Since strategic warfare is one of the central missions of the Air Force and a major item of its budget, decisions concerning strategic forces, including such details as the front ends of Air Force missiles, received attention from many sources. These included offices within the Air Staff and SAC, and to some extent members of the secretariat. Missile front end designs also reflected Air Force priorities for various strategic missions and had important and recognized implications for future force size. The introduction of a new front end could not be accomplished, therefore, without winning the consent of many different power centers within the Air Force. To win this consent took both time and energy on the part of the system's advocates.

The contrast between the speed with which the MIRV innovation was accepted in the Navy once SP was won over and the difficulties of achieving a consensus in the Air Force is particularly striking when compared to the previously-noted higher propensity within the Air Force technical community to conceive and propose the new system. This difference reflects what Sapolsky has called "a basic structural dilemma that makes the combination of creative and innovative organization extremely difficult to obtain."[70] Wilson has cast the recognition of this dilemma into a general hypothesis concerning innovation:

> The greater the diversity of the organization (in either its incentive system or its task structure or both), the *greater* the likelihood that some members will *conceive* major innovations, the *greater* the likelihood that some members will *propose* innovations, and the *less* likelihood that the organization will *adopt* the innovation.[71]

The organizations involved with the Air Force MIRV innovation, including DDR&E, the Air Staff, the Strategic Air Command, and BSD, its contractors, technical managers, and advisory boards, formed a very much more diversified structure than the organizations, namely DDR&E and SP, associated with the

Navy MIRV. MIRV was invented within the Air Force community and proposed for adoption more often and sooner than in the Navy community. The difficulty of achieving its adoption was significantly greater in the former than in the latter.

The strong and continuing involvement of the technical and industrial community is as evident in the consensus-building process for MIRV as it was in the conception and proposal phases. Pen-X, reports of the Air Force Scientific Advisory Board Nuclear Panel and Guidance and Control Panel, and the influence of the Livermore physicists all contributed to the growing momentum carrying the program forward. The ongoing development work at Autonetics and General Electric, including some company-funded development, the collaboration between the two and especially the strong influence exerted by Aerospace and STL over the direction of these efforts were major factors in establishing the feasibility of the MIRV concept.

The close working relationships between the service technical organizations and aerospace contractors is an example of a more general phenomenon, the blurring of the distinction between the private sector and the public sector that has occurred in the United States as a result of extensive government procurement of high-technology goods and services since World War II, especially for the space effort and national defense. Since government agencies have the mission responsibilities and the funds while technical expertise frequently resides in private industry, close cooperation is essential. Although hardware requirements are formally provided by the government contracting agent, they are frequently written by or coordinated with the firm that will eventually be contracted to do the work. Because very few companies exist in the United States that can provide the kind of specialized services and equipment required for a missile system and because the government is frequently the only customer for such products the public agencies and private firms develop a relationship of strong mutual dependence. The consequence is that the government exerts considerable influence and control over the operation and management of many companies and these same companies actually do much of the technical work that is the responsibility of government agencies. The distinction between public and private is even further blurred by the existence of such nonprofit, industry-oriented entities as the Aerospace Corporation that are hired under contract to manage government programs, and by the interconnection of industry, universities, and government agencies through a host of technical advisory committees.

Nonetheless attention must not focus entirely on the service technical organizations, their contractors and advisory structure. DDR&E played a central role in the MIRV innovation. Its effective control over the services' research and development budgets allowed it to encourage its own technical and policy choices and to discourage those with which it disagreed. The use of such leverage appeared repeatedly during the course of this research. The innovation of MIRV itself, especially within the Navy, was in large part the result of a conscious policy choice within DDR&E. The reorientation of the original Mark 12 reentry vehicle contract and the imposition of accuracy improvements in the Poseidon program, both in 1964 and again later when the stellar inertial guidance appeared feasible, were the result of DDR&E directives. Development programs sought by the services, such as the Air Force Mark 17 or the Navy Mark 3, had to be sold to DDR&E or they would not get funded. In short, because of the centralization of management control in OSD during the McNamara era and the Secretary's reliance on DDR&E for both advice and managerial direction of development programs, DDR&E became the center for decision-making authority on MIRV.

But, as important as DDR&E and the technical community were, they could not have advanced MIRV beyond exploratory development on their own. Acceptance by the Secretary of Defense was essential for the initiation of full-scale development. The involvement of McNamara himself, at least as early as 1964,[y] belies any claim that MIRV was the product purely of the technical community. It was just as much a product of McNamara's policy preferences. He saw the Minuteman MIRV as a means of reducing opposition in the Air Force and the Congress to a freeze on the land-based force and a reduction in manned bomber forces. He saw both Minuteman and Poseidon MIRV as a certain hedge against the possibility of a large-scale Soviet ABM deployment and as a system that would increase the available options in the event that deterrence failed.

From the point of view of the Pentagon decisionmakers, the 1964 decisions on MIRV and Poseidon were commitments to active development only, not to deployment. At that point they saw the programs as investments in future options. The development lead times were such that no deployment decision was required, and none was made. Nevertheless there seems to have been little doubt within the services that the systems would eventually be deployed. (On the Navy side this was stated explicitly by Secretary Nitze and CNO Admiral McDonald during the FY 1966 budget presentations.[74]) This is of course why opponents of the Mark 12 in the Air Force and, even more, opponents of Poseidon in the Navy resisted as strongly as they did. Even DDR&E Harold Brown thought that eventual deployment was likely.[z]

---

[y]There is some degree of uncertainty about just how early Secretary McNamara was aware of MIRV and how much attention he paid to it. For example, one source[72] considers Mr. McNamara's testimony before the Senate Foreign Relations Committee on the subject of the Limited Test Ban Treaty to have been a deliberate, although obscured, reference to MIRV.[73] Another source was convinced that if he had been aware of MIRV at that point, he would have been more cautious in his statements about the survivability of the Minuteman force.

[z]He told the House Appropriations Committee:

The decision to deploy is not yet made. But there is a strong presumption that it is a likely decision on the basis of our decision to proceed with a $1 billion development. My own view is that you do not proceed with a $1 billion development unless you think there is a high chance of deployment, and that is the situation.[75]

Once the decision had been made to begin engineering development of MIRV in 1964 support for the programs solidified rapidly. Despite the readiness of the MIRV program for major funding, relatively little pressure had been felt from below in 1964 and the decision to go forward had been taken primarily on the initiative of OSD. This was no longer true in 1965. Systems Analysis felt strong service pressures that year as it moved gradually toward authorizing deployment. The following summary by Herbert York is only a slight overstatement: "The decision to deploy MIRVs was made all but inevitable by the decision to develop them."[76] Although stopping the MIRV program became increasingly difficult after the decision to initiate engineering development, deployment was not quite inevitable. Had McNamara or his successors wanted to stop MIRV, and had they been willing to invest the time, energy, and political capital to overcome strong resistance from the services, DDR&E, and probably Congress, they might have been able to do so. McNamara did kill the B-70 and hold off Nike-Zeus and its successor for many years. However, neither McNamara nor any other official with sufficient authority had any interest in retarding the MIRV programs.

SOMETHING FOR EVERYONE

The task of tracing in detail either the development of a new idea, its gradual acceptance or the manner in which it transforms previous institutional practices is always very difficult. When the idea occurs to several different people in different places, but at about the same time; when these people are all part of a limited technical community that enjoys excellent communications; and when the adoption of the idea appears to demand only an incremental change in institutional practice, the task is probably impossible. Since these circumstances are those that exist in the case of MIRV, it is likely that the story presented in this chapter is incomplete. However, the central concern here is not so much with recounting history, as with understanding it. For that purpose the story is complete enough.

The most striking characteristic of the process that led to the MIRV innovation is the speed and ease with which it operated. The program proceeded about as fast as technology would allow. This is not because the technical community was given free rein to do what it pleased, but rather because all relevant centers of authority, including the Secretary of Defense, rapidly came to think that MIRV was a desirable system. Those who did not totally share this belief were soon won over, like the operational side of the Air Force, or were excluded from the decision-making process, like the Arms Control and Disarmament Agency (ACDA). In its formative years MIRV was a program that contributed to the objectives of all organizations and individual decisionmakers that participated in the innovation process.

To SP, BSD, and the technical community MIRV provided a

challenging new development effort and a means of extending their programs beyond the missiles then authorized. It also offered a solution to the technical problems involved in providing a high-confidence and cost-effective means of penetrating ABM systems. To the rest of the Air Force MIRV was a way of increasing the number of deliverable warheads, thereby permitting coverage of the expanding target list generated by the counterforce strategy, and freeing the large warheads for use against hardened targets. Eventually the Mark 12 MIRV even began to look attractive as a hard-target killer in its own right. It provided a war-fighting capability for precise surgical strikes against military targets within or near urban areas and for symbolic countervalue attacks against dams, nuclear facilities or other nonurban but important targets. Furthermore, the targeting flexibility of a MIRV bus would permit the use of nuclear weapons in precise and variable patterns for maximum effectiveness against a range of targets and the option to cross-target, that is to aim weapons from different missiles at the same target, would increase the overall reliability of the force.

In OSD the target flexibility, counterforce and war-fighting capability were desirable attributes of MIRV, but its usefulness as a hedge against the possible deployment of a large Soviet ABM system became more important. McNamara and his cost-conscious Office of Systems Analysis found MIRV particularly useful in their struggles to restrain the growth of the size and budget of the strategic forces. As Deputy Secretary of Defense Cyrus Vance wrote in 1966: "A capability to independently target several reentry vehicles from the same booster provides a substantial advantage in use of missile inventory, in flexibility of force operations, in penetration capability and cost."[7]

These perspectives are quite different and in some cases opposed. But it mattered little whether the different power centers could agree on underlying policy or priorities so long as they were unanimous in support of initiating and continuing development. That they were.

Chapter Three

Bureaucracy, Strategy, and Politics

Nowhere in official statements about MIRV do responsible officials, either military or civilian, suggest the very important role of the technical and industrial community in the process of innovation that was the focus of the previous chapter. In the budget statements of the President, posture statements of the Secretary of Defense and congressional testimony or public statements of defense officials, MIRV is explained in strategic terms and as a reaction to actual or possible actions by a potential enemy. There are probably two fundamental reasons for this reliance on strategic justifications for nuclear weapons policies.

First, senior government officials who bear a responsibility for the security and defense of the nation really are concerned with planning and procuring military forces that will enhance national security and otherwise serve the national interest as they perceive it. Broad questions of how best to structure the nation's military forces and how to provide a diplomatically valuable and militarily useful posture have real meaning to these officials. Whether they favor one or another type of strategic doctrine will, over time, influence the force structure. The strategic preferences of uniformed officials and less important civilian officials influence force planning as well. In developing any nuclear delivery system there are trade-offs among such variables as survivability, reliability, ability to penetrate defenses, deliverable megatonnage, accuracy, and cost. Choices must be made, sometimes at the DDR&E level, but often by the service technical organizations in conjunction with their contractors. To some extent the preferences of the current Secretary of Defense will percolate through the system and determine how these choices are made. But the preferences of the technicians and the services themselves will always be argued for and will sometimes win out.

Second, public officials are accountable to Congress and the public for their actions. They therefore feel obligated and are expected to justify their actions and expenditures according to some notion of national interest. This is true even when bureaucratic and political considerations have actually dominated a particular decision process. Public disclosure of internal bargaining or political maneuvering could both damage an official's credibility as a guardian of the public good and provide ammunition for his political opponents. Similar considerations apply for internal justifications oriented toward superiors and other bureaucrats rather than the public. Air Force officers, for example, simply cannot argue that they want a new manned strategic bomber because they prefer to fly planes than to sit in missile silos, or because the aerospace industry has all sorts of fancy aircraft designs and avionics that it would like to develop, or (even though they may strongly believe that the vitality of their organization is essential to the defense of the nation) because otherwise the Strategic Air Command's proportion of the Air Force budget or the Air Force's proportion of the defense budget would decline. Instead they must argue that the nation needs manned bombers for its defense, that building a new bomber would be more cost-effective over the long run than continuing to repair the old ones, and that all the fancy gadgetry is essential if the bomber is to perform its mission in the face of possible enemy countermeasures. No matter how important parochial interests actually are in determining policy, internal and public justifications must be made on the basis of national interest. This was particularly true in the McNamara Pentagon where the influential Office of Systems Analysis required that systems be justified on cost-effectiveness criteria to meet a given strategic objective.[1]

Strategic argumentation is certainly one of a number of techniques that bureaucrats regularly employ in the continuing competition for scarce resources. Any successful bureaucrat or administrator understands this role of argumentation, probably has used it that way himself, and strives to discover hidden as well as stated motivations of others, especially of those to whom he must allocate resources or with whom he must compete for resources. Nevertheless the degree to which strategic argument is used for advocacy can easily be overemphasized. The current tendency among students of the American weapons acquisition process is to consider either bureaucratic politics or the direct and indirect influences of the military-industrial complex as the primary determinant of weapons decisions. To do so incorrectly denigrates the importance of individuals in decision-making positions, their strategic preferences and views of the world, and their responsibility to determine policy according to their perception of the national interest. Politics, strategy, and bureaucratic bargaining, as well as technical opportunity and intelligence information all interact and contribute to the determination of weapons choices. In the case of MIRV, until about 1968, all these factors were mutually reinforcing.

STRATEGY AS BUREAUCRATIC ARGUMENT

The previous chapter emphasized the dependence of the Navy Special Projects Office (SP), the Air Force Ballistic Systems Division (BSD), and their supporting industrial contractors on a continuous stream of new missile developments in order to maintain their organizational vitality. The technical orientation and training of the personnel of these organizations tend to provide a professional incentive for an interest in new technology. As one engineer from a service technical organization suggested, although people may argue over whether improved accuracy is good or bad, in practice his organization sets accuracy goals based on what available technology can support at a reasonable cost. Organizations staffed by engineers and scientists, whether they are in the government or outside contractors, must provide new challenges in order to maintain morale and prevent a rapid turnover of personnel. When the end of one project is in sight, the organization will try to find another to replace it. Moreover, any official in the Office of the Secretary of Defense (OSD) to whom the health of the technical community is important will be sympathetic to these institutional pressures and to some extent be influenced by them in his policy decisions.[2]

Although everyone concerned with weapons development understands these realities, only rarely are they publicly expressed.[a] Instead, strategic arguments must be adduced or created by the services to justify their programs. In 1964, for example, the Mark 12 Task Group realized that the MIRV system it was developing could not be justified by any existing mission requirement. Its members made a conscious effort to find a strategic rationale. Counterforce targeting and growth of Soviet missile forces provided the solution. MIRV could be justified by the need for greater target coverage. Later that year, when BSD formed a series of panels[5] to prepare arguments to sell the MIRV program, strategic as well as technical considerations were included.

The technical community that supports the services must also provide strategic justifications for its technical suggestions. The Air Force Scientific Advisory Board Nuclear Panel's report, "Review of Advances in Design of Multiple Warhead Possibilities," of June 1964, argued that Livermore's small warheads would aid the counterforce mission by covering the large target list and would contribute to penetration by exhausting an opponent's ABM system. The weapons designers at Livermore Laboratory also felt obliged to generate strategic arguments to help them sell their small warhead. That, at least, was the interpretation given by a RAND Corporation expert on discrimination techniques of an invitation he received to brief the Livermore community on the advantages of using small multiple warheads rather than decoys to penetrate ABM systems.

---

[a]One instance when this concern became a public issue was during the debate over the Limited Test Ban Treaty.[3] In fact,

> the maintenance of modern nuclear laboratory facilities and programs in theoretical and exploratory nuclear technology which will attract, retain and insure the continued application of our human scientific resources to those programs on which continued progress in nuclear technology depends ...[4]

was one of the four safeguards on which the Joint Chiefs of Staff insisted in order to give their support to the Treaty.

The appropriateness of the strategic arguments is also important. In 1964 MIRV could be justified as a means of performing the counterforce mission, but by 1965 counterforce had taken second place to penetration as the major concern of the Secretary and his staff. From then on, MIRV had to be sold as a penetration device. This change in rhetoric meant neither that MIRV had become any less useful in fulfilling the requirements for counterforce nor that the Air Force and some people in DDR&E were any less interested in its counterforce capability. Although the service development organizations and the outside technical community can talk technology among themselves, when requesting approval of a new system from OSD they must argue not only that the system is technically feasible or even that it is cost-effective compared with other alternatives to perform a particular mission, but also that it fulfills a strategic mission that the decisionmakers consider important. Requiring that budgetary requests be justified in strategic terms should increase the leverage of senior decisionmakers over the bureaucracy below them and make the outcomes more responsive to their own preferences. McNamara and his Systems Analysis staff certainly realized this and tried to exploit it. Although they may sometimes have been successful, this technique would have been irrelevant in the MIRV case. It could be legitimately justified by any of the major strategic missions. Minor changes in the hardware development programs could accommodate major changes in the supporting arguments.

Organizations also use strategic arguments to seek organizational autonomy and to engage in or avoid roles and missions fights with competitive organizations. This may be well illustrated by examining the changes and variation of the strategic views within the Navy. During the B-36/Supercarrier debate of 1949, a Navy spokesman argued: "We consider that strategic air warfare, as practiced in the past and as proposed in the future, is militarily unsound and of limited effectiveness, is morally wrong, and is decidedly harmful to the stability of the post-war world."[6] By "strategic air warfare," at other times called atomic blitz, the Navy meant Air Force bombing from high altitudes using its proposed B-36, which would, of necessity, only be accurate enough for the destruction of urban-industrial or, in more recent terminology, countervalue targets. Instead the Navy advocated tactical air forces such as those carried by aircraft carriers, to be used for defense, for logistics, to attack military forces, and to provide air superiority. The arguments were clearly designed to strengthen the Navy's case for continued appropriations for naval air power against the expanding budget and strategic mission of the Air Force epitomized in the B-36.[7]

By the early 1960s the Navy's position on countervalue strategy had reversed.[8] Under the influence of SP, which was for many years almost the only part of the Navy that worried very much about strategic forces issues, the Navy was satisfied to have the Polaris force threaten only the enemy's urban-industrial centers. Not only did the combination of submarine navigation and guidance inaccuracies of this period and the use of relatively small nuclear warheads rule out the employment of Polaris for attacks against an opponent's strategic forces, (the counterforce mission), but SP also sought to avoid a direct confrontation with the Air Force, which by that time had appropriated the counterforce mission to itself. The Air Force was correctly perceived as the major opponent of the Polaris system. SP felt constant opposition as the Air Force sought more funds for its own strategic programs, total responsibility for the strategic mission, and operational control of all long range ballistic missiles.[9] Rather than confront this continual challenge, SP decided, especially in light of the Navy's stinging defeat in 1949, to take a low profile and avoid controversy if possible. Protecting the program and the organization's autonomy was the primary objective.

In order to avoid challenging the Air Force's highly-prized counter-force mission in the early 1960s, the Navy supported what was later called the strategy of assured destruction. "Assured destruction" is the shorthand term for the ability "to deter a deliberate nuclear attack upon the United States or its allies by maintaining at all times a clear and unmistakable ability to inflict an unacceptable degree of damage upon any aggressor, or combination of aggressors—even after absorbing a surprise first strike."[10] The degree of damage judged to be unacceptable to the Soviet Union was destruction of 20 to 25 percent of its population and 50 percent of its industrial capacity.[11] To fulfill this objective forces must be available to permit the attack of urban-industrial targets. The invulnerability of the submarine missile force made it a very high-confidence retaliatory capability and thereby, in SP's view, the ultimate defender of the nation's security. SP was said never to have set a technical goal that went beyond the assured destruction role. Both SP's initial lack of enthusiasm for the accuracy improvements that McNamara and DDR&E sought for Poseidon in 1964 and its opposition to the Mark 17 can be partially explained by this self-imposed restriction. One Naval officer associated with long-range planning for the Polaris force in the middle 1960s even suggested that SP had made a deal with the Air Force not to try to gain a counterforce capability.

Admiral Miller, head of the Great Circle Group within the office of the Chief of Naval Operations, and his staff were dissatisfied with the assured destruction strategy and did not share SP's desire to avoid a fight with the Air Force over the counterforce mission. They were reported to have been disappointed that SP did not deliver (purposely, it was claimed) a missile accurate enough for counterforce. In a series of studies, especially those dated August 1964 and November 1965 (known unofficially as Great Circle 1 and Great Circle 2), this group argued the merits of sea-based strategic forces. Sea-based missiles were said to have the advantages, among others, of mobility and invulnerability: they could make the Soviet's defense problem more difficult by attacking the Soviet Union from many different directions and would not attract enemy fire to the continental United States. For damage limitation, defined as the ability, "should deterrence fail and a war occur, to limit damage to our population and industrial capacity,"[12] the Great Circle Group argued the advantages of mid-course interception using sea-based interceptors and claimed that the shorter flight time of sea-based missiles relative to ICBMs gave them intrinsic advantages for destroying time-urgent targets.[13] These arguments were used to justify funding of Ballistic Missile Ships for the deployment of an ICBM on a surface ship, of the sea-based anti-ballistic missile intercept ship (SABMIS) and of counterforce options for Poseidon.[14]

The officers of the Great Circle Group realized that in order to expand the strategic role of the Navy they would have to take on the Air Force in a roles and missions battle. They were willing, even eager, to do so. But they could never overcome the unwillingness of Special Projects and the reluctance of most of the rest of the Navy to seek expansion of the strategic role, especially once the maintenance and modernization of their general purpose forces was hampered by the more pressing needs of the Vietnam War.

While SP's commitment to assured destruction partially reflected a real strategic preference of many of its officers, SP's Director, Admiral Levering Smith, was reported not to share this preference. On one occasion when there was no risk of confrontation with the Air Force, but support from OSD was at stake, SP clearly reversed itself. When interest in enhancing the counterforce capability of American forces first led OSD to explore the possibility of an accuracy-improvement program for the Polaris B-3 missile, SP cited a very high cost if a particular target objective was to be met. Much of this cost was for instrumenting the test range so that the accuracy of test missiles could be determined. While OSD wanted the accuracy improvements, it was unwilling to spend as much as SP specified. As a compromise, a couple of hundred million dollars were added to the Poseidon development program with the understanding that the accuracy improvements would be sought through a series of changes in specific subsystems, including the fire control system and the submarine navigational system, as well as the missile guidance,[15] and that they would be considered a development *goal*, not a *requirement*.[16] Privately, however, SP made its contractors aware that they should make every effort to meet the accuracy goal. While this is inconsistent with the supposed commitment of SP to a pure assured destruction strategy, the inconsistency was not apparent to the former SP officer who discussed it. The senior management of SP was evidently more interested in building support for the new missile than in rigorously holding to the no-counterforce dictum. It was felt to be in the long-term interest of the program to respond to the pressures for accuracy improvements.

Another way that SP used strategic argument was to preserve its technical independence. Since the early days of the program SP had tried hard to avoid relying on Air Force technology. Its unwillingness to use Air Force hardware had played an important role in the origins of the A-3 triplet warhead system[b] and led to its opposition to the use of the Air Force Mark 12 on

_____
[b]On this point see Appendix A.

Poseidon. Not only did the Mark 3 reentry system improve Poseidon's penetration capability, the argument that persuaded OSD of its value, but it also helped SP rid itself of the Mark 12. The same objective of avoiding Air Force reentry systems contributed to SP's resistance to the Mark 17 option for Poseidon, but in that case justification revolved around the counterforce issue: initially that a counterforce option should not be included in Poseidon and later that the Mark 3 system with the improvements in accuracy provided sufficient counterforce capability.

Of the ways in which strategy was used in the MIRV programs for bureaucratic purposes, namely program advocacy, expansion or protection of roles and missions, and maintaining organizational and technical independence, the last two have been illustrated only with Navy examples. The Air Force of course had been quite willing to engage in bureaucratic fights over the strategic roles and missions with both the Army and the Navy in the period when jurisdiction over long-range missiles was still unsettled.[17] When the early fights subsided, the Navy had managed to secure a strategic system for itself, but the Air Force had achieved the dominant strategic role. The onus, therefore, for challenging the status quo lay with the Navy. When that challenge was made, as it was with the expanded role of Poseidon, the Air Force responded, some say, by letting the cancellation of the Mark 17 go unchallenged and thereby undermining Poseidon's counterforce pretensions. The greater organizational and technical commitment to strategic weaponry within the Air Force shielded BSD from challenges to its technical independence and organizational autonomy. Because of its variety of ongoing programs BSD had greater involvement in reentry vehicle and missile technology than SP. This included its control over the ABRES program, which was supposed to support both services, but in practice was dominated by BSD personnel and interests. It seemed very natural for DDR&E to ask, the Navy to use a somewhat modified Air Force reentry vehicle. SP, unlike BSD, had constantly to differentiate its technology from that of the Air Force and to be on guard against Air Force encroachment on its own programs.

STRATEGY AS IDEOLOGY

While there can be no doubt that the military services regularly use strategic arguments to further their organizational goals, it is just as true that such arguments also reflect an honest concern for the welfare of the nation. Just as for anyone else, the belief structure of military men tends to reinforce their sense of professional importance and to justify their career to themselves. Just like all other participants, in the strategic debates since World War II military men believe that their own views are based on sound analysis and represent what is best for the nation. Their strategic preferences form the basis for individual action and thereby influence organizational policy. They form an ideology with respect to which policy choices can be assessed.

During the late 1950s and early 1960s the Air Force gradually abandoned its strategy of "optimum mix," which meant attacking a combination of military and urban-industrial targets, for the strategy of counterforce.[18] Many Air Force officers became persuaded that the only legitimate military mission for the strategic forces was actually fighting a nuclear war, primarily by engaging and destroying an enemy's war-making capacity. Threatening to destroy his society may be of central political importance as a deterrent, but carrying out that threat is of no military value once war has started. If deterrence fails, winning the war and limiting damage to the United States by destroying the enemy's forces should take priority. In fact, many Air Force officers would argue, without forces capable of really fighting a nuclear war and prevailing, the deterrent itself is not credible.

The Air Force, of course, recognized that many of the Soviet forces would no longer be available for attack if the United States used its weaponry only for second strike retaliation. Nonetheless, there would remain important military targets, such as air fields, air defenses, and residual missile forces, including those that could be fired only after the reload of launcher facilities.[c] There also seem to have been some officers in the Air Force who took seriously the possibility that the United States might strike first and initiate nuclear war, perhaps as a response to a Soviet attack on western Europe. Section 3-11 of the Air Force Manual, 101, United States Air Force Basic Doctrine, August 19, 1964, states: "Since we cannot preclude contingencies in which the United States may be the first to initiate the limited use of strategic force, our force posture and general war plans must consider the requirement for both first and second strike operations."[20] To the extent that the possibility of striking first was taken seriously, the forces required to prevent devastating retaliation against the United States, particularly after the Soviets began to harden and disperse their forces, would have been very large.

At least since the early 1960s, the Air Force and the Joint Chiefs of Staff (as well as OSD) have programmed the Minuteman force primarily for the counterforce mission. Certainly urban-industrial centers were targeted, and the Air Force would not have argued against doing so, but with a force the size that the Air Force wanted and even with the one they actually received there were many warheads excess to the countervalue mission that were available for counterforce targeting. One important advantage of the Minuteman force compared with strategic bombers or submarine-launched missiles is the ability to attack time-urgent military targets rapidly and accurately. Despite the decreased emphasis on the counterforce mission for the purpose of structuring the strategic forces during the middle and late 1960s the counterforce targeting requirements persisted. In discussing targeting strategy in 1968 with James T. Kendall, Chief Counsel for the Preparedness Investigating Subcommittee of the Senate Armed

---

[c]Some of the early Soviet ICBM launchers had a reload capability.[19] The denial of a second shot was a central component of the Air Force counterforce strategy.

Services Committee, General Earle G. Wheeler, Chairman, Joint Chiefs of Staff said: "Yes, you attack the urban industrial base, that is the population base and industry, but we also have always held to the view that we must attack those forces of the Soviet Union which are able to inflict destruction on ourselves and our allies."[21] In response to the question "What you are saying is that our war plans do allocate weapons for damage limitation or counterforce," the General replied, "They certainly do."[22]

The attractiveness of MIRV to the Air Force has always been determined primarily by its usefulness for counterforce targeting and other warfighting tasks. Both the original acceptance of MIRV by BSD and the early resistance to it by the Strategic Air Command and much of the Air Staff can be understood, in large part, as deriving from a commitment to counterforce strategy. Although MIRV was originally conceived as a means of assuring penetration of future Soviet ABM systems and this always remained an important asset of the system, its potential for increasing target coverage was immediately recognized and soon became the dominant consideration. The counterforce or "avoid-the-cities" strategy generated a greatly expanded target list compared to that derived from the old massive retaliation or even the optimum mix doctrine. To be included were not only Soviet ICBMs, airfields, air defenses, and nuclear storage depots, but also hundreds of medium and intermediate range ballistic missiles aimed at western Europe. Once this expanded list was actually drawn up in the early 1960s the Air Force saw a need for a very large number of deliverable warheads. But since BSD thought it was likely that the Minuteman force would be held to what the Air Force thought was a rather small number of missiles, MIRV provided the only alternative means of covering all targets. Most military targets were not hard. Even Soviet missiles at that time were deployed primarily in soft or semi-hard configurations. The relatively small Mark 12 warhead, delivered with accuracies foreseen in 1964, was expected to be quite effective against soft and semi-hard targets.

As explained in the previous chapter, the early resistance to MIRV in the non-technical parts of the Air Force derived from several concerns, all of them related to the counterforce mission. These included the possibility that a rapid acceptance of MIRV might damage the Air Force's case for a very large Minuteman force and the worry that the small Mark 12 might not be useful against hard targets. Since many Air Force officers did not understand or were not willing to accept that accuracy improvements could compensate for reductions in weapon yield or simply did not believe that accuracy would ever improve to the point where the Mark 12 would be usable against hardened sites, they insisted that in order to kill hard targets both large warheads and precision accuracy were required. In fact, fulfillment of even some of the optimistic accuracy projections of 1964, when the Soviets were first observed to be hardening their intercontinental missiles, would not have given the Mark 12 a very high single-shot kill probability. Air Force planners tended to assume that just as the United States had hardened its missiles, the Soviet Union would also. They could not see therefore that the Mark 12 would be useful for destroying a Soviet ICBM force projected out five to ten years in the future.

MIRV became more acceptable as its capability to perform the counterforce mission was perceived to be improving. After several years of trying, MIRV advocates, especially Glenn Kent, persuaded the Air Force that it would be better off with a mixed force of large warheads and MIRV than with all large warheads. The Mark 12 MIRVs could be used against the many soft targets, while the large warheads were reserved for hardened missile sites or command posts. Nevertheless, the precise ratio of the mix was always a matter of contention within the Air Force. Left on its own, the Strategic Air Command might have preferred a force of 80 to 90 percent large warheads. Only the presence of funding for the Mark 17 reentry vehicle made it willing to tolerate BSD's favorite, the Mark 12.

Another appealing advantage of the Mark 12, related both to counterforce and other warfighting tasks, was that if used to attack a target near a populated area it would cause less severe collateral damage than larger warheads. The need for a weapon that could be used in surgical attacks was stressed by Project Forecast. Reporting on that study in 1965, General Bernard Schriever, Commander of Air Force Systems Command, wrote:

> Our current intercontinental ballistic missiles are not well enough suited to surgically extracting military targets, with little collateral damage to the surrounding area. New systems must stress very precise target location and on-target controlled delivery.[23]

This is almost certainly a reference to MIRV. With sufficient accuracy, the Mark 12 MIRV could be considered a very useful weapon for such surgical strikes.

With the passage of time, expectations about the accuracy of the Mark 12 MIRV were repeatedly revised in the direction of improvement. No effort was spared in seeking such improvements. Some of the gain resulted from refinement of geodetic data about the location of targets relative to missile launch points. A special series of geodetic satellites were used in order to obtain improved targeting information. Advances in vernier rocket technology and inertial guidance technology contributed as well. Much of the improvement was the payoff from programs sponsored by the Air Force throughout the 1960s at the Instrumentation Laboratory (now called the Charles Stark Draper Laboratory) of the Massachusetts Institute of Technology and elsewhere intended to improve inertial components. The Mark 12 reentry vehicle itself was designed to have a very high ballistic coefficient and would degrade the system's accuracy only slightly.[d] As Air Force Secretary Eugene Zuckert said in 1965 when he was

---

[d] In fact, as test data for the Mark 12 were gradually accumulated, it became clear that, for a variety of reasons, its intrinsic accuracy was less than had been expected.

discussing the choice between improving missile accuracy or increasing warhead yield, "For both economic and technical reasons [the Air Force] would prefer to follow the former course."[24] DDR&E's summary of a major strategic forces study of 1964 projected an accuracy of only 1000 feet circular error probable (CEP) by the mid-1970s. Circular error probable is the distance from the aim point within which there would be a 50 percent probability of the warhead landing. A smaller CEP indicates a better accuracy.

Even though a single Mark 12 with a 1000 foot CEP would have only a 63 to 67 percent probability of destroying a silo hardened to withstand an overpressure of 300 pounds per square inch[e] in a target-rich environment it is clearly preferable to shoot three Mark 12s at three different silos than one Mark 11 or even one Mark 17 at a single silo. For example, if only 500 Minutemen are available to attack Soviet hardened missiles, the use of Mark 12 MIRVs is preferable to Mark 17s as long as there are more than about 535 hard targets to shoot at. This calculation assumes that a 1.5 megaton Mark 17 has a single shot kill probability of 1.0, that the Mark 12 is rated at .64, that Soviet silos are hardened to 300 psi and that the CEP of the missile is 1,000 feet. For a 1,500 foot CEP, a number frequently cited as being close to the accuracy of the Minuteman III in the early 1970s, the single shot kill probability of the Mark 12 is about .36 and the required number of targets goes up to about 1,190, still assuming the Mark 17 has a 1.0 single shot kill probability. The larger the number of hard targets over these breakeven points, the better the MIRV system would be. As the size of the Soviet missile force increased in the late 1960s, therefore, the Mark 12 looked ever more useful as a counterforce weapon. By 1967, when the rapid build-up of the Soviet ICBM force was only a year old, the size of the counterforce target list used for planning purposes had reached about 1,500.[f] Without MIRVs, therefore, the Air Force would have insufficient warheads on its missile force to be able to attack each target once.

---

[e]This single-shot kill probability, and those on which the following computations are based, were read from the RAND Corporation Bomb Damage Effect Computer. The more recently released RAND Damage Probability Computer that takes into account the increase in overpressure pulse duration with yield, would provide better estimates of the single shot kill probabilities. But at this writing the vulnerability numbers and K-factors for hardened silos needed to use the new computer have not been released. There would be relatively little difference in the single shot kill probability for a 170 kiloton weapon against a 300 psi silo. To avoid a possible underestimate of the capability of a 1.5 megaton weapon, the computations given below have assumed it has a 1.0 single shot kill probability.

It is important to point out at this point that single shot kill probability is far from the only important parameter for determining a missile's effectiveness for destroying hardened targets. Missile reliability, including particularly the ability of the guidance system to perform as expected, and, for a large scale attack, the precise tactics employed are also very important. The latter issues have taken on greater importance in the strategic debates of recent years because of the realization that the explosion of some attacking warheads can destroy other, subsequently arriving, warheads. Despite these reservations, single shot kill probability is still an important point of comparison for different systems.

[f]This was the size of the counterforce target list used by the Strat-X study in 1967.

By the time the Mark 17 was cancelled in 1968 most of the Air Force was not unhappy to see it go. Even the Strategic Air Command was reported not to have made a major issue of it. There were several reasons for this. First, given the concentration on the massive attack scenario that dominated strategic thinking during the latter McNamara years and the continuing growth of the Soviet missile force, second strike counterforce no longer looked very interesting. Following the initial Soviet attack, relatively few of their ICBMs would be left at which to strike; and even if the Soviets had tried to minimize civilian casualties in their first assault, their growing force of submarine-based missiles made significant damage limitation hopeless. Certainly planning to allocate one Minuteman missile to each Soviet counterforce target looked very inefficient. Second, the Strategic Air Command's influence over the Air Staff had significantly weakened and new personnel were more receptive to analytical argumentation. Third, funds were short and the expected advantage of the Mark 17 relative to the Mark 11 had significantly declined. Although its ballistic coefficient would be higher, its expected yield had dropped from about 2 megatons to about 1.5 megatons, making it not much bigger than the Mark 11. The latter, moreover, had been found to be "more accurate (and therefore, more effective against hard targets) than earlier anticipated."[25] Finally by 1968 the expected accuracy of the Mark 12 MIRV and therefore its expected single shot kill probability against a hardened silo had significantly improved. General Wheeler told the Senate Preparedness Investigating Committee:

> Generally speaking, we are in favor of the multiple-reentry vehicle program, depending upon, of course, increasing accuracy to give us the desired destruction.

> We believe that you can get a greater destructive power by going to the multiple-reentry vehicles, with the smaller warheads, presuming that we get the accuracies that are predicted [deleted].[26]

General James Ferguson, Commander, Air Force Systems Command, told the same subcommittee that "our projections of the effectiveness and the accuracy of the Mark 12, which is to be on the Minuteman III, were so close [to that of the Mark 17] that we felt that the Mark 17 was an unnecessary undertaking."[27]

In 1968, before the Minuteman III had been flight tested, there was still considerable spread in the projections of its eventual accuracy. But Air Force Secretary Brown made clear that even if the low estimate turned out to be the actual one, the counterforce capability of the Mark 12 would be "as good as what we have now."[28] To be as effective against hard targets as the earlier one megaton warheads, the accuracy of the 170 kiloton Mark 12 would have to be improved by less than a factor of two. Moreover, as General Wheeler pointed out, in the past the CEP of strategic missiles tended to decrease due to further component improvements even after they were deployed.[29] This pattern has indeed been repeated with Minuteman III. So satisfied was the military with the projections for the Mark 12 MIRV that by 1968 General Wheeler was even able to say that an increase in the Minuteman force was not necessary.[30] A similar theme was echoed again on September 22, 1970, when Air Force Chief of Staff, General Ryan, said, referring to the Minuteman III: "this missile, with a multiple independently targetable reentry vehicle, will be our best means of destroying the time-urgent targets like the long-range weapons of the enemy."[31] Especially as scenarios other than a massive urban-industrial attack returned to prominence after 1969 and because of President Nixon's emphasis on nuclear options other than the destruction of populations, the Air Force's interest in counterforce was rekindled. Although far from ideal for that mission in the view of the Air Force, the Minuteman III, with its Mark 12 MIRV, came to be recognized as a rather useful counterforce weapon. It was a major improvement over its predecessor.

Air Force officers certainly appreciated MIRV's usefulness as an ideal ABM penetrator, but this did not seem to have been a major determinant of their attitudes towards it. The Air Force was spending large sums of money to develop penetration aids and electromagnetic countermeasures, to harden re-entry vehicles against nuclear effects and to reduce their radar cross section and reentry time. Most officers seem to have almost taken for granted that Minuteman missiles would get through and that no ABM that the Soviets were deploying or were likely to deploy should be taken too seriously. Compared to the target coverage and hard target considerations, penetration seems to have been of relatively minor concern.

Air Force reaction to the small Mark 18 warhead is indicative of its ranking of priorities.[g] The major advantage of the Mark 18 was its light weight. By placing a large number of these small warheads on offensive missiles, the United States could readily exhaust Soviet ABM defenses. It was almost like putting a weapon inside a decoy, and would have been both more efficient and more reliable than true, unarmed decoys of a heavier reentry vehicle. Had the Air Force really believed that penetration of Soviet defenses was a serious problem it would have been more sympathetic toward the Mark 18. But instead, except for a small number of officers, primarily in BSD, who thought it should be developed, the Air Force reacted very negatively. Not only would much of the missile's payload have been consumed by the packaging structure at the expense of yield-producing material, but also it was simply too small to be tolerable. In a counterforce attack against a 300 psi silo a 50 kiloton warhead would have a single shot kill capability of about 37 percent with a CEP of 1,000 feet. With a CEP of 1,500 feet, however, this would decrease to only about 18 percent. Despite the fact that in a target rich environment even these small single shot kill probabilities might lead to higher effectiveness than if large, single warheads were deployed, it had to be the penetration argument or nothing that

---

[g]Mark 18 was the Air Force designation for a system based on the small warhead that Livermore Laboratory physicists were advocating. The Pen-X study used the designation Mark 100.

sold the Mark 18 to the Air Force. A development program did get underway but was soon cancelled for lack of funds.[32]

The reaction to the small warhead within the Navy was quite different. Since SP considered targeting the urban-industrial centers of the Soviet Union to be the primary mission of the Polaris fleet, much attention was given to how Soviet ABM deployments might reduce its effectiveness. In the 1964-65 period, when both intelligence reports and improvements in American ABM technology put in doubt the usefulness of the A-3 as an ABM penetrator, SP sought to optimize the ABM penetrating capability of its new missile. Unlike the Air Force, the Navy was not bound by a tradition of and commitment to large warheads. Studies in the mid-1950s had indicated the potency of fractional megaton warheads against urban centers[33] and all of the Polaris series missiles had carried warheads smaller than 1 megaton. Carrying up to fourteen small warheads in a MIRV configuration, therefore, did not excite doctrinal disputes in the Navy and was an ideal solution to the penetration problem. By the end of 1965 the Mark 3 reentry system employing the small warhead had replaced the Mark 12 in planning for Poseidon. After a period of design studies a development program was officially initiated in December 1966.[34]

The Great Circle Group and the JCS had a somewhat different view of the optimum configuration for Poseidon. They agreed that the Mark 3 should be used to provide assured penetration of possible defenses, but they also sought a counterforce capability using the Mark 17. Like the Air Force, they preferred a mixed force, with some Poseidon missiles carrying three Mark 17s.[35] Despite opposition to this plan from SP, the interest within OSD in providing Poseidon with a hard target capability kept the option alive for several years. When the Mark 17 was finally cancelled those in the Navy who had wanted the counterforce mission felt betrayed. It was probably at their behest that the Joint Chiefs of Staff protested the cancellation.[h]

At the same time that the Mark 17 was cancelled a development program for stellar inertial guidance was initiated for Poseidon.[i] Stellar inertial guidance could provide a number of appealing options to the system designer. By permitting the missile to fix its position after launch, it could be used either to relieve the stringent requirements placed on the submarine's inertial navigation system, to reduce the missile's CEP, or some combination of these two. In practice it was apparently to be used to improve accuracy. Navy Secretary Paul Ignatius indicated, "During the last year the decision was made to develop [deleted] to increase the accuracy of Poseidon. When these improvements are

---

[h]Deputy Secretary Nitze reported that "The JCS . . . recommended that the option for [deleted] reentry vehicle be retained [for Poseidon.] ." This clearly refers to the Mark 17.[36] The JCS did not record an objection to its cancellation as an option for Minuteman III.

[i]Nitze also reports that "the JCS concur in the development of a [deleted] system for the Poseidon missile," and that he has recommended "development of a more accurate [deleted] system for Poseidon."[37] These are references to stellar inertial guidance.

completed Poseidon will be effective both in the assured destruction role and in attacks against hard targets."[38] The Office of Strategic Offensive and Defensive Systems favored stellar inertial guidance because it could make sea-launched systems as accurate as land-based missiles and, despite the loss of the Mark 17, would still remove the Air Force's unique claim on the counterforce mission. SP, on the other hand, because it did not want to move in the direction of improved counterforce and perhaps because it preferred to use only well-proven technology, agreed to incorporate stellar inertial guidance only because DDR&E insisted.

STRATEGY AS POLICY DETERMINANT

The role of strategy is probably more important at the level of appointed cabinet or subcabinet officials than within the military services. These officials carry the responsibility both for guaranteeing the national security and for spending large amounts of public funds. While they do take account of domestic political constraints and strive to manage the bureaucracies below them, they are also influenced by their belief structure as it relates to strategy and the utility of nuclear forces. They must also consider the actions and possible actions of potential adversaries and face up to the fact that one day they might be called upon to use or to threaten to use the nuclear arsenal. In planning for such a time the President, the Secretary of Defense, and their staffs are unlikely to ignore the insights, incomplete as they may be, that strategic analysis can provide. Their strategic preferences and their perceptions of the national interest, therefore, are important determinants of weapons policies.

Occasionally new development projects are generated directly as a result of a decisionmaker's strategic perspectives. This was the case, for example, with the improvements in command and control, survivability and flexibility, that were introduced into the Minuteman system in the early 1960s. To McNamara, all these were critically important in his search for options between all-out nuclear war and doing nothing in the face of threats or low-level nuclear attack.

More often, however, strategic views are merely one of several criteria that a decisionmaker uses to choose among the vast panoply of programs that continually drift up through the system for his review. Not all new developments suggested by the technical organizations are funded, and even fewer receive adequate political and financial support to be expedited rapidly. Particularly during the annual budget crunch decisionmakers search for programs to discontinue or cut back. Any one of many excuses will do. Technical infeasibility and cost overruns, for example, frequently lead to a program's demise. But strategic perspectives, too, play a role in determining which programs survive and which do not. MIRV was one program that never lacked the strong support from Secretary McNamara and his staff. Although this must be attributed partially to the program's political utility discussed below, at least as important was the extent to which MIRV fulfilled their strategic objectives.

The fundamental objective for the American strategic nuclear forces during the McNamara period and since has been to deter a nuclear attack against the United States or its allies by maintaining nuclear forces that could ride out even a full surprise attack by the Soviet Union and still be able to retaliate overwhelmingly. In his early discussions of how to quantify this objective McNamara concerned himself with both civilian and military targets in the Soviet Union. Later he stressed particularly the ability to destroy urban-industrial targets. In the FY 1966 Posture Statement assured destruction, as this ability came to be called, was singled out as the first priority for the American strategic forces.[39] It has remained so to the present.

There were two sorts of potential Soviet weapons deployments that were perceived during the mid- and late 1960s to have the potential of undermining the American assured destruction capability: an extensive and effective ABM system to protect Soviet urban-industrial centers and offensive missiles of the type and number that might be capable of destroying most of the Minuteman force and strategic bombers in a preemptive attack. Although the desire to maintain a separate deterrent in each segment of the American triad (bombers, ICBMs and SLBMs) generated a concern that either of these actions might separately jeopardize the American deterrent, it was the combination of the two Soviet actions that was most worrisome. The possibility was considered that by means of a preemptive attack, the Soviets would destroy most of the ICBM and bomber forces and those submarines found in port and that their ABM system would then be able to prevent the residual American forces from causing overwhelming damage. If that were possible the American assured destruction deterrent would indeed be in doubt.

MIRV was a superb countermeasure to both of these possibilities. Simply by attacking Soviet targets with sufficient reentry vehicles, MIRV missiles could be certain to penetrate an ABM system. For this purpose MIRV was more reliable and more efficient than decoys, chaff or other penetration aids alone. Deploying more missiles with single warheads could accomplish the same result but at much greater cost. By substantially increasing the number of available warheads MIRV also provided a hedge against the vulnerability of the ICBMs and bombers. Not only would those Minuteman missiles that survived the hypothesized Soviet first strike be able to attack a larger number of targets, but MIRVed SLBMs at sea would, on their own, be able to cover many more targets than would the entire force without MIRVs.

The second major strategic objective of McNamara and his staff was to provide options for using the strategic forces if nuclear war actually broke out, that is, once deterrence had failed. At that point there would be little to gain from actually destroying an opponent's population, and if American cities had not yet been struck there might be much to lose by initiating city attacks. Rather, as McNamara said in June 1962:

The U.S. has come to the conclusion that to the extent feasible, basic military strategy in a possible general nuclear war should be approached in much the same way that more conventional military operations have been regarded in the past. That is to say, principal military objectives, in the event of a nuclear war stemming from a major attack on the Alliance should be the destruction of the enemy's military forces, not of his civilian population. . . . In other words, we are giving a possible opponent the strongest imaginable incentive to refrain from striking our own cities.[40]

This is the counterforce strategy discussed above. Several factors contributed to its espousal by the Secretary of Defense. It was an attempt to convince the NATO allies, particularly France, that American nuclear forces would really be used in their defense. By trying to remove American cities from the immediate risk of annihilation, McNamara hoped to strengthen the extension of the American nuclear umbrella to Europe. It reflected the fact that the United States probably had, in the early 1960s, the capability to execute a disarming first strike against the Soviet Union and the wish of some planners to maintain this capability as long as possible. It was meant to provide an incentive to the Soviet Union to avoid shooting at American and West European cities if nuclear war broke out. If the Soviets knew that the United States had options other than city destruction, they might be willing to exercise restraint. But it was also a statement of the strategic preferences of McNamara and his staff at that time.[41] They seem to have firmly believed that a strategic option to fight a nuclear war without attacking cities and the forces that would permit the implementation of that strategy should be created and maintained.

McNamara soon backed away from the rhetoric of pure counterforce strategy, particularly its first strike aspects. In large part this is attributable to the reaction of the Air Force, which used the counterforce doctrine to justify a long list of programs, including a very large Minuteman force and a new manned bomber.[42] Since McNamara was trying at that time to hold down the strategic forces part of the budget and to build up the general purpose forces, he was not willing to fund the Air Force's requests. Moreover, the Soviets gave no indication that they were willing to go along with "avoid-the-cities." Soviet spokesmen continued to insist that in the event of nuclear war cities would be attacked. Finally, as the structure of the Soviet force changed, counterforce was expected to become increasingly difficult and expensive. In January 1963 McNamara told Congress:

In planning our second strike force, we have provided, throughout the period under consideration, a capability to destroy virtually all of the 'soft' and 'semihard' military targets in the Soviet Union and a large number of their fully hardened missile sites, with an additional capability in the form of a protected force to be employed or held in reserve for use against urban and industrial areas.

> We have not found it feasible at this time, to provide a capability for insuring the destruction of any very large portion of the fully hard ICBM sites or missile-launching submarines.
>
> Fully hard ICBM sites can be destroyed but only at great cost in terms of the numbers of offensive weapons required to dig them out.
>
> Furthermore, in a second strike situation we would be attacking, for the most part, empty sites from which the missiles had already been fired.
>
> The value of trying to provide a capability to destroy a very high proportion of Soviet hard ICBM sites becomes even more questionable in view of the expected increase in the Soviet missile-launching submarine force.[43]

Despite this public disclaimer, McNamara and his staff maintained their interest in second strike counterforce, later subsumed under the more general concept, damage limitation. Through 1963 and much of 1964 a major study of alternative strategies for damage limitation was undertaken throughout the Department of Defense under the overall direction of Glenn Kent.[44] The results of a preliminary pilot study available during the summer of 1963 suggested that under a variety of assumptions about the nature of a major nuclear war, the United States probably would be able to limit significantly the amount of damage it would sustain. This conclusion was reflected in the FY 1965 Posture Statement. Although "it will become increasingly difficult to destroy a substantial portion of the [Soviet] residual forces," McNamara said,

> forces in excess of those needed simply to destroy Soviet cities would significantly reduce damage to the United States and Western Europe. And the extent to which damage to ourselves can be reduced depends importantly on the size and character of our own forces, particularly the surface-to-surface missiles such as Minuteman that can reach their targets quickly.[45]

OSD agreed with the Air Force that nuclear warfighting, including second strike counterforce, should be a primary mission for the Minuteman force. Systems Analysis personnel continued to study various targeting options and remained interested in improving missile accuracy and other means of improving the warfighting capability of the strategic forces. The significant improvements in accuracy and targeting flexibility built into the Minuteman 2 missile were partially a result of these interests in OSD.

There was, however, a gradual shift in emphasis. The Soviets were beginning to deploy more survivable forces. Intelligence estimates predicted that in the future most of their ICBMs would be deployed, like Minuteman, in hardened and dispersed silos. Their submarine-based missile force was also expected to grow and be modernized. These expectations significantly reduced the feasibility of and interest in second strike counterforce.[46] The completed damage limitation study, available in the fall of 1964, argued that although damage to the United States could be limited by buying additional offensive and defensive forces and by a nationwide fallout shelter program, once the Soviet forces were improved, the cost of doing so would be very great. Rapidly decreasing marginal return on investment would set in while the absolute level of expected casualties was still extremely high. Moreover, the cost to the Soviet Union of negating the effect of a given American investment for damage limitation would be considerably less than the cost of that American investment. The study also showed that while targeting one accurate and reliable reentry vehicle on each Soviet offensive missile could have considerable utility, targeting a second would be quite inefficient. Qualitative improvements in accuracy and reliability would be a more cost-effective means of enhancing counterforce capability than buying enough forces to double target.

McNamara and his staff in Systems Analysis seized on these conclusions and used them to argue against the deployment of a missile defense system and expanded bomber defense. The damage limitation study was frequently invoked to support their reluctance to invest heavily in either defensive damage limitation or extensive counterforce capability. The White House evidently agreed with McNamara's approach to strategic force planning. In his defense message to Congress in January 1965 President Johnson stated:

> Any comprehensive program [to limit damage in the event of a nuclear war] would involve the expenditure of tens of billions of dollars. We must not shrink from any expense that is justified by its effectiveness, but we must not hastily expend vast sums on massive programs that do not meet this test.[47]

Qualitative improvements in accuracy and reliability and MIRV, which is both qualitative and, in the sense of numbers of warheads, quantitative received renewed support, becoming a substitute for the deployment of additional Minuteman missiles. The demonstrated utility of being able to target one accurate, reliable warhead against each Soviet silo was an important factor contributing to OSD's decision to seek significant accuracy improvements for Poseidon. Particularly within DDR&E, where control over the budget for missile development programs resided, the view prevailed that any counterforce capability that was relatively cheap should be pursued. But Systems Analysis, while increasingly focusing on penetration capability as the central issue for force planning, did not oppose this approach. As Assistant Secretary of Defense (Systems Analysis), Dr. Alain Enthoven said in 1968: "Once we are capable of performing the assured destruction mission we try to improve the damage limitation potential of our forces. For example, we have gone to considerable trouble to make sure that our ballistic missiles are accurate."[48]

There is no doubt that the assured destruction criterion was less a strategy for conducting nuclear war than a management tool to help in structuring the strategic forces. It permitted the quantification of the nation's strategic requirements and was a means for holding the line against Air Force requests for larger forces. But it in no way constrained how the force might actually be used once deployed. McNamara never said that the forces would not be used in a counterforce mode. In fact, as the previously cited statement of General Wheeler makes clear, the targeting policy did not change with the rhetorical abandonment of a counterforce strategy. The desire for options other than striking cities remained strong although the assessment of how much damage could be prevented by attacking military targets changed very much.[49]

Both the Minuteman and Poseidon MIRV programs contributed to the counterforce and damage limitation missions. Not only did they receive support from OSD partially for that reason but many aspects of the programs were included specifically to enhance this contribution. Although initially very skeptical of the optimistic accuracy projections of the technical community, OSD planners realized that as their target list increased in length, Minuteman MIRV would be very useful for destroying the large number of soft targets, including soft military targets, and freeing the larger Mark 11 or Mark 17 for attacking hardened targets.[50] Later, as its accuracy improved, the Mark 12 was considered, by OSD as well as the Air Force, to be a useful weapon in its own right for attacking hardened targets. As has already been suggested, interest in counterforce led directly to the accuracy improvements and Mark 17 MIRV option for Poseidon on which OSD insisted in 1964. In late 1964 in one of the primary documents of the fiscal year 1966 budget cycle, Harold Brown wrote about Poseidon that technical studies had indicated that significant gains could be made in high-accuracy reentry vehicles and MIRVs. The high accuracy, he wrote, would be very effective against undefended hard point targets, and multiple warhead vehicles could potentially increase the effective size of the force against soft targets or, if the CEP were improved below 1000 feet, even against hard targets. A former senior DDR&E official reported that not only Brown but also McNamara himself had been a strong impetus behind the accuracy improvement program for Poseidon.

While from the perspective of OSD the Mark 17 program was partially an appeasement of the Strategic Air Command and the counterforce faction of the Navy, that is not the entire story. It also reflects the continuing interest in the counterforce mission within OSD. The slow rate of funding, however, suggests that the commitment to it was never strong; it was never more than an option program. When it was cancelled in 1968, it had not yet been flight tested. The Mark 17 was a prime target for cost-conscious budgeteers and was ultimately cancelled largely to save money. But, its strong identification in the services with the counterforce mission made its cancellation both a reflection and a symbol of the decreasing willingness of OSD to fund a program whose primary purpose was counterforce.

The juxtaposition in Deputy Secretary Nitze's congressional testimony of the cancellation of the Mark 17 and the initiation of the stellar inertial guidance development for Poseidon, suggests that the latter was a substitute for the former.[51] While it may have been intended in part as a means to reduce JCS resistance to the cancellation of the Mark 17, some OSD officials, particularly Ivan Selin, Deputy Assistant Secretary of Defense (Systems Analysis) for Strategic Programs, and Dr. Foster, were favoring it as a means of improving the counterforce capability of Poseidon.[52] Although the FY 1970 budget as left by the outgoing Johnson Administration cut back the stellar inertial guidance program, the motivation was almost solely financial. In a tight budget, other things took priority.

The Nixon Administration thought otherwise. Despite a cut in the FY 1970 defense budget of over $3 billion from the Johnson estimates, the stellar inertial program received an increase of $12.4 million to advance the date of the initial operational capability by about six months.[53] Only later, when the FY 1970 defense budget came under scrutiny again, was the program cancelled "in view of the serious fiscal situation."[54] But it seems unlikely that fiscal pressure can be the whole explanation for this cut-back. The amount of money involved was very small in FY 1970, and had it been deemed necessary an equivalent sum could have been readily found elsewhere. Secretary of Defense Melvin R. Laird had made clear earlier that he considered stellar inertial guidance to be "an important program."[55] Its cancellation must be partially attributed, therefore, to the rather strong congressional pressure that year to eliminate accuracy improvements that would improve the counterforce capability of American strategic missiles.

Because American defense officials have tended to disparage the utility of the Minuteman III as a hard target weapon since 1969, it is important to stress here that in earlier years the emphasis was the opposite. As late as 1968, for example, Dr. John Foster and Dr. Alain Enthoven both argued before a Senate Subcommittee that with the accuracies anticipated for the MIRV systems it would be more useful for counterforce than a single warhead on the same missile.[56] It is true that neither Minuteman III nor Poseidon were optimized specifically for the counterforce mission. Three Mark 17s on Poseidon would have made it a much better hard target killer than ten to fourteen Mark 3s. But, as Enthoven pointed out, efforts were made to offset the choice of smaller weapons that resulted from a concern for the ABM penetration mission by significantly improving accuracies.[57] Still, expectations and perceptions have changed. Estimates of the hardness of Soviet missile silos have increased markedly. The problems involved in really carrying out a successful countersilo attack have been recognized to be much more difficult than previously imagined. New technical opportunities in weapons design, reentry vehicle design, and accuracy improvement make the Minuteman III and Mark 12 technology appear rudimentary. Finally, in comparison to the counterforce potential (still far from realized) of the Soviet missile force, the current American systems seem rather paltry. But the fact that, from the perspective of the early and mid 1970s, the first generation MIRVs could not be considered particularly capable counterforce weapons does not alter the fact that through the 1960s as these systems were being developed the perceptions were quite different. The anticipation of significant improvements in counterforce capability was an important impetus for the programs and did influence their design characteristics.

In addition to his interest in limiting damage to the United States and its allies in the event of a major war, McNamara also sought nuclear targeting options other than the destruction of urban-industrial centers that would make the strategic forces more useful for diplomatic and military purposes. Not only did he feel that a flexible targeting doctrine and force posture would contribute to the deterrence of possible Soviet probing in western Europe and elsewhere but he also wanted ways actually to use the strategic arsenal in a militarily significant way if conventional war should escalate into a nuclear war. The credibility of American security guarantees to its allies, McNamara felt, required no less. President Richard Nixon shared these objectives. In the 1971 State of the World Message, he discussed the meaning of "sufficiency" for nuclear weapons:

> In its broader political sense, sufficiency means the maintenance of forces adequate to prevent us and our allies from being coerced. Thus the relationship between our strategic forces and those of the Soviet Union must be such that our ability and resolve to protect our vital security interests will not be underestimated. I must not be—and my successors must not be—limited to the indiscriminate mass destruction of enemy civilians as the sole possible response to challenges. This is especially so when that response involves the likelihood of triggering nuclear attacks on our own population. It would be inconsistent with the political meaning of sufficiency to base our force planning solely on some finite—and theoretical—capacity to inflict casualties presumed to be unacceptable to the other side.[58]

Subsequent messages continued to emphasize this same subject.[59] Shortly after becoming Secretary of Defense, James Schlesinger directed the Joint Strategic Targeting Planning Staff at Omaha, Nebraska, to increase the number of preplanned targeting options and enable the forces to be used in limited strikes for a variety of purposes, including against certain specific categories of targets.[60]

An important aspect of MIRV is the degree to which its introduction into the forces facilitated the sort of targeting flexibility that McNamara, and particularly Schlesinger, sought. Because the MIRVs have relatively small yield and their delivery accuracy is quite good, they enhance the ability to minimize casualties in a large strike if that were desired. They are also very useful for precise, surgical attacks, with limited collateral damage, against small numbers of military, civilian, or symbolic targets. Although the first generation MIRVs did not automatically provide the sort of nuclear options that might be useful for bargaining or for providing the Soviet Union with incentives to avoid the destruction of American urban-industrial centers in the event of war, together with adequate advanced planning and flexible, reliable command and control systems, they did contribute to this objective. Additional advances in system design, both contemplated and in development, will further improve this capability.

THE POLITICS OF MIRV

Besides meeting many of the strategic preferences of Secretary McNamara and his staff, the MIRV programs had significant political utility for them and for the Johnson and Nixon Administrations. In his efforts to keep down the size of the Minuteman force, to refuse funding for the Advanced Manned Strategic Aircraft and to delay the deployment of an ABM system, McNamara met strong resistance from the military and its congressional allies. The MIRV program both helped him in his fights with the Joint Chiefs of Staff and the service bureaucracies and provided a counter to the Administration's defense critics. As Soviet offensive forces grew in number and deliverable throw-weight, and following the signing of the SALT I agreements, MIRV came to be regarded as the capability that maintained American superiority over or parity with the Soviet Union.

Almost immediately upon assuming office in 1961 McNamara rejected the Air Force's requests for a very large number of Minuteman missiles.[61] In his first defense plan, presented with the FY 1963 budget, the programmed number was set at 1,200.[62] Then, for a brief period following the cancellation of Skybolt, an air-launched intermediate-range ballistic missile, the number was increased to 1,300.[63] In the FY 1965 budget it was again put at 1,200[64] and the following year the upper limit of 1,000 was finally established. One can ask about these numbers both why they are so large and why they are so small. In answer to the first question Arthur Schlesinger suggests that internal Pentagon politics probably dominated.[65] Feeling that he could hold out against the military on only so many issues McNamara may have seen a large number of Minutemen as the price for cancelling many other programs in his first few years. There is little doubt, for example, that the increment added to the plan in 1962 was intended to neutralize the military's opposition to the Skybolt cancellation. But that cannot be a full answer. There were real uncertainties in this period about how Soviet forces would evolve. Although the missile gap had turned out to favor the United States, no one could be sure whether or not the Soviets would eventually deploy a very large number of intercontinental missiles. Moreover, as long as a counterforce posture was desired 1,200 Minutemen did not seem to be an extremely large number.

Because the Air Force had wanted many more than 1,000 Minutemen one must also ask why the final deployment was not larger. Even if McNamara really believed in 1961 that he could, as President Kennedy was reported to have directed him, "develop the force structure necessary to our military requirements without regard to arbitrary or predetermined budget ceilings,"[66] he could not escape from fiscal constraints and what has been called the "great equation"[67] of the federal budget. As Crecine has pointed out,[68] although the defense budget ceiling may have been determined in the Pentagon during McNamara's tenure it was nonetheless a reality. In holding the budget to about $50 billion a year from FY 1962 to FY 1965 and in emphasizing general purpose forces in support of an overall strategy of flexible response, McNamara felt he had to restrain spending on the strategic forces. He also recognized that because of the sheer power of thermonuclear weapons, deployment of additional weapons would add little to military effectiveness beyond some point. Instead, he came to think, it would encourage an arms race in which both the United States and the Soviet Union would spend more and more resources without increasing the security of either. In order to hold the line on strategic forces, McNamara and his staff sought to compensate for their refusal to increase the number of missiles deployed by permitting, even encouraging, qualitative improvements. Such features as improved accuracy, reliability, survivability and range/payload characteristics, the ability to launch from airborne control centers and multiple-target storage in each missile[69] introduced with Minuteman II helped McNamara defend the reduction on the programmed force to 1200 in FY 1965. The final reduction in the program, made in the fall of 1964 for the FY 1966 budget, was closely coupled in OSD planning to the decision to begin development of the Minuteman II MIRV. In his FY 1966 Posture Statement McNamara said:

> On the basis of our analysis of the general nuclear war problem in the early 1970s, I am convinced that another 200 Minuteman silos are not required at this time. We now believe that we can markedly increase the "kill" capabilities of the Minuteman force through a number of qualitative improvements which now appear feasible. The Minuteman force presently planned for the Fiscal Year 1970 will have a total destruction capability of at least 30 to 40 percent greater than a force of 1000 Minuteman I. This is equivalent to adding 300 to 400 missiles to a force of 1000 Minuteman I. With the additional improvements that now appear possible, the destruction capabilities of the Minuteman force could be further increased in the future, if that appears desirable, by a factor of two compared with a force of the same size consisting of Minuteman I.[70]

The 30 to 40 percent improvement derived from the Minuteman II program, but the "additional improvements" is a reference to MIRV.

It would be an overstatement to claim that it was the decision to deploy MIRV that permitted McNamara to further cut back the programmed Minuteman force, but it certainly reduced the opposition. By providing more independently targetable reentry vehicles, MIRV would allow the Air Force to cover its growing target list, including semi-hardened and hardened missile silos, despite the cutback. Both Harold Brown and Secretary McNamara responded to congressional criticism of the cutback by explaining that MIRV would eventually be available to greatly improve the capabilities of the 1,000-missile force.[71]

In 1965 the MIRV programs and the missiles associated with them helped President Johnson respond to those who accused him of neglecting national defense and assisted Secretary McNamara in an acrimonious fight with the military. In the aforementioned special defense message to Congress Johnson announced a new program to develop a short range attack missile (SRAM) to be carried by strategic bombers and the Poseidon missile with "a series of remarkable new payloads."[72] At the time of the announcement the missile was still in the early planning stages. Contract definition studies had not yet begun. Special Projects personnel were reported to be quite surprised that the President would not only announce the development program, but also give as many details as he did about the missile's specifications when these were so far from firm. But Johnson had come under severe attack in the 1964 presidential campaign for not doing enough for the strategic forces. Among other charges made by Republican candidate Barry Goldwater was the one that Johnson's Administration had not introduced any new weapon systems.[73] In a *Foreign Affairs* article in January 1965, Hanson W. Baldwin, the military journalist of *The New York Times*, went even further. He accused McNamara and the Administration of cancelling too many programs, not initiating enough, and being hostile to innovative technical ideas.[74] Johnson's special defense message can be seen as an attempt by the President to reply to his critics, to show that he was not neglecting defense. The adoption of a new name, Poseidon, rather than just continuing the Polaris series was almost certainly intended to emphasize the missile's newness and its vast improvement over Polaris and to associate it clearly with the Johnson Administration.

As the FY 1967 defense budget was being prepared in 1965 one of the main issues was whether or not to fund the Advanced Manned Strategic Aircraft (AMSA), a new strategic bomber for which the Joint Chiefs of Staff sought a full commitment.[75] McNamara agreed to fund development studies at a low level, but he refused to commit the plane to full-scale engineering development. Moreover, he planned to retire the 345 B-52 C-Fs over five years and the two squadrons of B-58s in 1971. To replace these, he intended to add 210 FB-111As carrying the SRAM to the remaining B-52G and H squadrons.[76] This decision was strongly opposed by the Air Force and its allies in Congress. Congressional appropriations had consistently included more funds for manned bombers than McNamara had requested. That year he was not only frustrating a strong desire for AMSA, but he was also drawing down the existing bomber force. If not compensated, this would have resulted in a net decrease in the number of deliverable warheads later in the decade. The decision that year to deploy the Minuteman and Poseidon MIRVs facilitated the bomber decisions by preventing the decline of that politically sensitive indicator of force effectiveness. In fact, the MIRV deployments eventually caused it to rise several fold. The decision to deploy MIRV did not turn on this point nor was the refusal to fund AMSA contingent upon it, but the offsetting effect of MIRV was a consciously perceived political advantage. The decisions to delay AMSA, to buy 210 FB-111s, to reduce the number of B-52 and B-58 squadrons, and to deploy both Minuteman and Poseidon MIRVs were packaged in a way that was hoped would reduce the expected clamor over the bomber decision.

The next year the MIRV programs played an important part in the dispute over ABM deployment. McNamara did not want to deploy Nike-X but the development program had by then advanced to the point where he could no longer argue that another postponement of the deployment decision would not delay the date by which the system could be operational. In his FY 1967 Posture Statement, presented early in 1966, he emphasized that the Soviet Union could offset the effect of deploying Nike-X and that "beyond a certain level of defense, the cost advantage lies increasingly with the offense."[77] He nonetheless began to build a case for a light, anti-Chinese deployment.[78] Through 1966 the intelligence reports of Soviet ABM work continued and congressional and military pressure to deploy Nike-X became exceedingly intense.[79] One after the other, in both houses, the Armed Services Committees and Appropriations Committees voted funds for long lead-time procurement.[80] McNamara preferred to resist this pressure, but Johnson was evidently inclining to overrule him.[81]

On November 10, 1966, after a meeting between McNamara, General Wheeler and the President in which McNamara had argued for delay on the decision to deploy Nike-X, he tried in a press conference to decouple the question of Nike-X from that of Soviet ABM deployment. Anticipating that the recently completed national intelligence estimate assessing the Moscow ABM deployment would inevitably become public,[82] McNamara announced that there was "considerable evidence" that the Soviets were building and deploying an ABM system. As a response, he indicated, he would propose to Congress that Poseidon be produced and deployed,[83] thus linking the United States offense, not defense, to the Soviet ABM. Although MIRV was not mentioned in McNamara's statement and had not yet been officially acknowledged, the point could not have been missed by McNamara's congressional critics who were well aware of MIRV's existence and its advantages for penetration of ABM defenses. Moreover, through a series of apparently planned leaks, the essence of the MIRV concept was soon reported in *The New York Times*.[84]

Despite McNamara's statement, the decision to deploy Poseidon was not new in November 1966. While the pace of the development program did not require procurement of long lead-time items until the FY 1968 budget, the commitment to deploy the system whenever it would be available had been made the previous year. Many in the Navy considered it made in 1964 and McNamara himself said in February 1965 that he was "inclined to believe we should deploy it."[85] His announcement was a political maneuver, an attempt to relieve the pressure for Nike-X deployment and focus attention on advances being made with the offensive forces. Also by demonstrating that the United States had available a missile that could nullify the effect of a Soviet ABM, he could more easily argue that the Soviets would be able to overcome Nike-X.[86]

The timing and context of the official public disclosure of the MIRV programs was also chosen to provide maximum political effect. McNamara had insisted that MIRV be kept top secret so as not to encourage the initiation of a parallel Soviet effort. But with President Johnson's decision to deploy an ABM system, McNamara sought all possible means to prevent the initial limited deployment from growing into a massive defense against a Soviet urban-industrial attack. This goal was largely responsible for his accompanying his announcement of the deployment of an anti-Chinese system with a strong warning that expanding it into a heavy anti-Soviet defense would be counterproductive.[87] In an attempt to strengthen his argument that the Soviets could readily overwhelm a heavy ABM deployment, McNamara decided to discuss the advantages of MIRV in an interview with *Life*, published in the September 29, 1967 issue. He indicated that it was the expectation of having MIRV deployed that "makes us confident that we can overcome the Soviet ABM." And he added,

> But in a few years the Soviets could have their own MIRVs and that is one of the reasons we are pessimistic about deploying an effective, more extensive ABM against them. . . . The optimistic statements made by ABM proponents on both sides haven't taken such things as MIRVs fully into account.[88]

The fact that there was, reportedly, an intelligence report circulating within the Administration that claimed the Soviets were giving top priority to efforts to develop multiple warheads,[89] might have reduced McNamara's reluctance to discuss MIRV publicly and would certainly have reinforced his opinion about the futility of large-scale ABM deployments. To McNamara MIRV was not only a system to defeat the Soviet ABM, it was also one that could be used to reduce the domestic political pressure for a comparable United States deployment.

Through most of the 1960s the United States intelligence community continually underestimated the rate of deployment of Soviet ICBMs.[90] Beginning in 1966 and continuing for five years, the rate of Soviet deployment of ICBMs was quite rapid, while the United States' deployments leveled off in 1967. In light of this apparent effort by the Soviet Union to catch up with or surpass the United States in numbers of deployed ICBMs and the fact that, with their larger missiles, the Soviet Union had surpassed the United States in the total payload deliverable by missiles, Secretary McNamara sought to head off anticipated pressures for renewed missile deployments. He argued that because of its MIRV programs the United States could maintain superiority without increasing the size of its forces. In the FY 1968 Posture Statement he told the Congress: ". . . we should bear in mind that it is not the number of missiles which is important, but rather the character of the payloads they carry: the missile is simply the delivery vehicle."[91] Since the MIRV program was still secret, he could not be more specific in the public version of his statement. But the large number of warheads that the United States was planning to deploy was what he had in mind. This was made explicit the following year. In commenting on a one-year Soviet deployment of 380 ICBMs and on their advantage in available ICBM payload capacity, Mr. McNamara first reviewed the advantages for city, airfield or hard target destruction of a MIRVed missile with ten warheads of only 50 kilotons compared with a single warhead of ten megatons. He then went on to say:

> It is clear therefore that gross megatonnage is an erroneous basis on which to compare the destruction capability of two forces. And as I pointed out to the Committee last year, the number of missiles on launchers alone is not a much better measure. Far more important is the surviving number of separately targetable, serviceable, accurate, reliable warheads. But the only true measure of relative effectiveness of two 'Assured Destruction' forces is their ability to survive and to destroy the target systems they are designed to take under attack.
>
> In terms of numbers of separately targetable, survivable, accurate, reliable warheads, our strategic forces are superior to those of the Soviet Union. But I must caution that in terms of national security, such 'superiority' is of little significance. For even with that 'superiority'; or indeed with any 'superiority' realistically attainable, the blunt, inescapable fact remains that the Soviet Union could still effectively destroy the United States, even after absorbing the full weight of an American first strike.[92]

While trying to disavow all simplistic measures of strategic superiority, Mc-Namara recognized their political significance. The most important such measure, he claimed, is that in which the United States, thanks to MIRV, would stay ahead.

Such measures of superiority remained important, both bureaucratically and politically. In his FY 1970 Posture Statement Secretary of Defense Clark Clifford wrote: ". . . it is reasonable to conclude that even if the Soviets attempt to match us in numbers of strategic missiles we shall continue to have, as far into the future as we can now discern, . . . a distinct superiority in the numbers of deliverable weapons."[93] By the time the SALT negotiations began in 1969 the Soviets had deployed more ICBMs than the United States and by 1971 their total number of strategic missiles, including SLBMs, was greater than the American deployment and still growing. This disparity caused major difficulties during the negotiations and when the Interim Agreement on Offensive Weapons was presented to the Congress for endorsement. Without the ongoing American MIRV programs, then in the deployment stage, and the American lead of several years in MIRV technology the military would have been much more reticent in supporting the agreement, if they would have done so at all. Admiral Moorer, Chairman of the Joint Chiefs of Staff, stated that the Chiefs' endorsement of the SALT agreements was contingent upon congressional support of three assurances, two of which were directly related to MIRV deployment and MIRV technology. Assurance II specified "Aggressive improvements and modernization programs" and assurance III required "Vigorous research and development programs."[94] The primary congressional criticism of the SALT agreements was the advantage in numbers and deliverable throw weight of offensive missiles provided to the Soviet Union by the interim agreement. The Administration countered this criticism by explaining that these Soviet advantages were compensated for by the large number of American warheads.[95] Without the MIRV deployments the agreement, if it had been reached at all, would have been much more difficult to defend. As Paul Nitze, a member of the American negotiating team of SALT, told a subcommittee of the House Armed Services Committee, the American MIRV was "one of the principal offsetting U.S. advantages which made the inequalities favoring the Soviet side contained in the Interim Agreement acceptable to the U.S. side in 1972."[96]

These efforts by successive Secretaries of Defense and Administrations to use the MIRV programs to protect themselves from criticism and to relieve political pressure parallel, at a higher level in the government, the use of strategic argument by the service bureaucracies to protect their organizational autonomy. In both cases the arguments or policies are designed primarily to further the objectives of the individual or organization that makes them. While it is important to understand these essentially political aspects of the MIRV programs and to recognize their contribution in determining the pace and character of the programs, they should certainly not be emphasized to the exclusion of other equally important factors.

THE WOVEN FABRIC

Robert McNamara has said about the pressures on defense decisionmakers: "There is a kind of mad momentum intrinsic to the development of all new nuclear weaponry. If a weapon works—and works well—there is a strong pressure from many directions to procure and deploy the weapon out of all proportion of the level required."[97] Ralph Lapp has claimed that, "once technology became 'sweet' enough to permit packaging multiple warheads in a MIRV configuration, then this had to be accomplished."[98] The previous chapter traced in detail the organizational and technologic pressures in favor of MIRV. The purpose here has not been to deny the importance of these pressures, but, recognizing that the policy process is more complex than either of the cited statements would have us believe, to ask what other forces were at work. The decision to deploy MIRV was not made by a single policy choice at a particular moment in time. It was an evolving process requiring a myriad of separate decisions and activities. Along the way choices were made, such as the delay and eventual cancellation of the Mark 17, that went against the preferences of parts of the service bureaucracies. Other choices, such as the cancellation of the stellar inertial guidance program for Poseidon and the decision not to pursue the Air Force Mark 18 program, prevented, at least for a while, the exploitation of attractive new technology. To understand the full complexity of the decision-making process that determined these and other choices related to the MIRV programs, one must look beyond technology and the organizational interests of the military services.

There is no doubt that for the military, strategic preference blends with organizational interest until it is difficult to distinguish between them. Strategic arguments are employed in order to advance the programs that the technical organizations need in order to remain active, to maintain their technological and organizational independence, and to expand or protect their roles and missions. But strategic preferences also form part of the belief structure of military personnel and are thereby influential in their own right. To Air Force officers the primary measure of usefulness and desirability of MIRV was the extent to which it would advance their central mission, fighting nuclear wars. Their aversion to the Mark 18, their preference for the Mark 17, and their insistence on continually improving missile accuracies were directly attributable to their pursuit of this mission. As the Mark 12 MIRV was increasingly perceived to be useful for counterforce, its acceptability improved. Similarly, in the Navy the Mark 3 MIRV was oriented toward the preferred mission of the Special Projects Office, namely assured destruction. The primary advantage of the many small warheads was to penetrate a potential ABM system. Although Special Projects accepted accuracy improvements as an accommodation to and a means of gaining support from those who sought a counterforce capability for Poseidon, they resisted both the Mark 17 MIRV and the stellar inertial guidance.

If one adds together the ideological perspectives of the service bureaucracies, their organizational interests and procedures and the opportunities afforded by new technology, an explanation of the main features of the MIRV programs can be generated. James Kurth, for example, claims that the MIRV innovation "is best explained by bureaucratic process: bureaucratic doctrines, bureaucratic standard operating procedures, including in this case normal procedures for the research and development of technocratic interests, and bureaucratic programs for organizational preservation and growth."[99] Stopping there, however, omits the central role played by key decisionmakers, particularly Secretary McNamara and DDR&Es Harold Brown and John Foster.

One could just as easily and just as incompletely explain the MIRV programs entirely on the basis of the strategic and political objectives of these central decisionmakers as discussed in the previous two sections.

To adopt any of these partial explanations, the determination of technology, the inexorable drive of bureaucratic process or the preeminent role of central decisionmakers, as *the* explanation of the MIRV programs is to miss the richness and diversity of the decision-making process. All were involved and all must be included if an accurate explanation of the MIRV programs is to be given.[j] One would like to go beyond this realization, however, to make some judgment about which factor or factors were most important. That is a difficult task, not only because so many of the factors contributing to the MIRV programs were mutually reinforcing rather than competitive; but also because particular aspects came into prominence, receded and reemerged over time and in different ways for different actors in the process. It is so difficult in fact that one wonders whether any firm and definitive statement on the subject does not derive from ideological preference more than objective analysis.

The best that can be done is to suggest that at some times and at some levels in the government hierarchy one aspect was most important, and at other times and at other levels different aspects were. No single policy determinant predominated across either the span of time or the breadth of diverse organizations. Technical and organizational factors, for example, were much more compelling within the services, particularly the technical organizations, than in OSD, and within OSD they were stronger in DDR&E than in Systems Analysis or to the Secretary. Strategic objectives, on the other hand, were more compelling in their own right at the level of responsible decisionmakers. But, as discussed above, even their dominant strategic objective changed with time. To Secretary McNamara, moreover, the utility of MIRV as a means of controlling the bureaucracy was a major advantage in 1964 and 1965. By 1967 and 1968 he was trying, with less success, to use MIRV as an argument against the ABM advocates in Congress. Nonetheless it seems unlikely that either of these political purposes would have been sufficient on their own to guarantee McNamara's support for the programs. MIRV's role in domestic politics probably did predominate in President Johnson's mind. It was a counter to his defense critics and helped him delay an ABM deployment while trying to get the Soviets to agree to SALT.[101] In short, technology, strategy, politics, and organizational factors were all woven together in an intricate, unique and changing fabric. Until 1968 the main strands all tended in the same direction, carrying the MIRV programs forward.

---

[j]This point is completely missed, for example, in Ronald Tammen's attempt to test two theories of the strategic arms race by looking at the MIRV case.[100]

Chapter Four

Intelligence Information and Uncertainty

In the discussion up to this point, the role of Soviet weapons policy and deployments as a stimulus for the MIRV programs has taken a secondary position compared to domestic politics, strategic preferences, and bureaucratic advocacy. Yet, reacting to the Soviet threat is one of the primary official justifications for American strategic weapons policies, especially of MIRV. Most statements about MIRV by defense officials have justified it as a response to observed and expected Soviet ABM and offensive missile deployments. The mosaic of the decision process would be incomplete, therefore, without a detailed examination of this justification and of the impact of intelligence information about Soviet weapons development and deployment.

Three aspects of the Soviet strategic force posture had significant effects on the American MIRV program. First the hardening and dispersal of the Soviet ICBM force contributed to the gradual replacement of a strategy of counterforce with that of assured destruction, tempered by the desire to maintain limited second-strike counterforce capability. Second, the increased size of the Soviet ICBM force both generated a requirement for a large number of accurate warheads and was interpreted as threatening the survivability of the Minuteman force. Third and most important, Soviet development and deployment of ABM defenses, or of systems that were thought to be ABM defenses, seemed to challenge the credibility of the American deterrent, based as it was on the ability to inflict unacceptable damage on the Soviet Union even after absorbing a massive attack. If Soviet defenses could really prevent or be construed as being capable of preventing American missiles from reaching their targets, the credibility of the deterrent might be in question. To each of these challenges MIRV provides an appropriate response.

The extent to which intelligence information about the hardening, dispersion, and growth of the Soviet missile force contributed to changes in the strategic preferences of defense decisionmakers and the ability of MIRV to accommodate these changes have been sufficiently discussed in the previous chapter. Attention here will focus on the other two intelligence-related factors that had a direct influence on the MIRV programs.

STRATEGIC INTELLIGENCE AND ITS LIMITATIONS

The 1960s can be characterized as a period of information explosion in the intelligence field. The deployment in the early part of the decade and continuous improvement of observation satellites provided a great quantity of highly reliable information about the military forces of the Soviet Union.[1] When to this is added the land-, air-, and sea-borne radars that were used to observe and monitor Soviet long range missile tests and to examine the characteristics of their reentry vehicles, the electronic intelligence satellites, the large network of land-based and ship-borne communications monitoring stations and more traditional methods of espionage, the result was, compared to earlier periods, a veritable flood of raw data.

These data were collected, processed, and disseminated by the American intelligence community employing tens of thousands of people and sustained by a multi-billion dollar annual budget.[2] The Central Intelligence Agency (CIA), the Defense Intelligence Agency (DIA), the National Security Agency (NSA), the Office of Intelligence and Research (INR) in the State Department, and the intelligence staffs of each of the armed services all participated in these activities. The community's outputs were many and varied. For rapid distribution of new data there were both daily briefings for the President, senior Administration officials, and senior officers, and weekly, biweekly or monthly publications providing background information or dealing with major trends or matters of special interest. The time elapsed between the receipt of raw data and its availability to decisionmakers could be very short. For example, a few days after the arrival of a new set of satellite photographs at the National Photographic Interpretation Center briefers would fan out through the Defense Department and other interested agencies to report the information gleaned by the photo-interpreters. The President or the Secretary of Defense and their staffs had ready access to the community. The Director of Central Intelligence (who was also the Director of the CIA) not only was supposed to coordinate and guide the government's total intelligence effort but also to keep the President appraised of intelligence information. DIA reported to the Secretary of Defense through the Joint Chiefs of Staff and was available to respond to his requests. High level officials kept up to date on intelligence information, particularly as it bore on major or controversial matters.

For the estimating or forecasting of future Soviet capabilities and intentions there were two institutionalized mechanisms. The National Intelligence Estimates (NIEs) were discursive, non-quantitative documents providing short- to medium-term estimates on a wide range of subjects. They were published periodically, normally whenever previous estimates became outdated and while relevant to Defense Department planning and the annual budget cycle, were not tailored specifically for those purposes. The two NIEs of particular relevance to the MIRV programs were those relating to Soviet offensive and defensive strategic forces. Longer term quantitative projections, extending out to five or ten years, were contained in the National Intelligence Projections for Planning (NIPP). This document was prepared annually and was an important input to force planning and the budget cycle. Drawing on the analysis embodied in the NIEs, the NIPP provided numerical estimates of future military capabilities.

Because of the central role of these documents in determining the perceptions of Pentagon planners and thereby in force structure decisions, it is important to understand that they were the negotiated output of the entire intelligence community.[3] Although the Office of National Estimates, located in the office of the Director of Central Intelligence, both set the "terms of reference," defining the subject, content and structure of a national estimate, and did the drafting, background information and analyses were provided from the entire community. More important, each draft would be fully coordinated with all agencies in order to achieve consensus whenever possible and then be submitted, with all dissent and amendments, to the United States Intelligence Board. This Board was chaired by the Director of Central Intelligence and included representatives from CIA, DIA, State, NSA, the Atomic Energy Commission, the Federal Bureau of Investigation and, with observer status, the service intelligence staffs. A final reconciliation of conflicting views was sought, but if unanimity was impossible any participating agency could register a dissenting view in a footnote. The estimate was finally approved by the Director of Central Intelligence for publication and dissemination. The process for the NIPP was similar.

Although the participants in the writing of these documents were professional analysts who shared the same sources of basic data and the objective of making the final product as accurate and timely as possible, they differed in organizational affiliation, in perspectives, and frequently in values. As a result, the process involved not only rational analysis of data, but also different preferences for dealing with ever-present uncertainties and elements of bureaucratic bargaining. The right to express disagreement in appropriate footnotes was exercised regularly. The publication of a new National Intelligence Estimate or NIPP did not necessarily mean that the intelligence community was fully united on its contents. Disagreements frequently existed. Each service would sometimes leak its own estimates to the press or to a sympathetic congressman in order to mobilize outside support for its case in an internal fight that it did not appear to be winning.

Despite or perhaps because of the improvements in intelligence-gathering techniques and the rather substantial capability of the intelligence community to process and distribute information, the limitations of intelligence information deserve special attention. Even the flood of intelligence data that is continually directed at senior decisionmakers does not eliminate many very important uncertainties about Soviet weapons programs and Soviet intentions. Some of these uncertainties derive from, or are exacerbated by, the closed nature of Soviet society, but many are intrinsic to the available means of observation. For example, the accuracy of strategic missiles is extremely difficult to determine. Observers can know where a missile actually landed but not where it was intended to land. Although the observation of reentry vehicle shapes and speeds and extrapolation from the apparent precision of space missions can help bound the uncertainties, they cannot be entirely eliminated. Similarly, the capabilities of ABM or air defense radars and interceptors are difficult to determine by remote sensors. This fact was partly responsible for the years of controversy over the purpose and capabilities of the extensive Soviet air defense system known as the Tallinn line.

Much more important than the uncertainties involved in assessing current capabilities is the unknowability of future capabilities. Projections of the future must be made for planning purposes. Since the time span between the initiation of active development and the final deployment of new strategic systems tends to be about five to ten years, the planner's view must be a rather distant one. He must make estimates of what the strategic environment will be like when systems currently in early development are deployed. The difficulty inherent in such estimates is well illustrated by the fact that the intelligence community underestimated the rate and scale of future Soviet ICBM deployment not only while they were deploying relatively few each year but also after the rate of deployment increased significantly. Since the decision to close or slow down an assembly line and thereby terminate production and deployment of new missiles can be made rather rapidly Soviet leaders need not decide ultimate force levels very far in advance. American estimates, therefore, may have to anticipate the result of such decisions before they are made. This same quandry was recognized by Secretary McNamara. In the FY 1965 Posture Statement he stated:

> These longer range [at least five year] projections of enemy capabilities must necessarily be highly uncertain, particularly since they deal with a period beyond the production and deployment leadtimes of enemy weapon systems. We are estimating capabilities and attempting to anticipate production and deployment decisions which our opponents, themselves, may not as yet have made.[4]

Since military capabilities at any given time depend heavily on previous military research and development (R&D) programs, a knowledge of current R&D activities is extremely valuable in making projections. But information about weapons developments in their early stages is difficult to obtain, even with modern sensors. A system normally undergoes several years of advanced development before it is visibly tested and its discovery by the intelligence community must often await such tests. Since the time required between testing and initial deployment of a new Soviet system may be no longer than the time required to develop a counter to it, ongoing development programs try to anticipate the possible directions of Soviet activity. As a result, however, American planners tend to assume that the Soviets are engaged in any development program that the United States technical community has underway or has conceived of and are pursuing any technical avenue that has been identified as potentially fruitful or significant in the United States. For example, when it was realized in the late 1950s that the Soviets were actively engaged in ABM development, estimates assumed that they knew at least as much and were at least as advanced as the United States. The defense community reacted with a massive investment in penetration techniques, eventually including MIRV. Although such conservative projections have sometimes turned out to be false, and in retrospect one could sometimes argue that the United States has overreacted, decisionmakers have been willing to accept this risk. As DDR&E Dr. John Foster has said,

> Where threat information is adequate, we invest in amounts suffi-
> cient to meet the threat. Where information is inadequate and
> uncertainty high, we run some risks of overinvestment to insure that
> our capability will be adequate, that it is sure to fulfill our strategic
> objectives.[5]

There is also some concern that the Soviets may one day surprise the United States by exhibiting a major unanticipated technical breakthrough that provides them with a strategic advantage. Again in Foster's words,

> to avoid technological surprise, we must carry out vigorous, broadly-
> based research and exploratory development. We attempt to discover
> new ideas potentially relevant to national security. We test the
> feasibility of ideas to anticipate the worst that potential enemies
> could bring against us.[6]

Only by conducting a wide-ranging R&D program, he claimed, and by investigating countermeasures as each new opportunity is discovered, can the United States have reasonably high confidence that the Soviet Union will not achieve a major and important technical advantage by surprise. The United States has tried over the years to maintain what Foster has called a "margin of strategic safety," or a "margin of superiority" in strategic weaponry.[7]

Of course the urgency with which both investigative R&D programs and development of countermeasures must be pursued and the seriousness with which one would regard any Soviet technical advance depend critically on individual perceptions about the strategic balance. If one considers the balance to be very stable, is willing to relax the requirements that the strategic bombers, the Polaris/Poseidon force and the land-based missile force must be independently capable of serving as a deterrent, or accepts the idea that the possibility of only a few cities being destroyed would prevent an opponent from taking risks, the urgency of early reaction is reduced. Differences about the degree of acceptability of such assumptions have been at the heart of the strategic debate for two decades. Military men and policymakers have tended to take a very cautious approach to these matters. They have been unwilling, for example, to rely on the deterrent effect of the uncertainties that the Soviets would face in contemplating a nuclear attack, but insist that the United States must at all times and under all circumstances have complete certainty that the Soviets could not think that a disabling first strike against the United States were feasible or that they could emerge from a nuclear exchange as the victor in any meaningful sense.

Even after testing or early deployment of a new Soviet capability is observed, the uncertainties are still not fully resolved. Although the conservative assumption would be that the Soviets will deploy the new improvement or new system they are testing, this has frequently turned out to be incorrect. On the basis of observed testing of ABM components, some preliminary and limited ABM deployment and the deployment of some defensive installations whose capabilities were difficult to determine, the American intelligence community overestimated throughout the 1960s the extent to which the Soviets would move toward nationwide ABM defenses. Similarly, when the Soviets began testing multiple warheads, the projections of at least part of the intelligence community were that they would demonstrate and deploy a MIRV capability at an early date thereafter. This turned out to be quite wrong.

The lack of hard data about Soviet development programs and the assumption that they are or could be doing whatever the United States is doing sometimes create the impression that the United States is competing with itself in strategic weaponry. This was the case particularly in the offense-defense interaction of the 1960s. The defense-oriented community developed Nike-Zeus and the offense-oriented community developed light decoys, chaff and other techniques to penetrate it. Each improvement that one side made led to an offsetting change on the other side. When phased-array radar and the Sprint interceptor were introduced by the defense, heavy decoys and MIRV were developed by the offense. Nonetheless it is easier to see this aspect of self-competition retrospectively than at the time, when uncertainties loom so large.

Sometimes effort has been wasted because the Soviets did something different than expected. For example, the A-3 and the early decoys that were designed to be effective against Nike-Zeus were later considered inadequate to assure penetration of an extensively deployed Galosh ABM system. Sometimes things are not done simply because the American technical community is aware of an effective countermeasure. As Dr. Brown told the Senate Preparedness Investigating Subcommittee, "The United States decided . . . not to deploy the Nike-Zeus because its effectiveness was considered inadequate against U.S. penetration aids programmed for entry into the U.S. inventory before a Nike-Zeus system could be deployed (deleted)."[8] Other times, as in the case of the Soviet ABM deployment, the threat does not develop at all, or, like their ICBM deployments, only many years later than expected. When this happens critics claim that money and effort were wasted, and that the arms race was unnecessarily escalated. But at the time that the decision to develop or even to deploy a new system was made, the uncertainties may have been very large.

Intentions are even more difficult to discern than capabilities. To some extent intentions can be inferred from monitoring public statements of Soviet officials or by electronically intercepting communications. But several problems remain. The signals may be contradictory or ambiguous. Statements may be calculated to give a particular impression that does not necessarily reflect reality. Unless sufficient information is available to illuminate the internal debates of the Soviet consensus building process it may be very difficult to know which spokesman, if any, speaks for the nation. Finally, there may be no information at all about a particular question. Such a lack of information seems to have exacerbated the controversies about the Soviet intentions for upgrading the Tallinn system and their purpose in deploying so many ICBMs. In the latter case there seem to have been at least three schools of thought in the United States. One maintained that powerful internal bureaucratic forces were responsible for continuing Soviet deployments. Another feared the possibility that the Soviets were seeking a first strike capability. A third suggested that the deployments were merely part of a second strike damage-limitation strategy similar to that of the United States.[9]

The question of Soviet intentions at the time that the build-up was taking place may still be unresolved, but this has always been only part of the issue. As important as a potential adversary's current intentions and plans are the possible and likely changes in these intentions. Political intentions can change on a time scale that is very short compared to the lead times to develop nuclear weapon systems. Any planning based only on an assessment of intentions is therefore intrinsically uncertain. As a result, military planners and political leaders tend to rely much more on current and projected capabilities than on political intentions.[a] If the United States is prepared to counter the worst possible

---

[a]President Nixon has made this point himself. On April 18, 1969, he said,

As far as the Soviet Union's intentions are concerned, and I want to clarify one point that is made, the question as to their intentions is not something that I am going to comment upon. I don't know what their intentions are. But we have to base our policy on their capabilities; . . . [10]

threat, then the country's security will be unaffected, to the maximum extent possible, by capricious changes in political intentions. There are risks involved either way, however. Projections based on such worst case assumptions led to predictions in 1959 and 1960 that a missile gap would develop several years later, and may have encouraged the Kennedy Administration to authorize the very large (some would say excessively large) build-up of American missiles.[11] But senior military officers and responsible officials have tended to be conservative in their judgments and to hedge against the uncertainties of the future. Better, they have thought, to err on the side of too much than too little when national security or national survival is at stake.

INTELLIGENCE INFORMATION FOR ADVOCACY

The dissenting opinions of the various institutional units within the intelligence community that frequently showed up as footnotes to the National Intelligence Estimates have been readily seized upon by policymakers and advocates who found them either convincing or useful. The military, for example, preferred DIA's estimates of Soviet capabilities, which frequently credited them with more or better hardware and more malevolent intent than did CIA's estimates. The policy implications of this position tended to reinforce the military's requests for additional hardware, manpower or other resources. Both legislators and government officials that disagreed with official policy could frequently find a set of intelligence estimates other than those in the main text of a national estimate that more closely suited their predisposition and prejudices or reinforced their policy choices.[12]

Consider, for example, the debate in early 1969 over the Soviet intentions in building up their ICBM forces. In January out-going Secretary of Defense Clark Clifford said,

> It is reasonble to conclude that, even if the Soviets attempt to match us in numbers of strategic missiles, we shall continue to have, as far into the future as we can now discern, a very substantial qualitative lead and a distinct superiority in the numbers of deliverable weapons and the over-all combat effectiveness of our strategic offensive forces.[13]

Two months later, after a change of Administration and a Pentagon reevaluation of intelligence information, the new Secreatry, Melvin Laird, told the Senate Foreign Relations Committee, "With the large tonnage the Soviets have they are going for our missiles and they are going for a first strike capability. There is no question about that."[14] This opinion was evidently not based on any new evidence[15] and was not shared by the entire defense and intelligence community, although everyone had access to the same basic intelligence data.[16]

Although Dr. Foster said that "Mr. Laird's statements are based upon agreed intelligence data,"[17] he did not say that the National Intelligence Estimates themselves made such a prediction. Anti-ABM senators disagreed with Mr. Laird's conclusion. Senator Gore countered by saying that he had learned that "the national intelligence estimates does not concur with statements by Dr. Foster and Mr. Laird."[18] He was supported in this contention by Senator Fulbright.[19] Clearly the substantive argument relied not on the basic data nor even on the wording of an NIE, but on differing interpretations of the data and on estimates made by opposing advocates in the midst of the heated and highly polarized debate on ABM deployment.

Throughout the 1950s and 1960s intelligence information was used by advocates of a wide variety of programs to argue that the United States must match what the Soviets were doing. If the Soviets develop some weapon system, the United States, these advocates argued, must do the same. The argument often included the claim that the Soviets would achieve some military advantage if the United States did not match or exceed their actions and therefore that the American deployment was needed as military compensation. But the true matching argument claimed that important or perhaps intangible values, whether diplomatic bargaining advantage or the international prestige derived from a demonstration of technological superiority, would be sacrificed, if the weapon system in question were not deployed. A long list of weapons and military programs could be given that were supported by "matching" arguments. It would include the nuclear powered airplane, intercontinental bombers during the "bomber gap" period, intercontinental missiles during the "missile gap" scare, the resumption of atmospheric nuclear testing after the Soviet resumption in 1961, very large nuclear warheads, and ABM defenses. Two examples, both drawn from the efforts of Nike-Zeus supporters to secure deployment funds, should serve to illustrate the lengths to which advocates have gone in their political manipulation of intelligence information.

The following is the record of a discussion between Lt. General Arthur G. Trudeau, Chief of Research and Development, U.S. Army; Mr. Richard S. Morse, Assistant Secretary of the Army (Research and Development); and members of the House Committee on Science and Astronautics in February, 1961:

> **Mr. Miller:** Do you have any knowledge of any similar system that the Russians may be developing?
> **Mr. Morse:** Yes.
> **Mr. Miller:** That is a question that I withdraw now.
> **Mr. Morse:** I will stop.
> **The Chairman:** If there is nothing—
> **General Trudeau:** I don't think you should withdraw it.
> **Mr. Morse:** I said that I am not going to say any more.
> **General Trudeau:** This is a matter of concern. This could change the whole strategic balance if they come up with a system.

> **The Chairman:** Are they pushing the program?
> **General Trudeau:** You can be sure they are pushing it.
> **Mr. Ryan:** Without revealing it, do you anticipate when their system could be operational? Not revealing the date?
> **Mr. Morse:** May we have a short conference? (He confers with General Trudeau.) I would like to answer that this way: It is my opinion, based on the information which I have, that the Russians have a large, very large anti-missile effort, and have had for some time. I think I will stop there.
> **The Chairman:** Extensive?
> **Mr. Morse:** Very large.
> **Mr. Miller:** Too large.[20]

General Trudeau evidently saw an opportunity to support his case for Nike-Zeus by responding to an inquiry about the Soviet ABM program. Despite the severe limitations of security he would not let the matter drop and pushed it to the point where Mr. Morse had to reveal that the Soviets had an extensive effort underway. The desired impact was evidently made on at least some members of the committee.

In 1963 intelligence information about the Leningrad ABM deployment was apparently leaked to Senator Strom Thurmond, an avid Nike-Zeus supporter. Senator Thurmond had the Senate go into secret session during which he reported on the Soviet deployment and argued for the immediate deployment of Nike-Zeus. His effort was defeated by a concerted Administration effort, led by Senator Russell, then chairman of the Senate Armed Services Committee, and economy-minded Republicans.[21]

No evidence of the use of this type of argument for MIRV was found until 1969, even though the Soviets were reportedly thinking about "maneuvering warheads" as early as 1963[22] and some individuals in the defense community took the threat of Soviet independently targetable warheads very seriously. In September 1967 there was a newspaper account of an intelligence report circulating within the Johnson Administration concerning Soviet development of multiple warheads.[23] But if this information was leaked on purpose, it was intended to bolster McNamara's case against a heavy, nationwide ABM deployment, not to support the United States' MIRV programs. In May 1968 when Administration officials briefed the Senate Preparedness Investigating Subcommittee, they admitted that evidence existed of Soviet development work on multiples, but apparently did not use this to argue in favor of the American MIRV programs.[24] Even after the first Soviet multiple warhead test in August 1968 the official Pentagon response was reported to be "no comment."[25] This lack of a "matching" argument for MIRV suggests that unless a particular program faces opposition such a justification is unnecessary. It is, after all, not easy to sustain an argument based on political considerations and prestige. When controversy over the MIRV programs finally did develop a matching argument appeared.

During 1969 a disagreement developed concerning the nature of the

Soviet multiple warhead tests. On reappraisal of the evidence, military and OSD officials came to believe that the Soviet triplet warhead on the SS-9 was sophisticated enough to permit each one to attack a different Minuteman silo. Official statements and unofficial leaks about the SS-9 tests and their implications were primarily intended to bolster the Administration's arguments that the Safeguard ABM system was necessary to protect the Minuteman force.[b] A secondary purpose, however, was to reinforce the arguments of those in the Administration who favored continuation of the American program of MIRV testing.[28] and to undermine the case of congressional and non-governmental critics who were calling for a unilateral or bilateral moratorium on MIRV testing.

In response to a question about the resumption of MIRV tests, Secretary of State William Rogers told his June 5, 1969 news conference,

> Now, we are not going to delay all our military preparations in the meantime, [i.e., until there is a successful agreement with the Soviets on the limitation of strategic arms] any more than I expect the Soviet Union is. In fact, they are not. As you know, they have been testing their SS-9's in the Pacific right along.[29]

Since the Soviets were testing SS-9s with multiple warheads, Rogers suggested, the United States must continue to test its MIRV. Foster was more blatant in his use of the "matching" argument in his August 5, 1969 statement to the Subcommittee on National Security Policy and Scientific Development of the House Committee on Foreign Affairs. During a statement whose overall purpose was to argue against proposals for a MIRV test moratorium, Foster said,

> The things we do know about this mechanization [i.e., the SS-9 triplet warhead] are completely compatible with MIRV, even though they do not prove MIRV capability.
>
> My own judgment in this matter is that the Soviet triplet probably is a MIRV and that it has little other function than the attack of large numbers of hard targets. While they have not yet shown in flight tests all the performance necessary to demonstrate that fact to us, they may wish to deny us such information.[30]

Although the imminent Senate vote on Safeguard funding must have had some role in Dr. Foster's decision to make this statement, he was also implying that since the Soviets appear to be going ahead with MIRV, so must the United States. Later in his statement he suggested that "we must consider the possibility that the SS-9 triplet might be deployed on the basis of further extensive ground tests and without further flight tests."[31] It may be too late, he was suggesting, to prevent MIRV deployment, because the Soviets may already have gone so far in the test program that verification of a MIRV ban would be infeasible.

For the MIRV programs, advocates used intelligence information

---

bThis was, for example, clearly the intent of President Nixon's mentioning the Soviet multiple warhead tests during his June 19, 1969 press conference[26] and was conceded to be one of the motives for declassifying in the spring of 1970 several items about Soviet weapons, including a movie of a Soviet SS-9 multiple warhead test that was shown to newsmen on April 23.[27]

much more commonly in another way. During the debate of 1969 and 1970 MIRV advocates argued almost exclusively that MIRV was a compensation for or a countermeasure to the Soviet ABM system. The point here is not that the argument was untrue, only that it was incomplete. The argument was emphasized that could be least attacked by MIRV critics. By basing their case for MIRV on the need to penetrate future Soviet ABM systems, Department of Defense spokesmen could avoid discussing the system's advantages for offensive attack against the full Soviet target system, including strategic forces. Although, or perhaps more likely, because he was aware that the primary opposition to MIRV derived from its utility for counterforce attacks, a factor which was said to be destabilizing for the strategic balance, Dr. Foster's statement before the House Subcommittee on National Security Policy and Scientific Development tried to focus attention on Soviet ABM defenses and the need to penetrate them and denegrated the utility of American MIRVs for counterforce.[32] As has already been related, however, in speaking to a more sympathetic Senate committee the previous year, Foster had stressed the advantages of MIRV for counterforce.[33] The availability of intelligence information on Soviet ABM systems, the controversy over the feasibility of building a significant ABM capability into the Tallinn air defense system, and the uncertainties about future Soviet intentions in this area permitted Administration spokesmen to structure the debate on MIRV to their own advantage. So successful were they that many people came to regard ABM penetration as the single, overwhelming consideration relevant to MIRV deployment.

Although it had been a major justification prior to the public controversy, the argument that MIRV was needed as a hedge against the future vulnerability of the Minuteman force was not stressed during the MIRV debate of 1969 and 1970. There seem to be two explanations of this. First, the Administration was vigorously arguing that the potential ability of the SS-9 missiles armed with accurate MIRVs to destroy most of the Minuteman force required the immediate deployment of Safeguard to protect the Minuteman force. This was a blatant use of a compensatory argument to advocate a new system. The Administration's arguments were based on incomplete intelligence information and extremely uncertain intelligence estimates, about which there was considerable debate even within the intelligence community. To have stressed that MIRV was a substitute solution for the Minuteman vulnerability problem would have weakened its case that Safeguard was essential. Second, to argue either that Poseidon MIRV or Minuteman MIRV (to the extent that this would improve the capability of surviving missiles) would have been acceptable as a compensation for the vulnerability of the Minuteman force would have stressed their offensive advantages. Especially since the Minuteman force was widely understood to be targeted largely for counterforce attacks, this argument would have played into the hands of MIRV's opponents to whom its counterforce potential was a major drawback.

The advocacy of technological superiority for the United States, in which intelligence information on Soviet research and development programs played a central role, also affected the MIRV programs once they became centers of public controversy. Nuclear superiority over the Soviet Union has been a major political goal of American defense planners in the postwar period. After the Soviets surpassed the United States, first in deployed megatonnage and then in the number of missiles,[c] two important measures of nuclear superiority, successive Secretaries of Defense began to stress both the numbers of warheads and technological sophistication as the most important strategic measuring sticks. As explained in the previous chapter MIRV was the key to American superiority in the number of deliverable warheads. It also played an important part in the technological superiority argument.

In 1970 Pentagon officials suggested that the Soviet Union was investing more money in military R&D than was the United States.[34] Dr. Foster, who became the main protagonist in the debate on this subject in 1971, argued that the Soviet R&D effort had surpassed that of the United States and that if the current trend persisted, the American technological superiority would disappear "in the latter half of this decade." He predicted that the result of this reversal in technological leadership would be that "we would have to expect that the Soviet Union would surprise us with a series of major development programs."[35] The intention here is not to enter into the debate that followed Foster's statements about Soviet R&D,[36] but to suggest that in part his purpose was one of advocacy. Despite a planned decrease of $4 billion in the total new obligational authority of the FY 1971 defense budget compared with that of 1970, as revised by the Nixon Administration, the R&D line item in the FY 1971 program budget, which does not include a large amount for R&D of systems already authorized for deployment, was increased by over $500 million.[37] In FY 1972 the R&D line item was programmed to rise by more than $800 million compared to then current estimates of FY 1971 spending.[38] This made it by far the fastest growing part of the budget outside of manpower costs. Total RDT&E for the strategic forces was also increasing during this period due to the advanced development and test programs for Poseidon, Minuteman III, Safeguard ABM, and the Short Range Attack Missile and growth in the Undersea Long Range Missile Program, the Airborne Warning and Control System, the Site Defense of Minuteman and the B-1 bomber programs. In the face of growing congressional opposition to defense spending, these disproportionate increases in the RDT&E budget had to be justified. The arguments about the need for technological superiority served this purpose.

The MIRV programs had long been considered and referred to as important examples of American technological superiority. In 1969, for ex-

---

[c]Actually, if the number of strategic bombers and their payloads are included in the enumeration, as is very often not done, this Soviet numerical superiority is substantially decreased.

ample, Secretary Clifford, in addressing the question of American superiority in missile technology, mentioned accuracy, MIRVs, and penetration aids as areas in which the United States was ahead.[39] Despite its claims that the Soviets might deploy accurate MIRVs by the mid-1970s, it is clear that the Nixon Administration did not doubt the American technical lead in this area. The United States, after all, was deploying Minuteman and Poseidon MIRVs by 1970 and 1971 respectively. Because of this acknowledged lead in MIRV and accuracy technology and particularly because of the ongoing debate over the American MIRV and accuracy-improvement programs, any argument for maintaining technological superiority, especially in the face of the dire predictions of imminent Soviet MIRV deployments, was, by direct implication, an argument for continued MIRV development, testing and deployment.

As has already been suggested the fact of American superiority in MIRV technology was one important reason why the various power centers within the government bureaucracy could come to agreement in 1972 to support the interim agreement on offensive strategic arms and why the congressional opposition to it was not stronger. By the time the agreement was signed, the Administration's estimates of Soviet multiple warhead capabilities had been revised. In February Chairman of the Joint Chiefs of Staff, Admiral Thomas H. Moorer, said that the assessment of the Soviet SS-9 multiple warhead tests had changed. He reported that the triplet warhead, known as SS-9 MOD-4, "had thus far failed to demonstrate the actual achievement of [a MIRV] capability."[40] Dr. Foster's revised projections indicated that only with extreme effort could the Soviets deploy before the 1980s an accurate MIRV system that would threaten a large fraction of the Minuteman force.[41] The Administration was therefore able to argue that the numerical imbalance permitted by the Interim Agreement in favor of the Soviets was compensated by American technological superiority, in particular a lead of eighteen months to two years in MIRV technology.[42] Moreover, both Administration spokesmen and, through their three assurances, the military, argued that it was very important to maintain that superiority. It was, of course, recognized that the Soviets could eventually deploy accurate MIRVs as well and they were reported to have a MIRV development program underway.[43] So, although MIRV provided a significant technological lead, one that the Administration could exploit in order to seek support for the interim agreement, a vigorous development program was said to be necessary in order to retain that lead.

HEDGING AGAINST UNCERTAINTY

There are two ways in which intelligence information about Soviet strategic forces contributed to the decision, as opposed to the justification, to develop and deploy MIRVs. First, in the minds of defense decisionmakers, the MIRV programs were closely tied to their perceptions of the Soviet ABM threat.[d] Second, they were considered to be a hedge against the possibility that a large Soviet offensive missile build-up accompanied by qualitative improvements such as Soviet MIRVs, would weaken the confidence in the survivability of the Minuteman force. It has become fashionable in recent years to denegrate the importance of intelligence estimates in American weapons decisions and even to question the existence of an arms race in the sense of an interactive process.[44] Tammen, for example, claims that "the few inputs [to the MIRV development programs] that were related to Soviet weapons programs were so muted in influence as to be of little importance."[45] While the claim that MIRV was solely a reasoned response to perceived and anticipated Soviet activities can certainly not be sustained, to deny the existence of this dimension of the decision-making process for MIRV is to miss completely one of the central themes of the strategic weapons drama of the 1960s.

Throughout the late 1950s and into the early 1960s the combination of intelligence reports about Soviet ABM developments and the very vigorous Nike-Zeus development program led the technical community to envision a series of penetration techniques, including multiple warheads. In 1961 the observation of what was taken to be the initiation of an ABM system deployment around Leningrad and the Soviet nuclear test series, which included tests of nuclear blackout effects, existent ABM warheads, and tests that could have been intended for the development of a new, X-ray-intensive ABM warhead, led the intelligence and technical community to conclude that a large-scale ABM deployment might be imminent. This expectation continued through 1962, exacerbated by such inflammatory Soviet statements about their ability to shoot down intercontinental missiles as Premier Khrushchev's statement of June 1962 that Soviet anti-missile missiles could hit a "fly in outer space" and by the first observation of construction of a possible ABM site near Moscow. During this period projections for the number of ABMs that the Soviets might eventually deploy went as high as 8,000 or 10,000.

As a result of these fears several things happened that helped launch the MIRV programs. The interruption by DDR&E of the Mark 12 design competition and the program's subsequent focus on small multiple reentry vehicles was a direct reaction to observed Soviet ABM activity and to projections, based on the American program, of what they might eventually do in that area. Perhaps the major concern was about the large warheads that the Soviets had tested above the atmosphere. In 1961 a panel of the President's Science Advisory Committee under the chairmanship of Dr. Wolfgang Panofsky had examined the evidence obtained about the Soviet tests in light of whatever

---

[d]See Appendix C for a discussion of the intelligence information available to the United States about Soviet ABM development and deployment and for the sources of the information used in the following discussion.

relevant data could be derived from the American high altitude tests of 1958. Although little hard evidence was available, the panel apparently concluded that an exo-atmospheric, high-yield explosion designed to maximize X-ray flux would have a very large lethal radius, especially against reentry vehicles then deployed which lacked hardening against nuclear effects. This conclusion became widely known throughout the technical community and led directly to the inclusion of nuclear hardening in the specifications of the Mark 12 and all subsequent reentry vehicles. It also called into question the ability of the newly authorized Polaris A-3 triplet warhead to penetrate Soviet ABM systems. Separation of the A-3 warheads was so small that only one of the projected ABM interceptors could destroy all three. It was in searching for a solution to this problem that Lockheed engineers were led directly to the conception of a maneuvering bus to deploy decoys and reentry vehicles spaced much further apart.

There are several other respects in which the conception of a maneuvering bus was a direct reaction to advances in ABM technology. As early as 1958 the Bradley Committee had recommended the development of phased-array radar for Nike-Zeus.[e] Soon after, construction got underway of the Electronic Scanning Array Radar (SDAR) funded by the Advanced Research Projects Agency. This radar demonstrated the feasibility of applying advanced phased-array techniques to missile defense and led to the Army's instituting a phased-array development program associated with Nike-Zeus in June 1961. The traffic-handling potential of this new type of radar and improved computational hardware capable of rapidly reconstructing trajectories and predicting impact points greatly complicated the decoy problem. A missile defense system based on projected advances in these new components would be much more difficult to overwhelm than the older Nike-Zeus. In order to force it to shoot at decoys, great precision would be needed in their placement. The natural solution to the decoy and reentry vehicle placement problem, as Ballistic Systems Division and its contractors discovered through 1963 and 1964, was the use of a maneuvering platform to drop off reentry bodies on precisely calculated trajectories. Although a prototype of a primitive phased-array radar was observed at the Soviet missile defense test site, Sary Shagan, in the late 1950s, none was deployed in the Leningrad complex. Despite the fact that the Soviets lagged behind the United States in phased-array and computer technology they were expected to deploy systems with advanced components eventually.

The realization that the Griffon interceptor deployed at Leningrad was short range and therefore unable to carry an exo-atmospheric X-ray warhead seems to have accelerated the abandonment of reliance on decoys and the acceptance of the advantage to be gained by independently guided multiple

---

[e]The essential characteristics of phased-array radar that distinguishes it from conventional radar is the ability to steer the beam electronically rather than by physically moving an antenna. This permits both very rapid scanning and tracking of many objects simultaneously.

warheads. Some intelligence analysts apparently worried that the Griffon might have capabilities similar to the newly-designed American Sprint high-acceleration interceptor.[46] If that were true, light decoys that are automatically sorted from reentry vehicles by the atmosphere would be insufficient penetration aids. But, if heavy decoys were required, the use of several live warheads, accurately placed, would be a more efficient use of throw-weight.

By early 1963, however, the consensus of the intelligence community was that both the interceptors and the radars of the Leningrad system were almost useless against high-speed reentry vehicles delivered by intercontinental or even intermediate range ballistic missiles like the Polaris A-3. Nothing observed at the Moscow site that early seemed likely to be much better. At the policy-making level (but not within the technical community that developed penetration aids), there resulted a marked decrease in the concern about Soviet ABM and the urgency for deploying high effectiveness penetrators. According to one industry source, the Mark 12 program was almost cancelled during this period and the Polaris B-3 was put off for another year. For a brief time, since the lull in Soviet ABM activity corresponded to the period of maximum interest in counterforce within OSD, the major justification for MIRV became its ability to cover a growing target list without increasing the size of the Minuteman force.

This relaxed atmosphere changed in 1964. Construction of more advanced ABM radars and launcher facilities had been observed around Moscow, new high altitude interceptors were seen at Sary Shagan, and the first construction of what later grew into the Tallinn system had been detected. It appeared that although abandoning the Leningrad system, the Soviets were resuming their ABM deployment elsewhere, this time using much more advanced technology. The reaction to the intelligence information of these developments was swift and far-reaching. One response was the initiation of the Pen-X study, the significance of which was discussed in Chapter 2. More important was the recommendation of Harold Brown and Fred Payne of DDR&E, based on a study of American penetration capability conducted by Glenn Kent, that the large 74-inch Polaris missile be developed, using a MIRVed front end, and that MIRV decoys and chaff be developed for Minuteman. When McNamara approved these recommendations, the reorientation of the Mark 12 and B-3 programs to include MIRV capability had begun. In November 1964, just after the Galosh interceptor was first displayed in Red Square, the official orders were issued from OSD to reorient both missile programs.

From the perspective of OSD the 1964 decision to go ahead with the development of Poseidon and the inclusion of MIRV was motivated primarily by a desire to have a missile that would be able to penetrate a future Soviet ABM system with high confidence independent of the detailed characteristics of that system. The inclusion of the Mark 17 option and the emphasis on accuracy improvements, on the other hand, resulted primarily from a continuing interest in counterforce. The penetration arguments also played an important role in the decision to develop MIRV for Minuteman.[47] Although McNamara's desire to limit the total force size, the need for more warheads and the targeting flexibility offered by MIRV were also important contributing factors, the official public justification changed back to penetration. Although both the Air Force and the Navy shared OSD's concern about Soviet ABM deployment, other considerations predominated within the services. Special Projects primarily sought the support of OSD and the rest of the Navy for its new submarine-launched missile. The Air Force was more interested in counterforce.

The uncertainties about the capabilities of the Moscow system and about the extent of the Soviet commitment to ABM defense were very large in the latter half of 1964 and through 1965. This was particularly true of the Tallinn system which began to spread across the northwestern Soviet Union. Whether this was an extension of the Moscow system or some different type of ABM was initially unclear. The geographical location of the sites, first astride the corridor through which Minuteman missiles would have to enter Soviet air space in order to attack the industrial heartland of European Russia, and then across the corridor through which Polaris missiles launched from the eastern Mediterranean would pass, and the long-range nature of the interceptors suggested a system oriented toward ballistic missiles. Nonetheless, the initially deployed hardware did not seem to be designed for intercepting ballistic reentry vehicles. The capability of this hardware, and whether and how the Soviets might eventually improve it, were matters of continuing uncertainty and debate within the intelligence community. The Tallinn deployment also raised questions about the extent of the Soviet commitment to ABM defense. It was entirely unclear whether all major population areas, only European centers or just the Moscow area would eventually be protected. But this made a considerable difference in the type of forces that the United States would need in the future both to guarantee the credibility of its deterrent and to provide some second strike counterforce capability. The earlier proliferation of air defense installations in the Soviet Union and the level of resources that had been committed to air defense suggested that a similar pattern should be expected with missile defense.

This uncertainty, accompanied by a pervasive expectation that major Soviet commitment to ABM was imminent, acted as a strong stimulus to the MIRV programs. The decision to accelerate the Poseidon program in the FY 1967 budget, especially because a rapid development was opposed by almost everyone in the Navy outside the Special Projects Office, and OSD's agreement to replace the Mark 12 with the new Mark 3 must be seen, in large measure, as hedges against possible future Soviet actions.[48] The authorization that year of Minuteman III deployment was also part of a package designed to improve the penetration capability of American strategic missiles. The decisions in 1966 to raise the number of Minuteman IIIs programmed for introduction into the force and to increase the missile's throw weight (and thereby the number of reentry vehicles and penetration aids that it could carry) by including the new third stage[49] were also intended to improve its ability to penetrate potential Soviet ABM systems.

But MIRV was a hedge not only against potential Soviet ABM deployments. It was just as much insurance against the future vulnerability of Minuteman should Soviet offensive missile forces grow and improve. By 1964 the initial tests of the SS-9 and SS-11 had been observed. Although there was little if any evidence until 1966 of the rate at which these missiles would be deployed,[50] it seems likely that disagreements over intelligence projection developed the previous year. Perhaps as a means of protecting themselves against subsequent charges of having used optimistic estimates in their force planning, OSD analysts developed in 1965 and McNamara discussed for the first time in the FY 1967 Posture Statement, a so-called greater-than-expected threat. This threat included, as McNamara explained the following year, "an extensive, effective Soviet ABM deployment combined with a deployment of substantial ICBM forces with a hard-target kill capability."[51]

There seems to be no doubt that there was widespread concern within the Pentagon, among both civilian and military planners, that Soviet offensive deployments, possibly including Soviet MIRVs, might render the Minuteman force vulnerable to a first strike. The shroud of secrecy that was placed on the American MIRV programs was intended to reduce the possibility that they would follow the American example at an early date. As Deputy Secretary of Defense Cyrus Vance said in his memorandum of October 17, 1966 clarifying the security regulations with respect to MIRV:

> I do not want any potential Soviet MIRV capability to be accelerated by our lack of attention to proper safeguarding of information about the concept and its strategic advantages, or by inadequate security classification of our development and deployment intentions, as well as the engineering details of the MIRV program.[52]

The 1965 decisions to continue and, in the case of Poseidon, to accelerate the MIRV development programs were influenced by this concern. As Dr. Enthoven, Assistant Secretary of Defense (Systems Analysis) said in 1968: "One of the big factors in the Poseidon development decision made three years ago [i.e., in 1965] was the conclusion that Poseidon would be the most effective way possible of guaranteeing against the threat of accurate Soviet missiles."[53] If the Minuteman force were to become increasingly vulnerable, the best compensation would be to improve the assured destruction capability of the invulnerable sea-based deterrent. In fact, the decreasing confidence in the survival of Minuteman, the basic counterforce system, may have contributed to OSD's interest in improving the accuracy of Poseidon. But MIRVing the Minuteman force was also a way to compensate for its vulnerability. With three accurate and independently targetable warheads and penetration aids on each Minuteman III missile, that part of the Minuteman force that did survive the imagined Soviet counterforce attack would be a much more potent retaliatory force. Not only would it have a better chance of penetrating or exhausting Soviet ABM defenses but, given the projected accuracy, it would also be useful for second strike counterforce against the remaining Soviet force.

During 1967 much of the uncertainty about the Soviet ABM activity became resolved. Early in 1968 McNamara reported: "the majority of our intelligence community no longer believes that this so-called "Tallinn" system . . . has any significant ABM capability."[54] And, "It is the consensus of the intelligence community that [the Moscow] system could provide a limited defense of the Moscow area but that it could be seriously degraded by sophisticated penetration aids."[55] As reflected in these statements, the Soviet commitment to ABMs then appeared to be less strong than had been expected even the previous year. This view was further reinforced during 1968 when construction of the Moscow system was curtailed[56] and there were indications that due to technical difficulties and rising costs an anti-ABM faction was prevailing in Moscow.[57]

These changes in intelligence information and projections did not affect the MIRV programs. The FY 1969 Posture Statement makes clear that the deployment of Poseidon and Minuteman III was not in doubt.[58] This may be explained in large part by the natural coalescence of political and bureaucratic forces behind a major ongoing program. But that is not the full story. The uncertainties about future Soviet ABMs had not disappeared. The possibility still existed that deployment might be resumed, that the Moscow system might be extended to other cities, that the Tallinn System might be rapidly upgraded to have a significant capability against ballistic missiles, or that an altogether new system with improved components might be deployed.[59] The Soviets were apparently developing a new interceptor and taking steps to upgrade their ABM radar. Moreover, as anxiety about Soviet ABM deployment decreased anxiety about their offensive capabilities increased.

In late 1966, when both the Moscow ABM system and the Soviet ICBM build-up were advancing rapidly, a major communitywide, eighteen-month study called Strat-X was undertaken to consider possible American reactions to the growing Soviet threat.[60] Because of the mounting anxiety about the future vulnerability of the Minuteman force, this study focused largely on possible improvements to the American offensive forces. Besides the Undersea Long Range Missile System (ULMS), now called Trident (for which the study group did much of the early design work), Strat-X also considered mobile ICBMs, multiple shelter systems, a Ship Launched Missile System, and a number of super-hard silo arrangements, such as in tunnels under mountains.[61] By early 1967 McNamara was considering several measures besides the MIRV programs to reduce or compensate for the potential vulnerability of the Minuteman force. These included the procurement of additional Poseidon submarines, the development and deployment of a new ICBM with much greater throw-weight, construction of super-hard silos embedded in rock, and protection of the Minuteman force with Nike-X.[62] Although studies of a larger ICBM continued under the code name WS-120, development was never authorized. Development of a new superhard silo was initiated in 1968,[63] but was cancelled in 1970.[64] It was dropped because of its great expense and perhaps also because it was realized that in a competition between hardness and accuracy, the latter would almost certainly win out eventually. As a substitute, a much cheaper effort was initiated to harden the existing silos into which the Minuteman III was being emplaced.[65]

  McNamara did not favor an ABM deployment of any type, not even one that would protect the Minuteman force. Once he had to authorize one, however, it was configured to provide some protection to Minuteman bases. This was true also of the Safeguard system, introduced by the Nixon Administration to replace the earlier plan called Sentinel. Nevertheless, the planned number of interceptors was never very large and a deployment at two or even four Minuteman sites could have been rapidly overwhelmed, if not penetrated, if the Soviets deployed a MIRV front end optimized for that purpose on their very large SS-9s. Even the smaller SS-11s, used to attack Safeguard's radars, could have rapidly exhausted the system.[66] At any rate the restrictions of the ABM treaty and the Protocol of June 1964 permit the deployment of only 100 interceptors at one Minuteman site. If the full twenty radars permitted in the ABM treaty were deployed and if the system were flexible enough to permit selection of which silos to defend during an attack, a high confidence defense of a relatively small number of silos might be possible. Nevertheless the option of significantly reducing the vulnerability of the Minuteman force by deploying an active defense has been discarded as long as the present ABM Treaty remains in force. The important point here is that the gradual exclusion of other options that would hedge against future vulnerability of Minuteman gave increased importance to the MIRV programs. This was particularly true at the height of the congressional attempts to have the MIRV test program delayed in 1969 because each of the SS-9's multiple warheads were then claimed to be capable of attacking individual Minuteman silos. Although that conclusion was later reversed, there was little doubt that the Soviets would eventually deploy a system that would, at least on paper, threaten the Minuteman force.[67] The Poseidon and Minuteman III program were justified as insurance against such Soviet actions.[68]

  In part then the MIRV programs were a reaction to the intelligence information and intelligence projections concerning Soviet ABM and offensive missile build-ups. But the word "reaction" can only be used with great care. The United States did not wait until the Soviets had taken steps that required countermeasures, nor did it even wait until there was significant evidence that they would take those steps. Again, as Dr. Foster said in 1968,

> Our current efforts to get a MIRV capability on our missiles is [sic]
> not reacting to a Soviet capability so much as it is moving ahead
> again to make sure, that whatever they do of the possible things that
> we imagine they might do, we will be prepared. . . . we are taking
> action when we have no evidence (or very little evidence) on the
> other side of any such actions . . . [69]

It was the anticipation of potential Soviet actions that helped generate support
for MIRV. Although the Soviets did little more than hint at the possibility of a
large-scale ABM deployment, American defense planners felt obliged to hedge
against that possibility. Because the Soviets were deploying missiles that, with
accuracy improvements and MIRVing, could have been regarded as a potent
threat to the Minuteman force, means were sought to compensate. As it turned
out the second generation MIRVs may be deployed in the United States before
that Soviet force appears. But to have waited would have been to incur risks that
were considered unacceptable.

THE ACTION-REACTION CYCLE

MIRV has frequently been described as a prime example of an interactive,
action-reaction process driving the nuclear arms race. Because the Soviet Union
seemed to be deploying an ABM system, the explanation goes, the United States
reacted by developing and deploying MIRVs. The motivation of the early
inventors, the timing of the initiation of full-scale development, the changes in
the numbers and types of reentry vehicles that each system would carry and the
foregoing analysis of the motivations of senior decision-makers all point to the
important influence of intelligence information and intelligence estimates about
Soviet activities. The linkage existed, although it was far from the sole
determinant of the programs.

    But Soviet actions were sporadic and frequently confusing to
American intelligence analysts. The Tallinn system, that was such a cause of
uncertainty and concern, turned out not to be an ABM system at all. Although
Soviet offensive missile forces increased in number faster than expected their
ability to threaten the Minuteman force developed slower than expected. One
could conclude that to the extent that the United States reacted to Soviet
actions it did so as much or more in anticipation of what the Soviets *might* do
than in response to what they *were* in fact doing. Moreover this anticipation was
based largely on the presumption that the Soviets had knowledge and technical
capabilities similar to those available to American development programs. One
could argue therefore not that there was no reaction, but that the reaction was
as much self-generated as Soviet-generated.

    With hindsight it seems fair to say that MIRV was unnecessary as an
ABM penetrator, that to the extent that it was a reaction to Soviet ABM

activity, it was an overreaction. But decisions are not made with the advantage of hindsight. For one thing it is not impossible that the American MIRV programs, by providing some assistance to an anti-ABM faction in the Soviet Union, were partially responsible for the tapering off of Soviet ABM deployments. More important, however, without minimizing the central role of all the political, organizational, technical, and strategic factors that helped sustain the MIRV programs over their eight or so year development phase, the programs must be attributed, to a great extent, to the uncertainties inherent in intelligence information and intelligence estimates. But it was not just intelligence about Soviet ABM development and deployment, official claims of recent years notwithstanding. From at least 1965, and increasingly thereafter, the potential vulnerability of the Minuteman force played a very important role. It was particularly the combination of a potent first strike counterforce offense and a capable defense that worried American defense planners. The Minuteman MIRV would increase the retaliatory capability of those missiles that survived the hypothetical attack and even permit some second strike counterforce targeting. The Poseidon MIRV was the final guarantor of an effective and overwhelming assured destruction force and with Mark 17 or stellar inertial guidance could have assumed some of the counterforce mission of Minuteman.

Moreover, advocates, no matter what their motivation, were able to point to Soviet activities as a means of justifying the MIRV programs. The service technical organizations that needed new programs for their own organizational purposes could argue that MIRV was required to nullify Soviet ABM systems. Later, Administration officials could dwell on Soviet multiple warhead tests in order to discredit those who sought to delay or stop the American MIRV tests. They could also point to Soviet technical advances and to their numerical advantage in ICBMs in order to argue that American technological superiority must be maintained. In particular, this meant MIRVs, including the accuracy improvements, reentry vehicle designs and warhead advances that are indivisible components of MIRV. MIRV's role in a variety of political and bureaucratic disputes, the very mention of which might have weakened the case, did not have to be discussed because a convenient and acceptable justification was available in the Soviet ABM system.

Decisions on major weapons programs are rarely made for simple reasons and the MIRV decision was no exception. Had the Soviets not deployed the Moscow ABM system or the Tallinn air defense system; had they stopped their ICBM build-up at a much lower level; had they never deployed the SS-9 or never tested it with multiple warheads; the United States would probably still have developed and deployed MIRV. Too many other factors were pushing in that direction for the intelligence information to have been decisive. However, the fact that they did all those things and that they might have done many other things made the consensus to proceed stronger, the political obstacles fewer and perhaps the availability of the systems somewhat earlier.

Chapter Five

Controversy

For reasons discussed in previous chapters a firm consensus had developed within the defense community by 1965 that MIRV was an innovation that should be developed and introduced into the forces. The commitees of Congress with purview over military budgets and forces were informed about this intention and annually voted the requisite funds without dissent. The rest of the Congress went along, relying on the judgment of the specialists who sat on the Armed Services Committees and the Subcommittees on Department of Defense Appropriations. Up to 1965 even those within the government with responsibility for or special interest in arms control found some attractive features in MIRV and did not oppose the development decision. Almost as soon as it had formed, however, opposition to this consensus began to emerge. A small number of government officials and former government officials, many of whom were or had been affiliated with the Arms Control and Disarmament Agency (ACDA) came to question the wisdom of deploying MIRVs.

Although this opposition grew with time and eventually gained a sizable and vocal public constituency it always remained too weak to be effective. Initially it lacked access to high level decisionmakers; later, once planning began for the Strategic Arms Limitation Talks (SALT) with the Soviet Union, access was available, but the opponents were not persuasive. One might argue that the degree of accumulated momentum behind the MIRV programs would have made them difficult or even impossible to stop or even to restrain by 1969. But there is no direct evidence. No one with authority or responsibility shared the opponents' view that the effort should be made.

PRELUDE

Once the military services realized the strategic and organizational advantages of employing MIRV on their strategic missiles the only remaining motivations for opposing the programs were budgetary pressures and arms control considerations. The former was of some importance for Poseidon, but directed more at the missile itself (and later the stellar inertial guidance system) than at the particular design of the warhead delivery system. Although a MIRV configuration is much more expensive than a single warhead measured on a per missile basis, the higher effectiveness of a MIRV system more than compensates. Although costly, MIRV was cost-effective. Moreover, much of the additional expense was in the warheads themselves, charged to Atomic Energy Commission, not Defense Department budgets, and thereby relieving some of the financial burden from the individual services. Major opposition to MIRV had to emerge, therefore, and eventually did emerge out of a concern for arms control. But that did not occur until well into the development cycle.

As late as 1965 MIRV was perceived by almost everyone to be beneficial, not detrimental, to unilateral arms control and was essentially irrelevant to the subjects under active discussion in international arms control negotiations. By increasing the potency of those forces that would survive a first strike, MIRV, like hardened ICBMs and sea-based forces, helped reduce the fear of surprise attack that had been prevalent in the late 1950s. By greatly increasing the number of available warheads and thereby contributing to the implementation of a city-avoidance strategy, MIRV would presumably further the goal of reducing the damage to American urban-industrial centers if war should break out.[1] Particularly by assisting the Secretary of Defense to hold down the number of deployed Minuteman ICBMs, to refuse funding of the Advanced Manned Strategic Aircraft and to resist mounting pressure to deploy Nike-X, MIRV contributed to the primary objectives for unilateral arms control of the early and middle 1960s: restraining the size of the deployed offensive forces and preventing the deployment of ABM systems.

On the international front, agreements such as the Limited Nuclear Test Ban Treaty, the American-Soviet Hot Line, the Treaty on Peaceful Uses of Outer Space, the Latin American Nuclear-Free Zone Agreement, and the Non-Proliferation Treaty had little or no relevance to the Soviet-American strategic arms balance and did not affect the MIRV programs at all. Nonetheless they consumed much of the time and energy of those within the government with interest in and responsibility for arms control, particularly ACDA. Until 1964 Soviet-American discussions about strategic forces focused on comprehensive treaties for general and complete disarmament and were constantly bogged down in questions of timing and verification.

In 1964 the approach to Soviet-American arms control began to change. In January the United States proposed to the Eighteen Nation Disarmament Committee "a verified freeze of strategic nuclear offensive and defensive vehicles."[2] As explained by Adrian Fisher, Deputy Director of ACDA, on April 16, 1964,[3] this so-called Johnson freeze proposal would have included all offensive and defensive nuclear delivery vehicles and launch facilities. It would have frozen the numbers at then-current levels, prohibited qualitative improvements, and regulated testing. Since it was based, however, on verification of production, not of deployed systems, its implementation required on-site inspection of production facilities. Although it was, not surprisingly, rejected by the Soviet Union the plan was a major milestone in the gradual evolution of thinking about arms control within the United States. It was not only a departure from past attempts at comprehensive disarmament but also led ACDA and others to realize the advantages inherent in concentrating on the limitation and verification of deployed systems. As such it must be considered the first official step on the long road toward SALT.

Shortly after the first preliminary formulation of the Johnson freeze proposal, an advisory committee of government officials and outsiders, several of whom had been actively involved in the early nurturing of the MIRV concept, was established to look in detail at the qualitative aspects of the freeze. Dr. George Rathjens, Special Assistant to the Director of ACDA, served as chairman. The primary interests of this committee were possible improvements of ABM systems and ABM penetrators. The raising of MIRV as a highly effective penetrator before this committee seems to be the first official mention of the new system to ACDA personnel. In general they supported it as a means of preserving the security of the American deterrent in the face of possible Soviet ABM deployments. This was in part a reflection of the view then prevailing in arms control circles that ABM systems were detrimental and anything that would efficiently nullify ABM systems was useful. But beyond that the later arguments that MIRV could contribute to strategic instability or be detrimental to arms control efforts would have been difficult to sustain at that early date. So long as verification of possible arms control agreements was thought to depend on on-site inspection of production facilities, MIRV did not seem to complicate the procedure. Very few people foresaw the day when the system's accuracy would be good enough for the small American MIRVs to be capable of effective attacks against hardened ICBMs. Of those that did, even fewer regarded that prospect as undesirable. Moreover, no one thought that the United States could have any leverage in preventing the Soviets from developing and deploying MIRVs of their own. Despite the Johnson freeze proposal, the probability of engaging in serious negotiations about numerical limits on strategic weapons seemed virtually nil. Qualitative limitations would be even harder to agree upon. In the absence of these negotiations few people thought that the United States should exercise self-imposed qualitative restraint.

The very possibility that arms control might be feasible was exploited by the military and its allies as an argument in favor of MIRV. In 1963, for example, General W. Austin Davis, commander of the Ballistic Systems Division, argued that the formation of ACDA augured eventual agreement to limit the number of deployed offensive missiles. MIRV, he suggested, had better be well under way before that happened. A similar sentiment expressed in

Missiles and Rockets[4] after the Johnson freeze was proposed may reflect the view of at least part of the Air Force. The suggestion was made that under such a freeze, "increasing the number of reentry vehicles per missile would ensure continued U.S. superiority over the Soviets." It seems to have escaped the author's notice that MIRV would be prohibited by the qualitative restrictions of the Johnson freeze.

There were some reservations raised about MIRV prior to 1965. During the 1962 JASON summer study,[a] for example, one member identified exchange ratio, that is the number of an opponent's missiles that are destroyed by each missile fired, as an important parameter of strategic stability, suggesting that accurate multiple warheads might lead to first strike instabilities, particularly if an attacker had a capable ABM system. The next summer the same JASON member, with several others, again looked at long-term stability problems, this time in light of some very optimistic accuracy projections that were being suggested, and explicitly including the multiple targeting capability characteristic of the recently invented MIRV concept. Because no negotiated limitation of MIRV seemed feasible, the report that emerged from the effort recommended that a mutual ban of ABM systems be sought with the Soviets. The report also examined the implications of high exchange ratio, but because of top secret classification, the report was not widely distributed. The same general argument was repeated before a broader audience at an ACDA meeting in Aspen, Colorado, in the summer of 1964.

The possibility that MIRV might have adverse implications for the strategic balance was also suggested by Jack Ruina, who had recently gone to the Massachusetts Institute of Technology from the Pentagon where he had been Director of the Advanced Research Projects Agency. In an effort to look ahead and assess the significance for the strategic balance and arms control of new weapons that were visible on the horizon, Ruina gathered Dr. Freeman Dyson of the Institute for Advanced Studies, Princeton, Dr. Murray Gell-Mann of the California Institute of Technology, and Dr. Robert LeLevier of the RAND Corporation, all JASON members, for discussions based in part on recent briefings by the Aerospace Corporation. In a letter dated September 1964, addressed to George Rathjens and Dr. Charles Herzfeld, Deputy Director, Advanced Research Projects Agency, Ruina summarized their conclusions and suggested, among other things, that MIRV was the foremost new development in the offensive arsenal that needed serious consideration. He recognized that "given some limitations [to offensive force size] for any reason whatsoever, the possible use of MIRV can make a qualitative difference in capability," and recommended that

> a systematic study of the implications of MIRV under various limiting conditions for the U.S. and S.U. arsenals ought to be

[a]JASON is a prestigious group of scientists who work parttime on military-related problems under the auspices of the Institute for Defense Analysis.

undertaken. Perhaps this should be part of a more general study which tries to assess the effect various constraints in the form of treaty prohibitions, inspection requirements, etc., have on the arms race and what constraints tend to have the arms race become more or less stable.[5]

Although the communication of these thoughts to ACDA contributed to the reversal in its attitude toward MIRV, technical information received from the Aerospace Corporation was more important. As an outgrowth of the committee on the qualitative aspects of the Johnson freeze, Aerospace Corp. was put under contract to ACDA to provide information about anticipated technical advances. The commissioned report, delivered at the end of 1964, discussed MIRV in detail and seems to have provided rather optimistic accuracy projections for the system. With these data in hand there was a gradual realization by ACDA personnel, particularly within the Science and Technology Bureau, that a high exchange ratio would eventually be attainable using MIRV. They concluded that this would have a destabilizing effect on the strategic balance and might impede the negotiation of some types of arms control or arms reduction schemes.

Through the middle 1960s continuing Soviet refusal to consider any type of on-site inspection of arms control agreements and ACDA's ongoing study of the problem of verification altered the conception of how agreements should be structured. It was realized that on-site inspection was more difficult and less useful than had been previously thought. While this was true primarily of on-site inspection of unidentified seismic events, thought to be a necessary adjunct of a comprehensive test ban treaty, it applied also to on-site monitoring of fissile material or delivery vehicle production. Moreover the usefulness of observation satellites was increasingly realized, particularly as their reliability and capabilities improved. Attention shifted from agreements like the 1964 freeze proposal that would include restrictions on production to those that would limit the number of deployed delivery vehicles.[6] Such agreements could be unilaterally monitored.

To many ACDA officials the possibility of MIRV deployment seemed to jeopardize this innovative and otherwise feasible approach to arms control verification. It was presumed that no agreement could be reached that would be indifferent to whether or not MIRVs were deployed. But, once MIRVs had been tested and deployment begun it was thought that there would be no way short of on-site inspection to be sure whether any particular missile carried MIRVs or a single warhead. Satellites could be used to count missiles but not to tell what those missiles carried. Only by looking inside or by examining the front end with high energy radiation, procedures that would almost certainly not be acceptable to the Soviet Union, and probably not to the United States either, could one be sure how many warheads a missile carried. Unless the MIRV programs were stopped before extensive testing had been done, therefore, their very existence would make the achievement of bilateral arms control more difficult. They themselves would be very difficult to control or eliminate retroactively.

The problem of strategic instability was thought to be equally important. A study by the Weapons Evaluation and Control Bureau (WEC), using Pentagon computer models of strategic exchange, suggested that Soviet forces would be quite vulnerable to a first strike attack if the United States deployed its MIRVs. The Soviet forces assumed in this study, if they reflected intelligence estimates of that period, were considerably modest compared to what the Soviets actually had deployed by the time the American MIRV deployments were well underway. Nevertheless, the WEC study was reported to be quite influential within ACDA in generating opposition to MIRV.

It is not completely clear to what extent those with authority over the MIRV programs were aware of ACDA's concerns. The relations between ACDA and the Department of Defense were not at all close during McNamara's tenure.[7] He and his staff seem to have felt quite competent in dealing with arms control matters without outside assistance. ACDA had no input to the budgetary process and was not asked about its strategic views. It had no authority to comment on major planning documents such as the Draft Presidential Memoranda. One former senior ACDA official reported the ACDA did not even receive its own copy of Draft Presidential Memoranda. Unless there were informal contacts, therefore, there was no ACDA input to policy planning, not even on a subject as important to arms control as the decision to deploy the Sentinel ABM system.[8] The informal communication channels of the Johnson Administration also tended to close ACDA out of major policy decisions. The Committee of Principals, for example, which was a top-level interdepartmental committee for discussion of arms control matters, was all but dormant until it became involved in preparing a position for SALT.[9] ACDA Director William Foster, was not the type of administrator who takes the initiative in bringing new issues to the fore. Several of the internal ACDA studies that examined the adverse implications of MIRV were sent to the Pentagon, but they seem to have had little impact. For example, it was reported that the first time Cyrus Vance, who had been Deputy Secretary of Defense since 1964, was exposed to ACDA's thinking about MIRV was at a meeting of the ACDA General Advisory Committee in 1967.

Even within ACDA the MIRV question was far from dominant. ACDA personnel were primarily engaged in the laborious and time-consuming negotiations of the Non-Proliferation Treaty (NPT) up until its signing in 1968. The NPT was Foster's major interest. He left other issues very much to his deputy, Adrian Fisher. Moreover, most ACDA officials were of the opinion that an ABM ban, not a MIRV ban, had the highest priority in any strategic weapons limitation scheme. In the action-reaction model of the nuclear arms race that tended to dominate arms control thinking during this period, MIRV was seen primarily as a reaction to potential ABM deployments.

Outside of ACDA there was little interest in MIRV as an arms control problem. Within the office of the Secretary of Defense it continued to be viewed as a contributor to arms control objectives in that it aided the resistance against congressional and military pressures for more Minutemen missiles and Nike-X deployment. MIRV was not thought of as a subject for direct negotiations with the Soviet Union. McNamara and those on his staff who thought extensively about arms control negotiations focused almost exclusively on preventing the proliferation of ABM systems.[10] The one exception seems to have been Martin McGuire, a staff member in the Office of Systems Analysis. In 1965, when the decisions were being made to authorize continued development of the Poseidon and Minuteman MIRVs and to begin including them in future force projections, he tried to delay or stop the programs. He felt, given the available intelligence information about Soviet ABM programs and the relatively shorter lead times of MIRV deployment compared to that for extensive ABM deployment, that a decision to produce MIRV was premature and might stimulate a Soviet response unnecessarily. He thought that rather than going ahead at that time, the threat to do so in the future might be used in an attempt to induce the Soviets to enter serious arms control negotiations. He raised this possibility with the Assistant Secretary of Defense (Comptroller), Charles Hitch, in whose office Systems Analysis was still situated, but it got nowhere.

McNamara specifically pointed out in his FY 1968 Posture Statement that the Soviets might consider MIRV a threat to their land-based forces unless they further dispersed and hardened their ICBMs.[11] This does not, however, seem to have produced reservations about the MIRV program. The Soviets were, after all, taking precisely those actions that McNamara suggested. Most officials within Systems Analysis did not believe the optimistic accuracy projections being made for MIRV by DDR&E.[12] Although some realized that accuracy might eventually improve to the point where a later generation of MIRVs could successfully attack even a hardened missile force, they felt that such a possibility was too far in the future to be relevant to then-current force planning. It is interesting that these same officials were very worried about the potential vulnerability of the Minuteman force in the event that the Soviet Union deployed accurate MIRVed missiles. True, Soviet warheads and throw-weights, especially on the SS-9, were much larger than those of American missiles, but the Soviets were far behind in all aspects of accuracy-related technology.

The President's Science Advisory Committee (PSAC) and its panels, especially the Military Strategic Panel, although deeply involved in the ongoing internal debates about ABM, were not consulted about MIRV. The difference in the two cases is almost certainly the result of the noncontroversial nature of the MIRV programs and the fact that, unlike the ABM case, no one doubted that MIRV would work. There was no reason, therefore, for opponents to solicit a technical judgment from a prestigious PSAC panel in support of their policy preferences. Moreover, since President Johnson's Special Assistant for Science and Technology, Donald Hornig, had neither the strong interest in arms control and national security matters nor the close relationship with the President of his predecessors, PSAC's influence was slight and its opportunities to be heard were few.

Throughout the 1960s there was a rather small but active arms control interest group outside the government which included in a private capacity many who had held government consulting or advisory positions dealing with national security affairs and many former government officials who had had responsibility in that area. During the Kennedy Administration this community had excellent contacts and connections within the government. Some of those who had been part of the community in the late 1950s had joined the Administration. Under Johnson, however, after most of these had resigned and especially once the escalation of the war in Vietnam began, contacts were virtually severed. The almost universal commitment to working through official channels in the executive branch gradually weakened and the number of public activities and contacts with senators and congressmen gradually increased. The dominant interest of this outside community, once the Limited Test Ban Treaty was signed, was to prevent the deployment of the American ABM and, if possible, to negotiate a mutual ABM ban with the Soviets. This single issue captured the vast majority of their concern and attention.[13]

Lest the impression be given, however, that MIRV received no attention outside the government some of the infrequent examples must be cited. During 1966 and 1967 one former Defense Department official tried to arouse interest in Congress and in ACDA about how the American MIRV programs might look to the Soviets. He made his concerns known to several senators, including Edward Brooke (R.-Massachusetts), and Senate staff members and also to an official in the Weapons Evaluation and Control Bureau of ACDA. It is possible that these efforts contributed to the growth of congressional concern about MIRV and that they reinforced the apprehension that was by then very much alive within ACDA. The possibility that an American MIRV deployment might be interpreted by the Soviet Union as a first strike force and the stimulating effect that such a deployment, especially if accompanied by ABMs, might have on the arms race were raised by American scientists during a meeting of the Soviet-American Disarmament Study group in December 1967.[b] It is not possible to know what impact this discussion had on the Soviet scientists or whether it affected either the Soviet Union's offensive development programs or

---

[b]The first meeting of this group took place in 1964 as an outgrowth of the Pugwash conferences. It was felt that the multinational nature of Pugwash sometimes led to breaches in the confidentiality that the Soviets and Americans wanted in discussing issues of a bilateral nature and that purely private American-Soviet sessions would be useful. The American and Soviet groups were organized as the Committee on International Studies of Arms Control of the American Academy of Arts and Sciences and the Pugwash Committee of the Soviet Academy of Sciences respectively.

its approach to the MIRV problem at SALT. Nevertheless, the fact that MIRV was raised by the Americans does indicate that by 1967 it was a subject of growing importance to those who were involved in these meetings.

It is worth asking whether the extraordinary official secrecy that surrounded the MIRV programs until September 1967 was responsible for this absence of opposition. Certainly it was not lack of knowledge that prevented controversy within the government. It was precluded by the unavailability of mechanisms for those few government officials and advisors who questioned the MIRV programs to argue their case effectively. Although most legislators may not have known about MIRV until the daily press began to hint at it in 1966, or even until the official disclosure, the lack of attention given to all other weapons acquisition issues by senators and congressmen without positions on the responsible legislative committees strongly suggests that their reliance on these committees, not secrecy, prevented their attention from focusing on MIRV. Even the Subcommittee on Disarmament of the Senate Foreign Relations Committee, a center of opposition to ABM and eventually to MIRV, was apparently uninterested in MIRV as an arms control problem during its 1967 hearings,[14] although the Chairman, Senator Albert Gore (D.-Tennessee) explored the matter of accuracy-improvements with General Wheeler at the time.[15]

There were politically active opponents of nuclear weapons programs without security clearances and who therefore were probably unaware of the MIRV programs in the early years. Nonetheless, by early 1966, when articles started appearing in both *The Wall Street Journal* and *The New York Times* discussing multiple and maneuverable warheads,[16] the existence of MIRV must have become common knowledge among this attentive public. The actual term "MIRV" seems to have been first used in the daily press in January 1967,[17] but it had been used in aerospace journals since 1964.[18] If secrecy had been the inhibitor to opposition on the part of these outsiders that should have changed in 1966 or at least in 1967. But it did not. The real inhibitor was probably the centrality of the ABM question and the absence of any real chance during this period of engaging in strategic arms control negotiations with the Soviet Union.

The only case in which the evidence seems to suggest that official secrecy played an important inhibiting role to public criticism is in the editorializing of Robert Kleiman of *The New York Times*. Although his newspaper carried news stories mentioning MIRV much earlier he did not become aware of MIRV until shortly before McNamara's discussion of it appeared in the *Life* magazine interview.[19] Kleiman's first article about MIRV,[20] in which he discussed both the exchange ratio question and possible verification problems and expressed the hope that SALT might be able to head off this new technology, followed McNamara's announcement by less than two weeks. Had MIRV not been a secret program, Kleiman almost certainly would have known about it and probably would have written about it earlier. But it was not McNamara's announcement that set off Kleiman's anti-MIRV campaign. He did not write on the subject again until August 1968.[21] It made little sense, Kleiman felt, to call for MIRV's termination, so long as talks with the Soviets did not appear imminent, and he too saw MIRV as an asset in the fight against ABM.

If the development of public, congressional, and more effective official opposition to MIRV that began in 1968 cannot be attributed to the lifting of the security cloak, causes must be sought elsewhere, particularly in the changing political and social environment. It was the combination of technical advances, new intelligence information, changes in the mood of Congress and the country and the apparent imminence of arms control negotiations that led to the initial challenge to the MIRV programs. The outbreak of a full scale controversy also required a change in Administration.

Technical improvements in inertial guidance components increased the credibility of estimates that Minuteman III MIRVs would be useful weapons for attacking the Soviet land-based missile force. The stellar inertial guidance program and improvements in the navigation systems for ballistic missile submarines were expected to enhance rather significantly the counterforce potential of Poseidon. Moreover, there was little doubt that accuracies would continue to improve with time. It was not MIRV as a hedge against ABM deployment or MIRV as an efficient and effective countervalue weapon that attracted criticism. It was, rather, MIRV as an effective counterforce weapon that could either threaten or be perceived as threatening the destruction of Soviet land-based missiles. Without the accuracy improvements of the past and the expectation of future improvements, MIRV systems could not have been seen as a destabilizing force for the strategic balance.

The reduction in the apparent Soviet ABM threat seemed to undermine one of the central justifications for the MIRV systems and led to a weakening of the support for MIRV in the Congress and among the attentive public. Most intelligence analysts agreed by 1967 that the Tallinn System had no significant ABM capability and could not easily be upgraded to have such a capability. Although the military disagreed with the latter judgment, it was widely accepted in ACDA, the Congress, and among outside arms control advocates. Moreover, the Moscow ABM system was proceeding very slowly and was not being extended to other areas. It had the character of a system being used to gain operational experience and to experiment with new radar systems, not one that was intended to be a reliable defense of Moscow. No one doubted that the system, as deployed, would pose very little problem to American offensive missiles. In short, although the Soviets were continuing their R&D program on ABM components, it did not look as if they would soon deploy a large, nationwide system. The ABM part of the greater than expected threat was no closer to realization in 1968 than several years before and looked much less credible than it had then.[22] There seemed to be a debate between the pro-ABM and anti-ABM factions inside the Soviet Union.[23] The outside arms controllers were persuaded that, with their own help and encouragement (provided during Pugwash meetings and other informed contacts), the anti-ABM faction was winning out.[24] As their previous concern about the Soviet ABM diminished, both they and interested legislators were able to focus increasingly on the implications of MIRV as a counterforce weapon.

Senior Defense Department officials still thought that MIRV was necessary as a hedge against the possibility that the Soviets would change their minds on ABM, as a hedge against Tallinn upgrade or to deter both of these. They also saw MIRV, particularly on Poseidon, as a partial solution to the anticipated vulnerability of the Minuteman force and were acutely aware of the financial and organizational costs of delay. But arms control advocates and some senators saw, instead, the costs of continuing and the decreased need for high-confidence penetration capability. These critics were quite willing to rely on the existing Polaris force as a hedge against Minuteman vulnerability. They could therefore argue that MIRV was no longer needed, at any rate not soon. The change in expectation of Soviet ABM deployments, like the improvements in accuracy technology, was not sufficient to stir a controversy over MIRV, but was probably necessary to do so.

Equally important in catalyzing the debate were changing attitudes about the Administration, the military, and postwar history. Disillusionment with the Vietnam War engendered a new intellectual climate. A series of "revisionist" studies had reexamined the origins and development of the Cold War and concluded that the Soviets and Chinese were not the only ones deserving blame. The United States too had contributed to the tensions of the 1940s and 1950s. It had also pursued objectives and supported political movements abroad that were not always in the best interest of the majority of the population in Asian and South American countries. With such a view of the past, the Communist nations did not look so menacing as they once did. Moreover, it was now clear to informed observers that the concept of a unified world communism with policy dictated by Moscow was a myth. Even the domino theory was becoming discredited. The United States and particularly its military policy were seen as major contributors to the tensions and regional wars of the past quarter century. To many in Congress and among the non-governmental foreign policy elite the war in Vietnam was an abomination and the Administration that perpetuated it deserved neither loyalty nor sympathy. More radically inclined individuals saw the war as only the most recent in a series of misguided or malevolent policies which should be reversed.

Even among those who were not influenced by these changing intellectual attitudes, the Vietnam War was becoming increasingly distasteful by 1968. The number of Americans killed and wounded continued to rise; inflation was rampant and widely attributed to war costs; President Johnson's promised "Great Society" had evidently been sacrificed to the war effort; increasing disruption on the campuses and in the urban ghettos were indirectly attributed to the war. In 1968 a strong anti-war political movement split the Democratic party. All this reflected and encouraged a growing anti-militarism, a tendency to blame the military professionals and the civilian technocrats for the country's ills, to view government policy as a tool of the "military-industrial complex" and to disdain the very existence of weapons of war. Public spokesmen were increasingly willing to challenge the military's requests for funds, not only for Vietnam, but also for new strategic weapon systems. The main rallying point for these forces, aside from Senator Eugene McCarthy's presidential campaign of 1968 and the ongoing anti-war movement, was the ABM debate, focused on Sentinel in 1968 and even more strongly on Safeguard in 1969. Many individuals who first became interested in military-strategic matters through their concern about the ABM expanded this interest and began writing and lobbying against MIRV. But the MIRV controversy was never more than a minor skirmish compared to the bitter fight over ABM.

Despite the direct clash of Soviet and American interests, client states and military hardware in Vietnam, a movement toward talks with the Soviets on the mutual limitation of strategic weapons began in late 1966 and continued through 1968. Secretary McNamara and other Defense Department officials had become acutely aware of interactive effects in the strategic arms competition and convinced that the cycle of continuously rising force levels could be arrested only by means of bilateral agreement. During the review of the FY 1968 budget in late 1966, McNamara convinced President Johnson to hold off again on deploying Nike-X and to seek talks with the Soviets to the end of permanently eliminating ABM systems. After repeated delays and unaccepted American initiatives extending over a period of about eighteen months,[25] the Soviets finally signalled their readiness to begin. On July 1, 1968, on the occasion of the opening for signatures of the Non-Proliferation Treaty,[c] a joint announcement indicated that the two governments would "enter in the nearest future into talks on limitation and reduction of offensive strategic nuclear weapons delivery systems as well as systems of defense against ballistic missiles."[26]

The preparations for strategic arms limitation talks involved ACDA for the first time in policy planning for the strategic forces. Almost from the initiation of contacts with the Soviets, ACDA, particularly the Science and Technology Bureau, was an active participant in efforts to design a bargaining posture. A preliminary policy paper prepared in 1967 was a product primarily of ACDA and the State Department. ACDA was finally in a position, therefore, where it could communicate its reservations about MIRV at the highest level.

As the planning process got underway in early 1967, everyone agreed that the major issue was ABM, but there were no objections to discussing

---

[c]It may be, as one ACDA official suggested, that the Soviets considered the NPT a prerequisite to bilateral negotiations on strategic arms limitation.

offensive systems as well, as the Soviets evidently desired. ACDA officials and some of those from State argued that MIRV should be included in the basic negotiating position. Everyone understood, however, that the Joint Chiefs of Staff would strongly oppose any restriction on MIRV. ACDA staff members were apparently told that if they wanted to get agreement on a position including an ABM ban they should not press the MIRV issue. Fearing the loss of their credibility if they pushed too hard for what was clearly a minority point of view, ACDA did not insist. A proposal for a MIRV ban was merely appended as a possible option along with a bomber freeze and a prohibition of mobile systems. ACDA did generate a number of papers expressing reservations about MIRV and recommending that the subject be included at SALT. Some of these were sent to McNamara in an attempt to gain his support. But neither he nor his staff could be persuaded that MIRV was a central issue. He reportedly refused to consider the argument that MIRV might be destabilizing. Despite the exclusion of a MIRV ban from the basic posture, ACDA by no means abandoned its hope that it would be raised during the negotiations. In fact ACDA expected that the Soviets would be unwilling to ignore it. Since the first tests were still more than a year away, no one felt much urgency. The talks did not take place in 1967, however, and the MIRV programs remained unchallenged.

Energized by the prospects of SALT, the Military Strategic Panel of PSAC also began on its own initiative to think about preferred outcomes and the United States' bargaining position. Although by this time some panel members were quite opposed to MIRV, there was by no means total agreement. As a group, the PSAC panel made no pronouncement on the subject. Even if it had, however, the impact would have been minimal. By 1967 the stature and influence of PSAC and the President's Science Advisor had greatly decreased. Except for the participation of Spurgeon Keeny, who, as Hornig's staff assistant for weapons questions, worked closely with the National Security Council staff of Walt Rostow, the White House science advisory apparatus played no significant role in the internal planning for SALT. Several panel members, however, later became quite active in both the ABM debate and the MIRV controversy, relying on their PSAC experience in providing testimony to congressional committees and private advice to individual legislators.

The exclusion of the PSAC scientists from the internal planning of SALT was symptomatic of the estranged relationship between the scientific establishment, to which many outside arms control advocates belonged, and the Johnson Administration. Not only were there few people in the Administration who were interested in the views of this group, but dissatisfaction with the continued escalation in Vietnam was pervasive and on the increase within it. Many of those who had been active in Scientists and Engineers for Johnson-Humphrey felt disappointed, even betrayed, by Johnson's policy of escalation. As their alienation increased and their loyalty to the Administration decreased, many scientists who had been involved in military matters over the years lost their inhibitions against speaking publicly or seeking outlets outside the executive branch for their political activities.[27] The change of administration in 1969 made the turn to public advocacy even easier. Many of these scientists were Democrats by political affiliation and many had been associated with previous Democratic administrations. They had opposed the election of President Nixon, disagreed with his policies on many substantive issues, and felt no loyalty at all to his administration. Moreover, the termination of advisory positions freed several individuals from the obligation to refrain from public criticism.

Changes also took place within the Congress. During most of the 1960s military affairs and defense budgets were the exclusive province of the two Armed Services Committees, the Defense subcommittees of the two Appropriations Committees, and the Joint Committee on Atomic Energy,[d] the first four of which were chaired by conservative southern legislators who were sympathetic to the needs and desires of the military. Particularly Senator Richard Russell (D.-Georgia), who for many years chaired both the Senate Armed Services Committee and the Senate Appropriations Subcommittee on the Department of Defense, and Representatives Carl Vinson (D.-Georgia) and Mendel Rivers (D.-South Carolina), who were the successive chairmen of the House Armed Services Committee, were major advocates of military programs through the 1960s. Other influential senators, such as Henry Jackson (D.-Washington), who sat on the Armed Services Committee and chaired the Military Applications Subcommittee of the Joint Committee on Atomic Energy, and John Stennis (D.-Mississippi), who sat on the Appropriations Subcommittee on the Department of Defense and succeeded Senator Russell as chairman of the Armed Services Committee, often supported strategic weapons programs beyond the level requested by the Secretary. As with many highly specialized legislative areas, other members of the House and Senate tended to accept the recommendations of the specialized committees. Military matters were quite technical and most legislators not on the relevant committees were not cleared to have access to secret information. As a result, until about 1968 a small group of experts (called a "cabal" by one former Senate aide) most of whom were sympathetic to the military, exercised almost absolute control. Year after year the defense budget, allocating tens of billions of dollars, would take less time for passage on the floor of each house than the budgets of civilian agencies that were only a small fraction of that size.

Interest in arms control was centered in the Senate Foreign Relations Committee, which, aside from foreign military assistance, had no direct control over the defense budget. Almost every year the status of negotiations

---

[d]The House Committee on Science and Astronautics, the Senate Committee on Aeronautical and Space Sciences, and the Government Operations Committees of both Houses also made occasional forays into military and military-related matters, but they had no legislative authority in these fields.

and current problems were reviewed in hearings rather narrowly focused on subjects of timely interest such as the Limited Test Ban Treaty, the Outer Space Treaty, the Nonproliferation Treaty, and the various approaches to strategic arms limitations. Several members of the Foreign Relations Committee followed military affairs quite closely by means of their memberships in other committees. Senators Albert Gore (D.-Tennessee) and Bourke Hickenlooper (R.-Iowa) sat on the Joint Committee on Atomic Energy and Senator Stuart Symington (D.-Missouri) was a member of the Armed Services Committee as well as being a retired Secretary of the Air Force.

In the late 1960s the control exercised by the Armed Services Committees and the Defense Appropriations Subcommittees began to weaken, particularly in the Senate. The growing number of contacts between outsiders versed in military matters and certain senators, some of whom were not on the controlling committees, helped to build the senators' confidence that they could tackle military and strategic issues independent of the committee leadership. Some senators and congressmen added to their staffs individuals versed in military issues. The posture statements presented to the Congress yearly by Secretary McNamara provided detailed discussions of military programs and were read widely by senators and their staffs, thereby increasing their awareness of and enhancing their competence to deal with such matters. More important in sparking congressional opposition to military programs was the increasing dissatisfaction in both houses with the expense and cost overruns of military hardware and with the national policy in Vietnam and a feeling that Congress had abrogated its responsibilities in the fields of military and foreign policy. The latter was magnified after 1969, when the presidency and the Congress were controlled by different political parties. Many senators and some congressmen became more willing to challenge the President's authority and judgment in these areas. They saw that while the United States and the Soviet Union were moving haltingly toward SALT, a new round of expensive and, many thought, unnecessary and destabilizing weapons were about to be deployed by the United States. Those included particularly ABM and MIRV.

The number of legislators interested in military and arms control matters increased and other committees began to expand their traditional purview. The Joint Economic Committee began to take an interest in some aspects of the defense budget and both the Senate Foreign Relations Committee and the Subcommittee on National Security Policy and Scientific Developments of the House Foreign Affairs Committee began examining a wider variety of technical, strategic, and arms control issues including weapons procurement. Although none of these committees had legislative authority over the defense budget, their hearings served to educate the legislators and their staffs as well as the public. They all began to rely on the testimony of outside witnesses with special experience or expertise in fields of special interest. The increased knowledge and confidence of many senators and congressmen were demonstrated by amendments and floor fights on a variety of military-related issues.

The momentum of the new opposition took several years to build up. In 1967 the military appropriations bill including the funds to begin deployment of the Nike-X ABM system passed in the Senate with only a few dissenting voices.[28] The next year two amendments offered jointly by Senators John Sherman Cooper (R.-Kentucky) and Philip Hart (D.-Michigan) (neither of whom were members of the Armed Services Committee or Defense Appropriations Subcommittee) to deny funds for Sentinel ABM deployment received thirty-four and twenty-five supporting votes respectively.[29] By 1969 when President Nixon announced his decision to go ahead with a limited ABM deployment the opposition was prepared to fight hard. With the help and cooperation of a large number of scientists, many of whom had held full-time advisory or consulting jobs with the government,[30] they mustered fifty votes against Safeguard in a Senate vote without absentees.

It is interesting to note that despite this growing Senate opposition to ABM the first legislator to question one of the MIRV programs was a staunch supporter of the military, Senator Russell. In 1968 he questioned the decision to move ahead quickly on the Poseidon conversion program before the missile had ever been tested. Bitter memories of the troubles on the Navy's Tartar, Telos, and Terrier anti-aircraft missiles convinced him that the proven reliability of the Polaris system should not be jeopardized by rushing into a new and unproved technology. Despite the best efforts of Deputy Secretary Nitze, DDR&E Foster, Special Projects Office Director Admiral Smith and other Navy personnel, Russell cut the number of authorized conversions for FY 1969 from the six requested by the President to two.[31] According to Sapolsky, this was "the first congressional cut consciously made in an FBM[e] appropriation request (the preceding year there had been an accidental cut in an FBM-related measure)."[32] Again in 1969, despite the success of the test program, the committee cut the number of authorized conversions from six to four.[33] Although these cutbacks had no lasting effect on the program and probably did not delay it as much as Senator Russell had hoped, they were indicative of a changing attitude in the Senate: senators were more willing to take the initiative in opposing military programs.

Although many of the anti-ABM senators regarded MIRV and ABM as closely linked and were willing to oppose both, they made a tactical decision to defer a fight over MIRV. They feared that they could not win such a fight and that any attempt might divert attention and energy from the more important and more feasible ABM issue. Several felt that MIRV would be more vulnerable and easier to eliminate after ABM was defeated. ABM could be attacked on technical grounds and therefore the outside scientists could be

[e]Fleet Ballistic Missile (FBM) system is the official name for the Polaris system.

mobilized to testify and supply both arguments and information. MIRV, on the other hand, would have to be attacked from a purely strategic standpoint and that would be more difficult. Moreover, ABM had been a contentious subject for many years, and had become a major public issue the previous year when the Army began preparation of several sites near large metropolitan areas. Since there was already an active grassroots anti-ABM constituency in several places around the country, the political base would be larger than for a fight against MIRV, about which few people had heard. ABM was in every way a better target. Several of the anti-ABM senators did not agree with the decision to avoid taking on the MIRV programs and proceeded on their own. A similar effort was mounted in the House. It is largely as a result of their efforts that the MIRV programs became a public controversy in 1969 and 1970.

TO TEST OR NOT TO TEST

The first serious challenge to the MIRV programs finally occurred in 1968 as a result of the conjunction of the first MIRV tests and the imminence of SALT. Although opposition to MIRV had grown, primarily in ACDA, and increasingly in State, the challenge came from outside arms control advocates, the Senate and particularly from within the Pentagon itself. The efforts of the outsiders were public and ineffective, but did build a base from which a stronger opposition could be mounted in subsequent years. The Senate and Pentagon initiatives were private, uncoordinated and also unsuccessful.

When active planning for a SALT negotiating position resumed in the summer of 1968, several important environmental changes had taken place. First and most important, the decision to deploy the Sentinel ABM system had been made the previous September. Planning was now in terms of ABM limitations, not total prohibition. Second, the Joint Chiefs now provided a representative to the drafting group in the person of Major General R.B. Allison, later a member of the United States SALT delegation. Previously the chiefs had only commented on a completed draft position paper, but now ACDA and others felt the constant presence of the military point of view. Third, the MIRV tests were scheduled to begin in August.

Those ACDA personnel involved in SALT planning felt just as strongly about MIRV in 1968 as they had the year before, but they still feared that it would be a tactical mistake to push for either a MIRV ban or a delay in the tests. They were unwilling to risk losing in a major fight with the military. They still expected that the Soviets would raise the MIRV issue, and did not think that completion of a few tests in the meantime would make any difference. Once the Soviets raised it, they reasoned, the United States would have to take the possibility of a MIRV ban seriously and then ACDA could come forward with its previous analyses.[34]

The military and DDR&E strongly supported the continuation of the MIRV programs. The feeling was prevalent not only that the MIRV programs had been a crucial factor in inducing the Soviets to negotiate at all, but also that since the Soviets were engaged in a massive offensive missile buildup the ultimate extent of which was totally unknown, and since the United States had no offensive programs under way other than MIRV, stopping or delaying the tests would greatly reduce the Soviets' incentive to bargain. They also saw MIRV as a hedge against the upgrade of the Tallinn system, a possibility that both the military and DDR&E still claimed to be a serious issue. In fact this became a very contentious subject during this period.[35] The verification problems of a mutual MIRV test ban also raised problems. Since DDR&E and the military did not think that a verifiable mutual ban was feasible, they saw no reason not to go ahead with the tests. Moreover to delay the tests would be very expensive, since technical teams would have to be kept together and since the maintenance of Polaris submarines and the replacement schedules of older Minuteman missiles had been arranged with the expectation that the new missiles would be deployed. Finally, if SALT failed, which the military thought likely, MIRV would be, in their view, absolutely essential to counter the ever-enlarging Soviet missile force.

Management of the bargaining on the SALT position within the Department of Defense now fell to Deputy Assistant Secretary of Defense (International Security Affairs) Morton Halperin. Although his major problem was getting the Joint Chiefs of Staff and DDR&E to agree to a package including ABM limitation and quantitative restrictions on offensive weapons, Halperin also began to think about the implications of the forthcoming initial tests of Poseidon and Minuteman III. Although he did not think that the negotiation of a MIRV ban was likely, he did not want to preempt the issue by going ahead with the tests. If the Soviets should turn out to be interested in eliminating this new technology in which the United States had a very great lead and were willing to make interesting concessions to achieve that objective, Halperin thought the option should be available. After the first tests, he felt, such bargaining would be much more difficult. He saw no hope, however, of reaching agreement to delay the tests through the normal channels for discussing SALT-related matters.

Several people in State shared ACDA's opinion that a MIRV ban should be sought at SALT, but, unlike ACDA, they were willing to engage in a high-level fight on the issue of delaying the tests. They went to Secretary of State Dean Rusk and asked him to support such a delay, but they were turned down.[36] He was reported to be unwilling to go to the President in opposition to Secretary of Defense Clark Clifford or to interfere in what he considered to be a defense budgetary matter. The subject of a test postponement did come up at a meeting of the Committee of Principals, but with both ACDA and Rusk unwilling to push the matter, it just died.

As the chances were gradually fading that the MIRV tests would be delayed by agreement through official channels, an effort was made to circumvent the military opposition. Halperin and Ivan Selin, Deputy Assistant Secretary of Defense (Systems Analysis) for Strategic Programs, with the assistance of their staffs, decided to go directly to Clifford, who was the only one with authority to delay the tests. First they tried to discover when the tests were scheduled to begin and what the impact of a six-month delay would be. In response to their inquiries the services reported that the programs would be severely hurt: the costs of keeping the laboratories going would be high; there would be rescheduling problems and the overall reliability of the forces would suffer. Furthermore, testing was scheduled to begin almost immediately. One individual who was involved in the effort thought that the Air Force advanced the date of their first test in order to strengthen their case. Nonetheless, International Security Affairs and Systems Analysis drafted a plan that would permit a six-month delay in the first full-scale flight tests, while component testing continued, without delaying the deployment schedule.

This proposition was taken to Clifford and Deputy Secretary Paul Nitze. All the principal actors, including the Air Force, the Navy, the Joint Chiefs of Staff, DDR&E, and Systems Analysis were then involved in discussing the plan. The consensus was that a MIRV ban was probably not desirable; that it was quite unlikely that a mutual test ban could be negotiated quickly; that delay would be costly in terms of both resources and American security; and finally, that if, contrary to all expectation, a MIRV ban later seemed desirable as part of some overall SALT package, the fact that the United States had initiated MIRV tests would probably not be an impediment. There seem to be two underlying reasons for these conclusions. First the MIRV capability was considered to be compensatory for the unilaterally-imposed limitation of the American offensive forces in the middle 1960s and for the relatively small total throw-weight of the deployed missiles. The Soviets had been deploying missiles with very large warheads, had surpassed the United States in the total megatonnage deployed on missiles and were fully expected by most Pentagon officials to be building toward superiority in the number of missiles. A MIRV ban, therefore, would have to be accompanied by an equalization of numbers of missiles and available throw-weight in order to be acceptable. Second, the prevailing opinion was that taking unilateral restraining action was not the best way to induce the Soviets to negotiate seriously. Better to maintain the momentum of American programs and to bargain from a position of strength. Restraint, most participants felt, should be exercised mutually or not at all.

Clifford did not overrule this overwhelming Pentagon consensus as Halperin and Selin evidently hoped he would. In fact he seems to have agreed with it. He told a press conference on September 5 that in rejecting the suggestions to delay the MIRV tests and to defer or eliminate the Sentinel ABM he had assumed "that a position of substantial strength is essential and is the best position from which we can negotiate agreements that make the threat of nuclear war increasingly remote"[37] and that "I am confident that our decision to proceed with the very important tests of our MIRV principle does not prejudice the prospects that such talks would be fruitful."[38] He apparently did not feel required to seek presidential guidance on the matter of MIRV testing, but made the final decision himself.

At the same time that this internal effort was being made to postpone the MIRV tests, a similar initiative was taken by several senators and non-governmental arms control advocates. Senators Cooper and Hart, the sponsors of the anti-Sentinel amendments, and perhaps some other senators wrote to President Johnson asking him to postpone the tests, but to no avail. The arms control task force supporting Senator Eugene McCarthy's candidacy for the Democratic Party's presidential nomination prevailed on him to issue a position paper in early August calling, among other things, for delay in the Poseidon and Minuteman III deployments pending talks with the Soviets.[39] A Hubert Humphrey campaign task force under the chairmanship of Professor Marshall Shulman of Columbia University produced a draft of a speech opposing both MIRV and Sentinel ABM. The speech was never delivered, however. In fact, it was squelched because Spurgeon Keeny, then acting as a Humphrey advisor within the White House, felt that with all Humphrey's problems he would not be helped by making a rather theoretical speech about arms control. At the Republican National Convention during the summer of 1968, Kleiman tried to convince Nelson Rockefeller's advisors to oppose the MIRV tests, but to no avail. There was even a petition circulated within the scientific community and sent to the Pentagon urging that the tests be delayed.[40]

The efforts of the arms control advocates, of Senators Cooper and Hart and of Halperin and Selin were totally independent, and, in the latter two cases, quite private. Senate staffers who could reasonably be expected to have known about or helped draft the letter to President Johnson were not informed about it. A senior ACDA official who had been deeply involved in ACDA's own tactical decision about MIRV was unaware of both the Pentagon and the Senate initiatives. It is difficult to know if anything was lost by this lack of communication and coordination. Opinions from the outside arms control advocates were very unlikely to have made any impact within the government. Since ACDA had already decided not to push on the test issue and since the State Department officials had already failed to win Rusk's support, Halperin and Selin probably had nothing to gain from coordinating their efforts with either of them. Had Townsend Hoopes, then Undersecretary of the Air Force, known that civilians within the Office of the Secretary of Defense shared his reservations about going ahead with the MIRV programs, he might have been more willing to make an issue of it. A middle-level alliance might have been formed, but whether it could have been effective is doubtful. The nature of the Halperin-Selin strategy was to go outside normal channels around known centers of opposition, directly to Clifford. The strategy was probably a good one. Only a determined effort by the Secretary himself could have had a chance of overcoming the accumulated momentum of the programs. One can only speculate concerning the possible effect of interaction between this Pentagon effort and the senators' approach to the President. If Clifford had been told that some senators were writing to the President and the President had been told that some Defense Department officials favored delay, perhaps the chances of success would have increased. But the case is not very convincing.

By 1968 the military's commitment to MIRV was exceedingly strong. The programs were too far advanced, deployment schedules of Poseidon and Minuteman III were too integrated with the maintenance and modernization of existing systems, and too many other programs had been given up along the way for the military to forego or delay the new MIRVed missiles willingly. For delay to have been effected, the military would have to have been overruled. Only Secretary Clifford and the President had the authority to do this. In fact, Clifford probably could not have done it on his own. Had he decided to delay the tests, the military would almost certainly have appealed to the President.

There are two circumstances in which Clifford and Johnson might have overruled the military: if they were persuaded that the interest of the country clearly called for delay or if there was sufficient political pressure to counterbalance the political weight of the military. Both the senators and the Pentagon officials took the former approach trying to persuade Johnson and Clifford that the matter was important enough for them to withstand the military pressure. As mentioned above, Clifford does not even seem to have been convinced himself that delay was a good idea, never mind being sufficiently convinced to be willing to lead a crusade against the military. Johnson tended to stay aloof from the bureaucratic bargaining that accompanied the preparations for SALT. He preferred to receive the unanimous position of the government rather than be told about disagreements and make his own decisions.[41] On the MIRV tests the weight of opinion, as Johnson must have perceived it, was clearly in favor of going ahead. Even if the senators had told him that several Pentagon officials disagreed with this opinion, his perception of the consensus would almost certainly not have changed.

There was no chance of providing a political counterbalance to the military. ACDA had decided not to try and Rusk had cast State's lot on the matter with the Joint Chiefs. In the Senate, Cooper and Hart had been defeated in their attempt to stop Sentinel in June and no one can doubt that they would have done even worse in an attempt to get the Senate to suggest a delay in the MIRV tests. In fact, if Clifford had decided to delay the tests the military might have been able to mobilize more active supporters in Congress to help their own cause than Cooper, Hart, and others could have mobilized against it. Outside arms control advocates were still not united in the belief that MIRV was a high-priority issue. Many individuals continued to view MIRV primarily as a useful argument against Sentinel.[42] As the date of the first tests approached, some outsiders, including Kleiman in *The New York Times*, denounced the apparent decision to go ahead. But they had no leverage to make those inside either listen to their statements or care about them. Given the environment of 1968 and particularly the policy preferences of the major political actors, the effort to delay the MIRV tests was bound to fail. Failure had little or nothing to do with the lack of coordination between those who opposed the program. Under the circumstances, Halperin and Selin seem to have made a rather good try.

On August 16 the tests went ahead as scheduled. Both were described as complete successes.[43] The only concession that was made to those who tried to delay them was to subdue the subsequent announcements. International Security Affairs successfully argued that a dramatic announcement of the type the services would have preferred might harm the prospect of the talks. They won agreement to a low profile approach. This is reflected, for example, in *The New York Times* reports.[44]

Whether or not the Soviets would have insisted on discussing a MIRV ban in 1968, as ACDA thought, will never be known unless they one day decide to reveal their own thinking about SALT in that period. On August 20, 1968, the very eve of the planned announcement that talks would begin, the Soviet Union invaded Czechoslovakia. Johnson felt that his planned visit to Moscow and the anticipated SALT negotiations must be delayed as a result. For a while the Soviets pressed for the initiation of talks while the United States waited for western emotions about the invasion to die down. By the time Johnson was ready, the Soviets were no longer interested. They evidently had decided to wait until the Nixon Administration took office.[45]

In the months following the invasion MIRV ceased to be an issue in the Administration. The test question was settled. The military must certainly have felt vindicated when within a week after the first tests SALT was delayed and the Soviets tested a multiple warhead system of their own.[46] The Administration's attention was focused on whether or not there would be talks at all. Reopening the question of a MIRV ban was simply not timely.

It has been suggested that a MIRV ban may have been a casualty of the Soviet invasion of Czechoslovakia.[47] While no one can be sure, this seems unlikely. Even if the Soviets had been interested enough, despite the initiation of American tests, to offer major concessions in exchange for a MIRV ban, the United States probably would not have agreed. The inability to build any significant support for a delay in the tests strongly suggests that agreement on a MIRV ban would have been equally impossible to achieve. Of course the issue would not have been settled during Johnson's tenure. The decision still would have fallen to the Nixon Administration. But, as will be seen in the next section, the acceptability of a MIRV ban was no greater then.

MIRV AND SALT

The debate over MIRV testing resumed in 1969 and continued into 1970, heating up considerably. There were two major stimulants of the debate during this period. The most important was the planning for and then engagement in strategic arms negotiations with the Soviet Union. Second was the very bitter and highly polarized fight over the Safeguard ABM system, compared to which the MIRV debate was a relatively minor skirmish. The major impetus came from a small number of legislators, particularly Senator Edward Brooke (R.-Massachusetts), who believed, despite the explicit decision of his like-minded colleagues to avoid diverting attention from the ABM fight by focusing attention on MIRV, that every effort should be made to prevent the deployment of MIRV or at least to delay it in order not to preëmpt the possibility of its elimination through SALT.

When the Nixon Administration assumed power in January 1969 it inherited the commitment of its predecessor to begin negotiating on strategic arms limitations with the Soviet Union, the growing public outcry over existing plans to deploy nuclear-tipped antimissile missiles near major population centers, and the ongoing test programs for Poseidon and Minuteman III. Neither the President nor his Special Assistant for National Security Affairs, Henry Kissinger, was in a hurry, despite urging from Moscow, to plunge into talks on a matter of vital importance with a nation that they both fundamentally distrusted. Lengthy and detailed planning was prerequisite. A better sense was needed of what Soviet interest and perspectives were in the strategic forces area.[48] The Soviets, after all, were then deploying ICBMs at a rate of over 200 a year and, despite the fact that they were about to surpass the United States in total number deployed, showed no evidence of slowing down. An independent evaluation was needed by the new Administration into American strategic priorities and military requirements. Such an evaluation was initiated by National Security Study Memorandum Number 3, entitled "Military Posture," that was issued the day after inauguration. It called for a thorough review of the military programs of the United States, both strategic and general purpose forces.[49] Moreover, strategic arms limitations was only one of a variety of issues about which understandings were wanted with the Soviets. It was felt that SALT should wait until contacts on other matters were moving forward.[50]

ABM was a more pressing issue. A halt was called in Sentinel ABM deployment and a high-priority National Security Council review initiated. On March 14, 1969, President Nixon announced the decision to deploy, now under the name Safeguard, a slightly modified version. This announcement sparked an intense public and congressional debate, culminating in the dramatic Senate vote five months later in which the program barely avoided defeat.

The MIRV test programs were not similarly interrupted and were not subject to an intensive and separate review. They were, however, a major factor in the general evaluation of strategic programs and the planning for SALT that was formally initiated by National Security Study Memorandum 28 on March 14.[51] Not surprisingly, verification became a central issue in the ongoing discussion of including a MIRV ban in the American SALT position. With the test programs moving steadily along, ACDA officials now felt that time was running out on the possibility of banning MIRVs. They urged that the Administration accept Soviet invitations for an early commencement of SALT and conduct its review in parallel with the talks' early stages.[52] State Department participants in the interagency discussions did not share ACDA's feeling that MIRV was a keystone to SALT. ACDA, State, and the Central Intelligence Agency all seemed to believe that multiple warheads tested so far by the Soviet Union were not true MIRVs and were distinguishable enough from true MIRVs that unilateral verification of a MIRV deployment prohibition was feasible by prohibiting MIRV testing.[53] This position was later supported by a report of ACDA's General Advisory Committee.[54]

The military and most civilian officials in the office of the Secretary were no more willing to tolerate a suggestion that MIRV deployment be delayed or bargained away than they had been in the past.[55] They argued that the SS-9 Mod-4 multiple warhead system then being tested was, as Newhouse puts it, "for all practical purposes, already a MIRV,"[56] because it could be used to attack several Minuteman sites. Unilateral verification of a deployment ban was therefore said to be impossible. Dr. Foster appointed a panel of experts under the chairmanship of Daniel Fink (a former Deputy DDR&E and subsequently an executive at the Missiles and Space Division of General Electric) to examine the verification problem and other issues. This panel's report supported the Pentagon's position and was reported to have caused the President to worry that he would be severely criticized if he opted for unilateral verification of a MIRV ban and the Fink panel report were subsequently leaked.[57]

Because of this disagreement over the verifiability of a MIRV ban, an interagency MIRV panel was established in April with Kissinger as chairman. By July a report was produced laying out available data and identifying areas of disagreement.[58] Although this panel and their overall involvement in SALT issues forced both Kissinger and his staff to deal with the MIRV issues, there seems to have been a sense among proponents of a MIRV ban that no one at policy levels in the Administration took seriously the problems that continuing MIRV testing entailed. A participant in the State Department, on the other hand, thought that Kissinger perceived a choice between concentrating on reaching agreement with the Soviets on ABM or on MIRV and opted for the former.

ACDA again stood alone in its opposition to the MIRV programs, but now its visibility was much greater than in 1967 and 1968. As active planning for SALT began ACDA had the responsibility for organizing and orchestrating the interagency process.[59] Although this role soon passed to the National Security Council staff, giving Kissinger essential control, ACDA was still represented on the verification panel and other interagency committees that formed the framework for discussion, compromise and concensus-building. On an organizational chart of the decision-making structure for SALT, ACDA now had equal rank with State, Defense, and the Joint Chiefs of Staff.[60] In fact, however, ACDA's influence was never very large. One participant who had moved from ACDA to Defense reported that because of zealous advocacy of early negotiations in the first months of the Administration, ACDA lost much of its credibility with Kissinger and his staff. Without their confidence ACDA's impact on policy decisions could only be minimal.

The Administration's feelings about a unilateral moratorium on MIRV tests, a proposal sometimes suggested in the press and occasionally in the Congress, was spelled out by President Nixon in his July 7 press conference:

> We are considering the possibility of a moratorium on tests as part of any arms control agreement. However, as far as any unilateral stopping of tests on our part, I do not think that would be in our interest. Only in the event that the Soviet Union and we could agree that a moratorium on tests could be mutually beneficial to us, would we be able to agree to do so.[61]

If, as seems likely, the Administration's view is reflected in a formal submission presented by the Office of the Secretary of Defense to the House Subcommittee on National Security Policy and Scientific Developments, the official explanation for this position was that a unilateral moratorium would not be in the interest of the United States or be likely to elicit a comparable Soviet moratorium on multiple warhead testing. Even if a mutual moratorium resulted from an American initiative, it was felt, this "would not advance the prospects of the SALT negotiations."[62] The same Pentagon document suggests that there was a strong feeling within the Administration, particularly because of the uncertainty about Soviet plans for their own missile programs and Soviet objectives for SALT, that the only appropriate forum to raise the subject of a mutual moratorium was during formal negotiations and that the only appropriate means of instituting it was a formal agreement. As stated in that submission:

> . . . a moratorium would forego the protection normally expected in a formal agreement and thereby set a precedent for very loose verification that would be inadequate for a durable agreement. Such an arrangement would suggest something about our verification requirements—with respect to both Soviet ABM capabilities and MIRV development and deployment—that could in fact hamper success at reaching a viable arms agreement. If we were unable to

> monitor a moratorium adequately, the result would be more rather
> than less suspicion and tension. In addition, the Soviet Union could
> place us in the position of having to choose between either breaking
> the moratorium on the basis of evidence that might not be
> sufficiently convincing to the general public or risking a serious
> strategic imbalance.[63]

Even a supposedly limited-duration moratorium was said to be disadvantageous because it would probably cause the United States to bear the burden of termination if no permanent agreement had been reached upon its formal expiration.

Only hinted at was the fact that MIRV, like the Safeguard ABM, was considered crucial to the American bargaining position. While the Soviets were moving ahead rapidly with their offensive buildup, MIRV and Safeguard were the only American programs in progress. It was felt that iı the United States appeared to be willing to forego either one, the Soviets might feel no incentive to bargain seriously. At the very least the American bargaining position would be severely weakened by either a unilateral moratorium on MIRV testing or a strong demonstration, such as a Senate or House resolution to that effect, that part of the government was anxious to avoid deploying the MIRV missiles. Not admitted at all was the strong linkage between winning congressional support for Safeguard and taking a firm stand on the MIRV testing question. Any wavering from the Administration's expressions of alarm about the SS-9 multiple warhead tests would have weakened its case for Safeguard.

In June President Nixon announced that the United States would be ready for SALT in August.[64] At that point it was the Soviets' turn to stall again. They may not have wanted to seem too anxious or, as a State Department official suggested, they may have been expressing displeasure over Nixon's trip to Rumania. At any rate, talks did not begin until November 17, 1969, by which time the Minuteman III test program was more than half completed. Given the Administration's general suspicion of Soviet motives at SALT, its conclusions about the disadvantages of decoupling MIRV from other SALT issues, the determination of the military to see Poseidon and Minuteman III deployed, the vigorous Soviet missile deployment programs and the acceptance of the military's view of the verification issue, it is not surprising, despite the urgings of both ACDA and State Department officials, that the possibility of a mutual MIRV test moratorium was not raised at the opening session of SALT. Nine bargaining packages were reported to have emerged from the initial planning process for SALT:[65] five permitted MIRV and four banned it. But none of these were to be presented at round one. The Administration, evidently with Soviet concurrence, chose to engage only in exploratory talks at first. The subject of MIRV was to be raised in a preliminary and noncommittal way,[66] but any proposal for a MIRV ban would be held in abeyance until round two.[67] The

United States apparently did raise the subject of MIRV as one of several qualitative improvements that could be discussed, but not as a matter requiring urgent attention. Contrary to the expectation of ACDA officials, the Soviets were reported to be unwilling or unauthorized to discuss such matters.[68]

This failure to raise the possibility of a MIRV ban at the first round in Helsinki does not in itself prove that the Administration had decided against eventually pursuing that course. Substantive proposals were to be presented for the first time at the second round of negotiations. Four options emerged from the planning process within the American bureaucracy. One of these included a prohibition against MIRV testing and deployment to be verified by national means.[69] It had stayed alive through the bargaining in the working groups, but did not survive the White House review. In an action that must have been realized essentially to rule out the possibility of a MIRV ban, President Nixon, reportedly with Kissinger's support,[70] amended the option to include on-site inspection.[71] After the SALT agreements had been signed, Kissinger described the revised proposal as follows:

> We have made two proposals, two linked proposals, one is a ban on the testing of MIRV, this we are prepared to monitor by national means of inspection, and second, a ban on the deployment of MIRV for which we asked for spot-checks on on-site inspection. Now we considered the test ban absolutely crucial because we could have been somewhat more lenient on the frequency of on-site inspection if there had been a test ban on MIRVs because without testing, by definition, it is not easy to deploy them. It is, in fact, impossible to deploy them.[72]

The question that this explanation leaves unanswered is why, if deployment is "impossible" without tests and a test ban could be verified unilaterally, could not the United States have been satisfied, as proposed in the original plan, with only unilateral inspection?

The answer seems to be twofold. First, for reasons already outlined, Nixon and Kissinger shared the military's reluctance to bargain away the option of deploying MIRV. Second, they may not have been as convinced in 1970 as Kissinger apparently was two years later, either that the Soviet Union could not deploy a MIRV without testing beyond what it had already done or that national verification could provide high-confidence assurances that the Soviet Union was not in fact testing a MIRV device clandestinely. It has been suggested that since the National Security Council staff lacked technical competence, Kissinger may have initially relied on DDR&E's judgment about these things, but later changed his mind.[73]

It must not be forgotten that the SALT negotiations were two-sided. Newhouse emphasizes that the Soviets were not interested in a MIRV ban either.[74] This was corroborated by several individuals interviewed who were in

OSD at the time and the Soviet reaction to the American proposal also seems to bear it out. Predictably they rejected a ban with on-site inspection, but their own suggestion was a production ban without any inspection,[75] which they must have known would be equally unacceptable to the United States. The fact that they did not respond with a suggestion for a testing and deployment ban without on-site inspection, which the United States would have at least had to have taken seriously, suggests that they were glad to let the issue drop.

Some proponents of a MIRV ban disagree with this conclusion. One congressional source who followed these matters closely at the time contends that the Soviets were indeed interested in negotiating a MIRV ban during the second round, but were not prepared to discuss ridiculous suggestions like on-site inspection of MIRV deployment. There had been private contacts between some legislators or their aides and officials from the Soviet Embassy in which Soviet interest in a MIRV ban had been affirmed.[76] An article in the Soviet Defense Ministry's newspaper, *Krasnaia Zvezda*, also implied the same thing.[77] According to an editorial in *The New York Times*,[78] the Soviets were split on the MIRV issue with the military opposing a ban and at least part of the civilian leadership favoring it. The editorial claims that signals had been sent to the Administration indicating that a ban might be negotiable, but that the subject would have to be raised by the Americans. Informal contacts with individual Soviet officials employing well-established channels for discussing arms control issues produced mixed signals, some suggesting that the Soviet Union might be interested in a MIRV ban and others suggesting that because the United States was so far ahead in MIRV technology the Soviet Union would not be interested. It is possible that with greater informal encouragement from the Soviet side, those Americans interested in a MIRV ban would have pushed harder and been able to make a more credible case. But, in the same way, to gather any momentum within their bureaucracy Soviet advocates of a MIRV ban may have required reinforcement from the Americans. Because of the nature of the Soviet decision-making process, the Soviet delegation often found it easier to get a proposal accepted in Moscow if it was an American initiative. As it turned out, the mutual reinforcement only helped the anti-MIRV-ban factions on both sides.

By the time the second round of SALT was underway in April 1970, the first flight of Minuteman III missiles was being deployed and the conversion of the USS James Madison to carry Poseidon missiles was almost complete. On June 19, the Strategic Air Command took over operational control of the first ten Minutemen III.[79] On August 3, eleven days before negotiations recessed, the first Poseidon missile test from a submerged submarine was conducted.[80] The second round of SALT was probably the last chance, therefore, (if there really was a chance at all) of negotiating a MIRV ban. But no serious attempt was made to narrow the differences. From then on it was clearly understood at the negotiations that any mention of a MIRV ban was a ritualistic exercise not to be taken seriously. During the spring of 1972, shortly before the Moscow Summit, the head of the American delegation, Gerard C. Smith, one of the leading proponents of a MIRV ban, decided to make one last try. Upon inquiry he was told by his Soviet counterpart, Vladimir Semenovich Semenov, that the Soviet Union would be receptive to an American proposal for a MIRV ban. Lt. General Royal B. Allison, the military representative in the American delegation, was subsequently told the opposite by his Soviet counterpart, Lt. General Konstantine Trusov, and the idea was dropped. Agreement on MIRVs was not something that was barely missed at SALT I or that just kept eluding the negotiators. Neither side really wanted such an agreement and neither side really tried to get one. Those initiatives that were made have been described by several participants as purely exercises in public relations.

There is little doubt that other than the debate and congressional action on ABM, almost all the influential discussion and debate about strategic arms control and strategic weapons, including MIRVs, was carried on within the Nixon Administration during its first few years in office. With one minor exception the public debate on MIRV testing and MIRV accuracy was, as President Nixon termed Brooke's Senate Resolution, "irrelevant"[81] to the formulation and substance of national policy. All the speechmaking and writing of MIRV opponents inside and outside the Congress, all the editorializing, all the testimony at congressional hearings,[82] all the behind-the-scenes maneuvering[83] that finally resulted in passage of an amended version of Senator Brooke's Senate Resolution 211, while perhaps contributing to public education and building the Senate's competence and interest in dealing with complex weapon system and national security issues, did not in any important way inhibit or even delay the MIRV deployments. It is even difficult to judge the degree to which the resolution's supporters were determined to influence the Administration's policy. Despite the claim by an active participant that the purpose of the resolution was to say "to the President in advance of negotiations, here's where we think you ought to go, and we are ready to view sympathetically this kind of a package," such nonbinding Senate resolutions are frequently used primarily, as Jonathan Medalia points out, to let senators get "on the record and off the hook."[84] Nor was any help forthcoming from ACDA to congressional and public opponents of MIRV.[85] While sharing the perspectives and frequently agreeing with the policy recommendations of these opponents, ACDA officials chose not to risk their credibility in the internal debates by becoming associated with these external efforts.[86]

Because of their certainty, in 1969 and 1970, that they could not come close to mobilizing a majority and because a major defeat would have damaged their credibility in the ABM fight, Senate anti-MIRV forces did not even suggest adopting the approach being taken in the ABM case, that is refusing to appropriate money for the MIRV programs.[87] In 1971 when Senator Hubert Humphrey (D.-Minnesota) and Representative Donald Fraser (D.-Minnesota) suggested that all funds for MIRV deployment be placed in escrow until "the President and the Congress jointly determine ... that the Government of the Union of Soviet Socialist Republic's testing and deploying of its own MIRV system and other action necessitate the further testing and deployment of the United States' MIRV as a guarantee of the United States' retaliatory capability,"[88] they were soundly defeated. By then anyway, the momentum of congressional efforts to influence the SALT negotiations had largely dissipated. Because of the essential irrelevance of this congressional and public debate to the decision-making process, it need not be examined here in detail.[89] The single exception to this otherwise total ineffectiveness, one example of temporary responsiveness, and one example of apparent effectiveness are worth considering, however, since they suggest the degree to which congressional and public pressure can have influence over weapons programs nearing the deployment stage. The key objection to MIRV by its opponents was that the utility of the system for attacking hardened missile silos could, either upon deployment or when accuracies were further improved, cause the Soviet Union to perceive their land-based missile force as vulnerable to an American first strike. That this Soviet perception might develop and that it might result in a reduction in strategic stability were certainly suggested by the Administration's (particularly Secretary Laird's) graphic claims during the ABM debate that the Soviets would soon be able to destroy most of the American Minuteman force with their SS-9 MIRVs and that dire consequences might result. The efforts of the MIRV opponents were directed toward inhibiting the capability of American MIRVs to destroy Soviet missile silos.

The only change actually made in the MIRV programs that partially resulted from criticism was the cancellation of the stellar inertial guidance development for Poseidon. But even in this case the external criticism was not the only factor. The cut was actually made during a budget review, whose purpose was to reduce outlays in the 1970 fiscal year. Special Projects Office (by then renamed the Strategic Systems Project Office, SSPO) moreover had never been particularly enamoured with the stellar inertial guidance program and the Air Force was delighted to have another chance to arrest the Navy's encroachment on the counterforce mission. Without these internal forces providing incentives to cancel the program, one wonders whether congressional and public outcry would have been enough. No evidence could be found of any other accuracy-improvement programs, for Minuteman III for example, being terminated or refused funding.

One little-known effect of the opposition to the hard target capability of MIRV was the effort of SSPO (responsive as always to criticism of its programs) to determine whether the cross-range maneuvering capability could be removed from the Poseidon bus in a way that would be verifiable to the Soviets. Although DDR&E apparently did not feel that this was feasible, SSPO engineers thought they had a way. Although this effort went on for about a year, the entire subject was just dropped when congressional interest waned.

One effort that appeared to be a success for Senator Brooke in fact had no effect. On his initiative the Senate Armed Services Committee reduced the funds for ABRES in the FY 1971 military authorization bill from $105 million to $100 million and included the following language in the committee's report:

> This reduction related to efforts in support of any future hard-target kill capability. Those efforts which are pointed toward a strictly retaliatory objective which can be met with substantially less accuracy and more modest yields than needed for the counterforce mission are to be fully supported.[90]

This reduction in funding survived the Senate-House conference on the bill and, with the language of the Senate Armed Services Committee's report serving to indicate Congress' intention, was enacted into law. Shortly thereafter the director of ABRES briefed the military officers associated with the SALT delegation. It was said at that briefing, somewhat proudly according to one member of the audience, that ABRES programs would not be affected in any way by the funding cut and prohibition against developing reentry systems able to destroy hard targets. Everything that had been planned or in progress previously was continued normally.

Several conclusions seem to emerge from this discussion of congressional impact on the MIRV programs. It is extremely difficult for a minority of senators or congressmen to influence significantly a weapons development program in its advanced stages, even if the cause is aggressively pursued both in the Congress and in the offices of the executive branch. What is required is success in a major and dramatic vote in which the opposition of the majority is clearly expressed. This almost happened in the ABM case in 1969, and if it had, would surely have stopped the program, at least for a while. It did happen in the case of the supersonic transport aircraft. While this was not a military system, it shared many of the technical, organizational, and political characteristics of large development programs for military hardware. In order to achieve minor and marginal successes, as in the case of the stellar inertial guidance cancellation, congressional advocates need allies within the executive departments or operating organizations. Without the willingness of the Navy development organization and the impetus of budget economies it seems very unlikely that the stellar inertial guidance program would have been cut. It also seems to be much easier to affect programs at an early stage in the development cycle than later. The stellar inertial guidance was not yet at an advanced stage in 1969 and the relative ease with which the ABRES funding cut was legislated reflects, in part, the fact that ABRES concentrates on research and exploratory development rather than the design and engineering of operational systems.

The military services can find ways to circumvent even the explicitly-stated intention of Congress as the ABRES office apparently did in FY 1971.

Small amounts of money can be reprogrammed; definitions and descriptions can be changed so that proscribed activities can be carried out under different names and different mission requirements. To be effective at all, therefore, the Congress must be extremely persistent. The time frame of government bureaucracies is rather long. They expect to be operating long after the attention of legislators or administration officials who may become temporarily interested in their activities has moved on to other things. The effort to find an acceptable way of removing the cross-range capability from the Poseidon MIRV was sustained only as long as congressional interest was high, then it was simply dropped. In order to ·significantly affect a program like ABRES continual oversight would be necessary, including a sustained effort to make sure that legislative direction was being followed. A single piece of legislation without serious followup could not be expected to be effective.

TOO LITTLE TOO LATE

Why was controversy over MIRV so late in coming and why, once it came was it so ineffective in influencing the course of the programs? The answers are complex. MIRV began and was nurtured by the technical community without the participation of political decisionmakers. In the mid-1960s when the MIRV development programs were gaining momentum, resources and organizational support, and had received the close attention of Secretary McNamara and his staff, there was little reason to oppose them. Because of their cost effectiveness and utility in performing a variety of military missions, opposition could only come from arms control considerations. Few people with interest in or responsibility for arms control foresaw that accuracies would increase to the point where small warhe ds would be useful for destroying hardened targets. Those who did foresee this development either saw it as desirable, felt it would not happen soon enough to be relevant to the Poseidon and Minuteman III programs or had little opportunity to communicate their concern about it to responsible officials. Even if the latter group could have done so, however, the development programs would almost certainly have continued unimpeded. MIRV was just too good. It contributed to the solution of too many political problems of the Administration and the civilian authorities in the Pentagon. It was too useful a hedge against possible future developments in Soviet ABM systems and offensive missile forces. It fit too well the McNamara rhetoric of assured destruction as well as suiting his residual interest in second strike counterforce.

By 1968, the argument that MIRV might lead to strategic instability was finally heard at decision-making levels within the government and was becoming accepted by a broad group within the non-governmental community interested in strategic matters. Even a number of ABM supporters outside the government opposed MIRV deployment. By 1969, congressmen and senators had joined the MIRV debate. Nonetheless very little changed. Those with authority over the programs chose not to delay or suspend the testing, not to delay or suspend deployment and not to raise the question of a MIRV ban at SALT at an early date or in a way that might have encouraged Soviet acceptance. MIRV continued to serve important political and strategic purposes. The perspectives of the military, the National Security Council staff, and the President about the process and desired outcome of SALT were very different from those of MIRV critics, both inside and outside the government. Equally important, by 1968 the programs were so far along, so many resources had already been invested, so many other things had already been foregone in deference to MIRV, so interdependent were the expected deployment of the new missiles and the continued viability of the whole deterrent force, and so much organizational and personal prestige within the services relied on the timely and successful completion of the programs that delay or cancellation was considered truly intolerable by the military.

Unlike the B-70, cut back during its engineering development phase, MIRV was not an expensive program adding little to the overall capability. Unlike Snark, Regulus II or Navaho cruise missiles, MIRV was not about to be made obsolete by new technology. Unlike a variety of space-based and land-based missile defense systems, MIRV could not be challenged on cost-effectiveness and technical grounds. Unlike the Sentinel and Safeguard ABM systems, MIRV did not have a long history of controversy and did not raise difficult political problems like "bombs in the backyard." MIRV was technically sound, cost-effective, and unquestionably a major improvement over previous strategic offensive systems. In short it was vulnerable to no argument or attack other than the possibility that its deployment might lead to strategic instability and generally contribute to the nuclear arms race. This was a view that was certainly not universally accepted and an argument that was rather difficult to make. To the extent that the argument may have been accepted by the military and civilian leadership, it was far outweighed by MIRV's advantages. The Air Force, for example, preferred to deploy its own MIRVs than seek to prevent a comparable Soviet deployment that would increase the vulnerability of its Minuteman force.

Those in Congress and outside the government who opposed MIRV were unable to win their case by argument and had insufficient strength to win it through a political contest. There was no chance at all that either the Senate or the House would vote to cut funds for the MIRV program. Even the ABM, against which a massive assault was launched, was funded. It seems likely in fact that if the Administration had, totally uncharacteristically, decided to delay or suspend MIRV testing or deployment and if the military had subsequently taken its case to the Congress, as it surely would have, the pressure generated to resume the original schedule would have beeen at least as great as the pressure mounted against that schedule. Even those minor incremental achievements of the critics were hardly more than cosmetic and partially subverted by the organizations charged with responding to them.

Chapter Six

Propositions and Implications

One would perhaps hope that in concluding this case study it could be set within the framework of a well-established theory or, at least, a widely accepted model of the weapons acquisition process. Unfortunately that is simply not possible, not because of the lack of candidate models and theories, but because of their inadequacies. As James R. Kurth complained in 1971, despite the proliferation of theories to explain the weapons acquisition process two fundamental problems remain for the analyst of any particular and actual historical case: *a posteriori* over determination and *a priori* underdetermination.[1] Retrospectively, several alternative explanations always seem, logically and plausibly, to be sufficient explanations for the observed outcome. But none of the theories alone, nor even a combination of them, is sufficient to permit reliable prediction of future policies. Among the theories suggested in the rather extensive literature on the weapons acquisition process are—bureaucratic politics emphasizing the importance of intra-governmental conflict, bureaucratic process emphasizing the crucial role of standard operating procedures of large organizations, technological determinism suggesting that technical feasibility is not only a necessary characteristic for a weapon system to be deployed but is frequently a sufficient characteristic, systematic strategic analysis focusing on the needs and interests of nation-states viewed as unitary actors on the world scene, action-reaction arms race pointing to the interaction between Soviet and American weapons programs, and the nature of the American political and economic system. The latter includes such notions as the military-industrial complex and the cooptation of the Congress, or at least key members of Congress, by the military and its industrial allies.

The critical point missed by most analysts of weapons programs is that all or most of these explanations can have some validity for the same weapon system either simultaneously or over its lifetime. The real world of policymaking is complex and multifaceted. Large numbers of actors, both individual and institutional, have stakes in and participate in the decision-making process for any expensive or important weapon system. Each has its own interests and perspectives, its own routine procedures and style of operation, its own political environment. Bureaucratic process, bureaucratic-corporate alliances, the nature of the economic system, and bureaucratic politics are influential to a greater or lesser, but constantly changing, degree for all weapon systems. So are strategic and policy preferences of senior decisionmakers, the actions of allies and potential adversaries, uncertainties inherent in intelligence information and estimates of an adversary's future actions, executive-legislative politics and many other components of domestic political processes.

Both the partial applicability and the inadequacy of each of these separate models or explanations has been demonstrated for the MIRV case. The importance of strategic doctrine can be seen in the initial Air Force resistance to MIRV and in the process by which its acceptability gradually increased. At the level of the office of the Secretary of Defense the demise of the Mark 17, the replacement of the Mark 12 by the Mark 3 for Poseidon, and the impetus for accuracy improvements for Poseidon can be understood in terms of a rational analysis of military needs moderated by budgetary constraints. The role of uncertainty and the impetus of action-reaction cycles can be seen in the overwhelming concentration on the penetration problem in the early and middle 1960s. Particularly in 1963 and 1964 the early development program for MIRV was largely and consciously paced by the perception of Soviet commitment to the anti-ballistic missile systems.

Bureaucratic process played a key role in the early formation on the MIRV concept within the technical community, both military and contractor, and in its early gestation until DDR&E became fully committed. The workings of the military-industrial complex are evident in the extent to which industry was seen to conceive and suggest new ideas to the service technical organizations and in the closeness of their working relationships. Bureaucratic politics largely explains the Navy's reluctance to encroach on the Air Force counterforce mission, the different manners by which MIRV achieved acceptability in the two services and the extent to which the Secretary of Defense used MIRV to buy off the Air Force opposition to his restraining their strategic programs. Other aspects of domestic politics, including executive-congressional power struggles, and the internal politics of Congress are needed to explain the initial lack and subsequent ineffectiveness of the opposition to MIRV, the timing of the public announcements of the Poseidon deployment and the existence of MIRV, and the role of MIRV testing in the planning for SALT I.

No single-factor explanation—not the popular notion that MIRV was a reaction to Soviet ABM; not Tammen's[2] reliance on domestic factors as the primary determinants; not Kurth's contention that MIRV is "best explained by bureaucratic process"[3] and "also can be fitted into a broader economic analysis";[4] not York's[5] and Lapp's[6] insistence that MIRV deployment was inevitable once its feasibility was recognized—captures the full complexity or illuminates the interaction between and fluctuations in the many separate strands that together produced the MIRV programs. Their common failing and the origin of Kurth's *a posteriori* overdetermination is a seemingly innate preference on the part of analysts for neat, single-valued explanations and a common, but not universal, reluctance to deal with historical evidence in all its richness. The *a priori* underdetermination derives from the inherent impossibility of predicting in advance how the many threads, even if they are correctly identified, will weave together as history unfolds.

General predictive theory is simply not possible in this field, in the author's view. It is not just that the analysis of government decision-making, and for that matter most of social science, is exceedingly complicated. High complexity also characterizes many physical systems that can, nonetheless, be understood quite well theoretically. But in physical systems one can frequently identify a definite hierarchy of importance among the factors producing the complexity. Understanding can be achieved by taking successive approximations that capture first the essence of the problem and then systematically expand the degree of complexity taken into account. With systems comprised of people and institutions, on the other hand, although variables describing the system can usually be identified, it is frequently impossible to know *a priori* which ones will be of greater and which of lesser importance in a given situation. Circumstances are rarely even close to similar between historical cases that are well understood and future cases. Institutional and personal interests change; personalities, ideology, and structural relationships fluctuate widely. Controlled and reproducible experiments are almost always impossible. One should simply not expect to be able to create social theory that is anything close to as comprehensive or predictively useful as is theory in physics or chemistry. The problem derives not from a lack of research or a paucity of case studies to serve as a data base (the claims of some social scientists notwithstanding) but from the very nature of human personality and human society.

What then should be the tasks of an analyst of an historical case study? The first is to bare the inner workings of a decision process, identifying the various strands and showing how they converged and diverged, overlapped and intermingled to produce the observed outcomes. The hope would be to sensitize the reader to the range of variables that can be important in such cases and how they can interact. The second is to suggest some generalizable propositions or hypotheses about the interrelationships of these variables that may on the one hand be testable by other scholars and on the other be useful to policymakers. The preceding chapters tried to fulfill the first task for the case of MIRV. Here the discussion turns to the second.

PROPOSITIONS

Proposition 1. *Without adequate political support a weapons innovation cannot survive to be deployed as part of the force structure.* This is not to suggest that political support is sufficient to guarantee the health of a weapons program, nor that the nature of the required support need remain constant over the program's lifetime. The creation of any major weapon system is a political as well as a technical process. As Sapolsky correctly pointed out in concluding his study of the Polaris program,[7] political uncertainty can be as debilitating as technical uncertainty for a government organization responsible for the development, and sometimes more so. Support, be it active or passive, must come from controllers of needed resources, and all or most potential sources of significant opposition. The important individuals and organizations will vary from case to case. In some instances, Congress, or at least some influential members, may be crucial allies, but in others Congress may act merely as an automatic budget ratifier and therefore be almost irrelevant. During the early stages of a program the requirements for support may be rather modest. But as the need for resources grows the degree of support must grow commensurately.

In the initial stages of the MIRV program only the technical community was involved and gave support. But a broader consensus was quickly forged among all relevant centers of power and resources: the Air Staff, Ballistic Systems Division and Strategic Air Command within the Air Force, the Special Projects Office within the Navy, DDR&E, Systems Analysis and the Secretary of Defense within the Office of the Secretary, the aerospace contractors who supported the Air Force and Navy strategic missile programs, the Atomic Energy Commission laboratories who would have to design the nuclear warheads and other members of various governmental technical advisory committees whose acceptance both legitimized the programs and nurtured their growth. Other potentially important and interested participants, particularly the President, the Bureau of the Budget, and the Congress either actively or passively ratified decisions made without their direct participation. This consensus was based on neither an agreed strategy nor shared priorities. Rather, everyone saw that development and deployment of MIRV would further his own interests and policy preferences. It did not matter that these were disparate and frequently conflicting. The existence of the consensus was essential, however, for the relatively unencumbered advance of the MIRV programs.

The addition of new and increasingly critical participants to the decisions on MIRV testing and deployment after 1967 does not contradict the basic proposition that continuing political support is necessary to the successful completion of a weapons program. It would be a mistake to focus on the opposition to MIRV as the central feature of the programs' existence at any time. Although strongly felt and sometimes well articulated, this opposition never had a significant political base. In fact it was precisely the strength and cohesiveness of the support for MIRV in the Pentagon, in the successive administrations, and in the Congress that prevented the opponents from having any but the most superficial impact on the programs.

Proposition 2. *The management, techniques, and style of the Secretary of Defense affect the degree of control he exercises over the weapons acquisition process and his policy preferences can affect the type of weapons developed and deployed.* A secretary like Robert McNamara, whose staff becomes involved in detailed force planning and weapons trade-offs, will be more effective in influencing the ultimate nature of the force structure than one who acts only as an arbiter of disagreements that are not ironed out at lower levels. This is not to argue that the outcome will necessarily be more desirable in one case than another, especially since there exists wide disagreement about what is desirable, but only that the degree of influence of various policy preferences are liable to be different in each case. But even McNamara's rather assertive style was less effective in giving him control over weapons choices than may be thought. Because the Office of Systems Analysis had no authority over development expenditures for systems not yet programmed for deployment and because a decision to enter engineering development was not considered a commitment to deployment, it was DDR&E and the technical community that acted as the major source of inputs to McNamara on weapons development decisions. Therefore, options were curtailed and the perspective of his advisors was unnecessarily narrow. Had Systems Analysis or some other organization with fewer pro-technology biases played a more central role at this critical decision point, the options may have been more broadly defined. That, of course, is not to say that the outcomes would have necessarily been different.

But still there can be little doubt that McNamara's own policy preferences had a major impact on the MIRV programs. It was his concern that the Soviet ballistic missile defense might jeopardize the American deterrent that led to authorizing engineering development of MIRV in the FY 1966 budget. It was his desire to improve counterforce capability that led to the accuracy improvement program for Poseidon. It was his opposition to an expanded Minuteman force, new manned bombers, and ballistic missile defense systems that made MIRV such a politically advantageous system. While his advisors in Systems Analysis and, especially early on, in DDR&E may have structured the issues for him and even recommended the ultimate course of action, the decisions that were executed were McNamara's and their purpose was to further the goals that he thought at the time were worth pursuing.

Proposition 3. *The critical event in the life of a weapon system is the decision to enter into engineering development.* If congressional support is uncertain, the appropriation of engineering development funds can replace the decision within the Pentagon as the critical event. For MIRV this decision was made by the Secretary of Defense in November 1964. It was implemented by subsequent directives from his office and funded without difficulty in the FY 1966 budget. Previous to this event there existed a number of competitors for the same military missions. In the Air Force there was still hope for a much larger Minuteman force, (a hope that was quelled once and for all with the decision to move ahead on MIRV), the strategic alternative of relying exclusively on large warheads and the technical alternative of putting a separate guidance system in each reentry vehicle. In the Navy the alternatives were a single warhead or a multiple reentry vehicle system without individual guidance capability. Before this decision no consensus existed that MIRV was the direction of the future in strategic missilery and, as reported in Chapter 2, the Office of the Secretary felt little pressure to proceed at that stage. True the Ballistic Systems Division was pushing hard for funding of MIRV, but this effort was not shared by most of the Air Force and was not paralleled in the Navy. Indeed in the latter case the initiative came primarily from the Office of the Secretary of Defense.

The decision to begin engineering development was at once a recognition that consensus was emerging on MIRV and a major impetus to creating it. Once the course was charted other things began to fall away. P-Ball was abandoned; the Mark 17 was funded, but at a very low level and only temporarily. In the competition for resources sacrifices were made and cutbacks accepted by the services in order to preserve the vitality of the MIRV programs. Institutional and personal stakes in the program were accumulated; plans were made and schedules set based on the anticipated deployment of the new systems whenever they would be ready. Only one year after the engineering development decision was made and less than half way into the first fiscal year of its funding, the Systems Analysis office felt considerable pressure from the services to continue the advancement of the programs. Termination became increasingly difficult (although a slowdown of the Minuteman MIRV program did occur as a result of technical problems and budgetary pressures). By 1968 the services were arguing that planning for the expected deployment of the new missiles was so integrated with the routine maintenance of the deployed forces that cancellation or significant delays would jeopardize the very integrity and credibility of the nuclear deterrent.

In their study *Technology, Economic Growth and Public Policy*, Nelson, Peck, and Kalachek address this same subject in a general context. They point out that

> in cases where these costs [i.e., of moving from development into a market test] are high and the costs and risks of development low, the classical break between invention and innovation may be quite meaningful. Where middle and late stage development costs and risks are high and where some production capacity is built in the course of development, the break between achievement of a roughly worked out concept and the decision to initiate major development may be more important.[8]

Since the latter conditions apply to complex strategic weapon systems, it is the transition into engineering development not the decision to deploy that marks the natural division point in a system's life cycle.

This is not to argue that major weapons programs cannot be terminated once they have entered the engineering development stage. There are many examples to show this is possible. The point, rather, is that termination is relatively simple before the commitment to engineering development and becomes increasingly difficult thereafter. Programs can be cancelled at any point and an example could probably be found of a cancellation at any stage one chose to mention. But the cost to the decisionmaker, barring unusual circumstances such as catastrophic technical failure, rises steeply at the point of the engineering development decision and would normally be very great by the time deployment begins.

Proposition 4. *The technical community plays a central role in the weapons acquisition process.* This community includes industrial contractors, the service technical organizations, DDR&E, and, to a lesser extent, the network of technical advisory committees. By initiating exploratory development of new weapons systems and subsystems and through its own allocation of effort and resources it can both structure and significantly influence the choices of the services and civilian decisionmakers. As was seen in Chapter 2, this community is more likely to conceive of and propose innovative ideas to the extent that it is complex, diversified, decentralized, loosely coordinated, and tied together by an efficient communications network. The Air Force technical community, centered around the Ballistic Systems Division, with its broader range of interests, more numerous contractors, looser control from the center, and reliance on Aerospace Corporation and STL Inc. for general systems engineering and technical direction and on outside scientific advisors as channels of information and linkages to DDR&E, satisfied those criteria much more fully than the Navy community centered around the Special Projects Office. The rate of invention and proposal of innovations was significantly higher in the Air Force.

The role of DDR&E deserves special attention here. With both staff responsibility to the Secretary of Defense and operational authority over the research and development budget, DDR&E has a major impact on weapon system choices. It is ultimately to DDR&E that the services must sell their proposals for new programs and it is to DDR&E that a service technical organization can appeal to circumvent or overrule resistance elsewhere in the service. Depending therefore on the style and preference (which may change from issue to issue) of the Director and his staff, DDR&E can be either a stimulator or a dampener of technological innovation. In fact it has played both roles and frequently plays them simultaneously on different issues. There seems to be little disagreement, however, that of the first three Directors, York tended to be more of a dampener and Foster more of a stimulator of innovation.

Proposition 5. *Strategic preferences and intelligence projections can have important impacts on weapons choices.* Although they are frequently used for bargaining or other essentially political purposes by both senior decision-makers and organizations with parochial interests, they nonetheless form important elements of the belief structure of all actors in the policy-making process and are therefore very influential. The time span from conception to deployment of any major weapon system is close to a decade. Over that period of time it will almost certainly be challenged either on the basis of technical viability, need or cost effectiveness. The system, if it is to survive, needs a credible justification. The justifications that are most widely used and most readily accepted are that the system fulfills a desired strategic mission or is a reaction to a perceived or anticipated threat.

Several examples of the impact of strategic preferences on the MIRV programs have been discussed. Although the Mark 3 warhead provided a convenient way for Special Projects to avoid using an Air Force reentry system on Poseidon, a different solution to the commonality problem would have been sought if Levering Smith and other senior officers in Special Projects had shared the Air Force and Great Circle Group's concern with counterforce targeting. Had the Air Force been more concerned with the problem of penetrating ballistic missile defenses and less fixated on counterforce, the Mark 18 reentry system might very well have survived. Had McNamara's high level of interest in counterforce been sustained the Mark 17 might have been more fully funded and eventually deployed. The notion of MIRV itself was so readily accepted largely because it was a system whose deployment could advance so many different approaches to nuclear strategy that almost everyone came to see it as fulfilling his preferences.

Intelligence information influences strategic weapons programs by permitting an evaluation of what the Soviet force structure is likely to be in the future. This is important from a military perspective because the effectiveness of programmed forces can be measured against the anticipated threat. In this sense MIRV was, in part, a reaction to Soviet ABM deployment. The Soviet Union was widely expected to deploy an extensive ABM system and MIRV was a means of assuring the effectiveness of American forces if they did. That the expectation proved incorrect is irrelevant to its impact on weapons decisions while it was held. But intelligence information is also important from a political perspective. To those who worry not only about actual military effectiveness but also about relative size and apparent strength, intelligence estimates provide convenient standards against which to measure future American force deployments and then to argue for superiority, parity or whatever is preferred. In this sense MIRV was intended to counteract the growing numbers of Soviet ICBMs. As the Soviets pulled ahead in deployed delivery weight on ICBMs and then in numbers of ICBMs, the American lead in numbers of deliverable warheads, provided by MIRV, became increasingly important in domestic debates on weapons policy and ultimately in the strategic arms limitation agreements of 1972.

The uncertainties inherent in intelligence estimating also influence weapons choices. Not only can partisans of parochial views find or create estimates that reinforce their own policy preferences, but prudent guardians of national security tend to hedge against the possibility of mis-estimation and unanticipated technological breakthroughs. Planning must be done, weapons choices made, and development programs run despite the uncertainties. Indeed it is frequently argued that research and development are useful tools for intelligence gathering. But there is a danger implicit in hedging against uncertainty, in maintaining what Dr. John Foster has called a "margin of strategic safety."[9] The extensive research and development programs that are maintained in order to reduce the risk of technological surprise generate both potential threats and real countermeasures. As a hedge against the realization of these threats, the countermeasures may be actively pursued. At first they would be considered option programs. But if they have important political and strategic advantages, if they gain the support of important sections of the services and the technical community, if they assist in bureaucratic arguments or help maintain the vitality of organizations, and if they are technically both feasible and interesting, they soon generate a large constituency and assume a life of their own. From then on it may matter very little what the Soviets do; the program is propelled forward by other forces. Particularly when there is considerable overlap of development and procurement and when deployment schedules are closely calculated to correspond with or to replace maintenance of existing systems, a reduction in the apparent threat need not affect the program at all.

Despite all these other factors, advocates can still argue their case based on the Soviet threat. Uncertainties are always large, especially those about future intentions. Particularly because of the lead time constraints, they can say, options must be exercised early. Eventually, the sunk costs are so great that the program must be completed merely to justify the investment. (Despite the economists' claim that such costs should not affect current decisions, politicians do not always act accordingly.) Moreover, since old systems must be replaced eventually, the added expense of replacing them sooner rather than later may not be large. In the end perhaps the United States will have moved ahead and bought another system which later, with hindsight, will turn out to have been unnecessary. "The risk" as Foster himself has suggested, "is not that we will be caught without adequate capability, but that we may have excess capability."[10] Some people would say that this is an accurate description of what happened in the case of MIRV. Others would point to the greater than expected Soviet build-up of its ICBM forces and suggest that the deployment of MIRV as a hedge turned out to be most fortunate.

Proposition 6. *Mechanisms exist by which Congress can influence weapons acquisition decisions.* By repetitive and reinforcing actions Congress can set general policy guidelines and identify special issues of concern. This was the case, for example, in the early and mid-1960s when frequent additions to the

Pentagon's budget and continued pressure on the Secretary exerted by both responsible congressional committees and individual legislators made clear that Congress wanted to spend more rather than less on strategic forces. It was in this atmosphere that MIRV was introduced and received unquestioned congressional support. Congress can also make specific cuts in or additions to particular programs. In the latter case there is no guarantee that the money will be spent in the way Congress wishes. In the former, although few cases exist from which to draw conclusions, it is safe to assume that if the system were strongly supported by the Pentagon, forcing delays or perhaps the purchase of fewer copies of a weapon would be easier than outright cancellation. Finally, even a minority of legislators can sometimes be influential on a relatively minor matter if they can find and support an ally in the executive branch who will fight the case internally. Thus, with the help of internal opponents in Special Projects and budget-conscious officials in the Office of the Secretary, congressional opponents of accuracy improvements were accommodated by the cancellation of Poseidon stellar inertial guidance. The victory was temporary, however, since the new Trident submarine-launch ballistic missile will carry a similar system. But, as seen in Chapter 5, without allies willing to support a cut in the accuracy-improvement programs of ABRES, even a direct instruction from the Senate Armed Services Committee could be ignored. In keeping with proposition three, it seems to be easiest to find internal allies to oppose a program when it is in the early development stage.

Proposition 7. *The Arms Control and Disarmament Agency and special interest groups gain influence only through the sufferance of more central actors.* Whether opposing or supporting a program neither ACDA nor any non-governmental group seems to be capable of becoming a major participant on its own. Not until ACDA became involved in planning for the Strategic Arms Limitation Talks in 1967 did it begin to participate in decisions affecting the strategic forces and not until 1969, under the formal committee structure of Henry Kissinger's National Security Council staff, did ACDA have any voice at all in actual weapons choices. Even then it had influence only to the degree that it could convince Kissinger and the President that its recommendations should be adopted as national policy. The non-governmental opponents of MIRV, unlike the anti-ABM forces, had almost no political base from which to influence Congress or the President. They relied on a publicity campaign and personal contacts with Kissinger and sympathetic legislators. Except to the extent that they reinforced and encouraged the efforts of Senator Brooke and his supporters, their efforts were ineffective. They simply could not find a sympathetic ear within the Pentagon or the National Security Council where the decision-making authority was centralized.

Proposition 8. *Significant unilateral reduction in the rate of modernization of the American offensive strategic forces would be very difficult to achieve.* This is a corollary to what has gone before. The institutional incentives of the aerospace industry, the military services, and DDR&E to continually generate new possibilities are so powerful, the need for civilian decisionmakers to hedge against uncertain but possible Soviet actions are so high, changes in perceptions about strategic requirements so likely, and countervailing forces so weak that the possibility of unilateral restraint appears quite dim. This does not mean that proponents of new systems can afford to be complacent nor that opponents should give up in despair. Arguments will continue over particular systems as they always have and choices will continue to be made between them. But the overall rate of innovation and the annual expenditures on improvement of American offensive strategic forces seems unlikely to fall significantly without comparable restraint by the Soviets and formal understandings between the two countries.

IMPLICATIONS

Given any set of assumptions about the purposes of development programs for strategic weapons, important policy implications can be deduced from these propositions. The basic assumption on which the following is based is that strategic weapons development programs in the United States should enhance the nation's security in a manner consistent with the strategic preferences, political judgments, and informational requirements of the Congress, the President, and those to whom the President delegates his responsibility for national defense and foreign policy. To the extent possible this goal should be fulfilled efficiently and in ways that do not encourage strategic arms competition with the Soviet Union. Unnecessary weapons should not be bought, but those that are needed in the pursuit of national policy should be available when needed and procured as inexpensively as possible. No assumption is made here about which strategies and policies are preferable nor about the rate of innovation or new weapons deployments that might be desirable. For illustration purposes both rapid and slow rates will be considered.

It might be hoped that all of these goals for the weapons acquisition process would be mutually reinforcing. In practice, however, they frequently conflict. A rapid rate of innovation may be inconsistent with minimizing costs and reducing the risk of an arms race. A slow rate of innovation may be inconsistent with the need for intelligence-related information and with the ability to produce new weapons rapidly when needed. One important corollary to the above assumptions, however, is the need to have a high degree of responsiveness to political will built into the weapons acquisition process.

Without significantly altering the organizational and incentive structure of the technical community, little leverage is available for changing the rate of conception and proposal of innovations. Changes could be made by increasing or decreasing the diversity and complexity of this community or by altering the communications network that ties it together. But in order to assist in intelligence operations, to hedge against uncertainty, and to assure the health of the technical community so that its services will be available when required, it would seem unwise to reduce significantly the research and exploratory development programs that result from and generate new ideas. In any event changes in the rate of conception and proposal need not have any impact on the rate of adoption of new ideas. Systems and subsystems that are ultimately deployed are only a subset, sometimes a small subset, of innovative ideas that are conceived and proposed. Furthermore, although these activities were more restrained in the Navy's Special Projects Office than in the Air Force Ballistic Systems Division, the Navy's ballistic missiles are not less sophisticated and have been deployed in no fewer versions than those of the Air Force. If the number of new proposals were increased or decreased, the result could well be only a compensating decrease or increase in the likelihood of acceptance of each idea with the overall pace being little affected.

A more appropriate place to cut back, if that were the preference, or, in any case, to seek greater responsiveness would be in the adoption phase of technical innovations. There is always a selection process at work within the services during this phase. Neither the Navy nor the Air Force can or wants to adopt all the innovative ideas suggested by their technical organizations for the offensive strategic forces. By raising or lowering the budget of each service and by structuring the budgetary process to discourage or encourage intra- and inter-service competition, the selection process could be made more or less permissive. In either case, if the services themselves are permitted to make the selections, the structure of the deployed forces will eventually reflect the priorities of the military rather than those of elected and appointed, but ultimately responsible, civilian decisionmakers. If the strategic and political preferences of Congress and the President are to be reflected in weapons choices, less prerogative should be given to the services.

A Secretary of Defense or a congressional committee that wishes to maximize its flexibility and keep open the option of terminating or significantly altering the design of major weapon systems should pay close attention to weapons development programs. Exploratory development and even engineering development should not always be expected to lead to a deployed system. Parallel and competitive development programs should be funded in order to increase the number of available choices to decisionmakers and, by generating competition for resources and discouraging the early formation of strong allegiances, to reduce service pressures for deployment commitments. Competitive bidding for single development contracts does not have the same result. Not only is the degree of competitiveness frequently much less in practice than in theory,[11] but also the flexibility of decisionmakers is not enhanced during the development stage itself. To the extent possible exploratory development should be organized along specialty lines, advancing technology in a wide variety of areas, but not oriented toward particular weapon systems. A commitment to initiate engineering development should be delayed and competition should be maintained as long as possible, in some cases even through the prototype or test phase. Flexibility could also be increased by reducing the overlap between engineering development and production. In the case of a system that is intended to replace an existing one, maintenance and sub-system modernization of the deployed hardware could be much less tied to the deployment schedule of the replacement than was the case in either MIRV program.

Special consideration should be given to those programs nearing the engineering development phase. Management techniques, such as major review and concept justification papers, are needed to institutionalize an examination of the design, cost, and mission justification of any major system about to be funded for engineering development. This could be done within the Pentagon (but only if the Secretary or his delegated subordinate plays an active part) and, with appropriate changes required by military security, revised versions of these papers could be made public. A legal requirement that these documents be presented to the Armed Services Committees of Congress would both insure their being taken seriously within the Pentagon and provide a regularized procedure for timely legislative review of weapons programs. Despite a very substantial mobilization of effort against the ABM at the time when a deployment decision was about to be made, the effort failed. That late in the process is almost always too late. This is especially true of innovations perceived to be mere improvements in existing forces rather than new systems. In the past the services and often the Congress have interpreted a decision to engineer a qualitative improvement to be almost equivalent to a decision to deploy it.

One could go further and institutionally separate the early development of a weapon system or sub-system from the engineering development and procurement phases. Early development could be contracted on its own, preferably to several competing companies, and another round of bids would be solicited later for the engineering development phase. In order to prevent the recipient of the early development contract from having too great an advantage in the second round, the results of the early development would have to be made available to all interested and qualified contractors. In order to guard against companies bidding unreasonably low in order to win the contract, a review of progress and costs should be conducted before a production contract is issued. This procedure is consistent with, and even an extension of, the notions of fly-before-buy and milestone contracting instituted by David Packard when he was Deputy Secretary of Defense.[12] To go one step further, however, and conduct all early development work within the services and government installations would probably stultify the innovation process too much.

As already mentioned these procedures to enhance flexible management and responsiveness of weapons programs to political will sometimes cost money and time. Increasing competition beyond the engineering development stage, delaying the decision to enter engineering development and institutionally separating exploratory development from engineering development and production might lead to both cost increases and delays. This need not be a decisive argument against their adoption however. Some additional cost and delay should be accepted in order to enhance the control of central decisionmakers over the weapons acquisition process. On the other hand, some of these procedures may make savings possible. A decrease in the amount of concurrent development and production would probably reduce overall costs by lowering the number of expensive design changes to be incorporated into an operating production line. If it led to a better designed product, a competitive development program might also reduce total life-cycle costs. In some instances trading cost and time for controllability might ultimately lead to savings by means of eventual cancellation of systems or subsystems.

The role of DDR&E deserves the special attention of the Secretary of Defense.[a] The Secretary should seek a DDR&E who shares his own approach to technical innovation. He could probably make the office less reflective of industry priorities by insisting that candidates for positions within DDR&E be individuals who have had experience in managing technological programs but not, as most DDR&E personnel working with strategic forces have indeed been, engineers with aerospace contractors or subsystem manufacturers. The Senate, too, since it has the responsibility for confirming Directors-designate, should recognize the degree of influence of DDR&E and review candidates with more care. In order to enhance the flexibility of the Secretary of Defense a strong institutional counterweight to DDR&E should be maintained within the Office of the Secretary. Systems Analysis under McNamara is a fair model, but substantially more contact with development programs and some control over the research and development budget, starting at least with engineering development, would be essential for an effective balance to DDR&E. Senior defense officials can be effective restrainers or even managers only if they are sensitive to the speed with which their options narrow and constituencies form behind weapons systems and programs in late development and only if they both institute and use managerial techniques designed to permit their direct intervention in the critical lifecycle decisions of major systems.

The critical significance of political support to the continued existence and health of a weapon system development program has implications for both promoters and opponents of weapons programs. Congressional and non-governmental advocates should seek the support of influential power centers within the Pentagon. Internal promoters would be well advised to consciously

---

[a]The function and operation of the DDR&E as an organization would also be a useful subject of scholarly study.

strengthen their base of support. In the case of Polaris, the Special Projects Office invested large amounts of effort and manpower in promoting and protecting its program. In the case of MIRV the support was less sought after and promoted than fortuitous and automatic. It was nonetheless very strong. Opponents, on the other hand, should choose for targets those systems for which the internal base of political support is most narrow. In principle, it matters little whether the internal weakness results from technical deficiencies of the system, arguments over strategy, competition for resources or fights over roles and missions, so long as it exists. Any sort of internal challenge to a program's existence or serious claim to its resource base makes it vulnerable to external attack. But in practice, technical deficiencies seem to arouse maximum opposition in Congress and from non-governmental interest groups. From this perspective the decision of 1969 to challenge the ABM system instead of MIRV was a sound tactical judgment. Because of serious technical uncertainties, a long history of controversy and great expense ABM was a better target.

The final policy implications relate to the need of responsible decisionmakers for both intelligence information and ways to hedge against uncertainties. The inherent uncertainty in intelligence estimation, both in the validity of any single expectation and in the breadth of possible disagreement over any particular estimate, pose serious problems. Modern intelligence systems have greatly reduced these uncertainties, but have far from eliminated them. While it is important to realize that investment in intelligence capability may generate savings elsewhere by reducing the need to hedge,[13] intelligence technology or techniques should not be expected to reduce uncertainties to anywhere close to zero. As former Secretary McNamara pointed out,[14] the long lead times required to deploy modern weapons programs require the United States to plan for a time so distant that the Soviets themselves may not yet know what their force will look like, or, if they do, they could certainly revise their plans between now and then. Other means must therefore be sought to narrow or counteract these uncertainties.

Arms control agreements can, but need not necessarily, help. The 1972 treaty prohibiting ballistic missile defense certainly diminishes the uncertainty in that area of strategic competition. While it is important to be able to verify compliance with the treaty, as long as it is in effect and lived up to there need be no expectation that the Soviet Union will deploy a missile defense system. The 1972 interim agreement on offensive weapons is less useful in this regard. It is of limited duration and permits, even encourages, continued weapons deployments both in those categories not covered by the agreement and as qualitative improvements in controlled categories. Extrapolating from the Vladivostok agreement in November 1974, the only basis at this writing for speculation about an eventual replacement of the 1972 interim agreement, there is reason to be optimistic concerning future reductions in uncertainty. The anticipated formal agreement, if it takes the form specified at Vladivostok, will be of longer duration, leave fewer categories of weapons uncontrolled, and put upper bounds on the number of strategic weapons that can be deployed. Qualitative improvement, however, may again remain largely unconstrained. One measure of the value of any future arms control agreement should be the degree to which it reduces uncertainty in the projection of the future strategic environment.

In unilateral force planning the problem is to minimize simultaneously the risk of being caught by surprise and the risk of deploying unnecessary weapons. This can indeed be a dilemma since some development programs that are desirable as a hedge against uncertainty may gain enough political support to become full-fledged, but perhaps unnecessary, deployed systems. If competition were increased in weapons development, if management techniques were improved and, particularly, if great deliberation were required before committing a new innovation to engineering development, the chances of a program advancing by the weight of its own momentum would be decreased.

Appendixes

Appendix A:
Early Consideration of
Multiple Warheads

The first significant discussions of multiple warheads seem to have occurred in the late 1950s in connection with the problem of penetrating Soviet ABM systems. Until about 1957 the technical problems that occupied the community concerned with ballistic missile defense (BMD) were primarily those of guiding a single interceptor close enough to a single incoming warhead to be able to destroy it. This was a one-on-one duel (the popular phrase at the time was hitting a bullet with a bullet), a tremendous simplification of the actual BMD problem as seen from today's vantage point, but nonetheless a great technical challenge for the 1950s. As projections of radar, interceptor, and nuclear technologies gradually advanced to the point where the one-on-one problem looked solvable, attention began to shift towards offensive countermeasures. In recognition of the difficulties for the defense that would result from the offense's use of various penetration aids, the Director of Guided Missiles in the Office of the Secretary of Defense, William M. Holaday, established a technical committee late in 1957 to investigate the problems. It is probably fair to say that the motivation for establishing this committee was at least twofold. First was the desire to delineate the technical problems that the American defense would have to face in order to be effective against an attack specifically designed for penetration. Second, and equally important, was the goal of outlining opportunities for improving the penetration capability of American offensive forces against a future Soviet ABM. These two objectives were closely interdependent.

This Reentry Body Identification Group, or Bradley committee, after the chairman, William Bradley, submitted a preliminary report dated January 30, 1958 and a final report dated April 2, 1958. For the offense the report pointed to the probable feasibility of using decoys, chaff, booster fragments, small radar cross-section reentry vehicles, nuclear blackout, and multiple warheads to overwhelm the slow, mechanical radars upon which

Nike-Zeus relied.[1] For the defense it stressed particularly the potential use of phased-array radars for handling heavy traffic. Coming as it did during a period of rapid technical advances, the Bradley report was remarkably influential. It established a preliminary agenda for technical activity over at least the following five years, including the extensive work on decoys, reductions in radar cross-section and multiple warheads.[2]

The offense-defense duel as fought within the technical community was largely American technicians against each other. Although the Soviet Union was known to have an active ABM development program underway (see Appendix C), insufficient information was available to provide a design threat for those working on decoys and other offensive countermeasures. In practice, therefore, Nike-Zeus, the Army's first generation ABM system, was used for this purpose. Year after year the Army's request for deployment authorization for Nike-Zeus was refused because conceivable offensive countermeasures could easily overwhelm it. In congressional testimony in May 1960, Jack Ruina, Assistant Director of Defense Research and Engineering for Air Defense and previously a member of the Bradley Committee, listed among the reasons why Nike-Zeus should not be deployed

> the probability that the enemy can, without prohibitive cost to himself, provide for nearly simultaneous arrival of multiple targets, either decoys or perhaps even true warheads. Then it is clear that in its present design the Nike Zeus's firepower can be rather easily saturated.[3]

The same theme recurred in an April 1961 staff report requested of DDR&E by Secretary McNamara: "The bleak outlook [for ballistic missile defense] arises because of the enemy ability through the use of penaids (decoys, low radar cross-section warheads, multiple warheads) to ensure our destruction at a cheaper cost to himself than it costs us to counter his move."[4] During the summer of 1961 a group headed by Jack Ruina, this time as director of the Advanced Research Projects Agency (ARPA), prepared a report to be used by the Secretary as a basis for the FY 1963 budget decision on Nike-Zeus.[5] As part of their analysis the Ruina group pitted Zeus against the Polaris A-3, then in development, and a technical projection of 20 reentry vehicles on the Titan II. The former did quite well against Zeus, the latter totally overpowered it.

Multiple warhead schemes became an integral part of new missile designs. As early as 1957, for example, engineers at Convair considered the possibility of putting several warheads or decoys on the Atlas missile. Even Project SLAM, a proposal for an intercontinental supersonic low-altitude missile powered by a nuclear ramjet engine and never much more than a gleam in the eyes of its proponents (primarily, it was reported, Dr. Ted Merkle of Livermore), was anticipated to be capable of carrying multiple warheads.[6] By 1960, officers within the Nose Cone Division of the Ballistic Missile Division, Air Force Research and Development Command had conceived of a family of multiple warheads—the Mark 12, 13, and 14 for Minuteman, Titan II, and Atlas/Titan I respectively. In none of these early designs for the use of multiple warheads was there serious consideration of employing separate guidance for each one. The purpose was simply to provide an effective means of penetrating ABM defenses of the Nike-Zeus type. This did not require very sophisticated technology.

Despite this concern for penetration, the first deployed multiple warhead missile, the A-3, was primarily motivated by other factors. In order to produce the A-1 and A-2 on accelerated schedules, several of their technical objectives had been sacrificed, including the missiles' range and the size of their warhead. The Special Projects Office retained the objective to produce a missile with 2,500 mile range and a one megaton warhead. The A-3 was to fulfill this objective. However, at the time that the A-3 was being designed, the nuclear test moratorium prevented the testing of a new warhead. Several courses of action were available to Special Projects personnel. They could have used the warhead being developed for the Air Force Mark 11 reentry vehicles. However, they felt strongly that this warhead was not optimized to satisfy their requirements, that the risks of unexpected degradation of the entire American deterrent as a result of unforeseen problems with the warheads would be too high if both Minuteman and Polaris used the same weapon, and that they wanted a Navy, rather than an Air Force, warhead. The Atomic Energy Commission proposed scaling up a 200 KT warhead that had already been tested. But Special Projects did not want to rely on a weapon that had not been tested in its operational configuration. Finally it was possible to use three of the 200 KT warheads in a multiple mode. Simple calculations soon convinced both Special Projects planners and Lockheed designers that three smaller warheads would be as effective in inflicting damage as one larger one; some people even claimed they would be better.

If the A-3 front end had been designed only to maximize damage, however, it could have been a simpler device than it actually is. The ability to penetrate a Nike-Zeus-type ABM system was also built in. The separation of the three reentry vehicles was made large enough so that even when fired from minimum range, one Zeus-type interceptor could not destroy all three. The footprint of the three warheads also had to be small enough, however, to be effective against an urban target from maximum range. Since the separation was by fixed, mechanical means, the precise footprint would be a function of the actual distance that the missile traveled, but it was on the order of mile.[7] Although Zeus, the interceptor against which the A-3 was designed, was an endo-atmospheric interceptor, its relatively slow speed required a commitment to interception before the target reentry vehicle entered the atmosphere. Light decoys were therefore very effective in confusing and overwhelming it. For this reason the A-3 had the option of carrying two reentry vehicles and a decoy package instead of the usual three reentry vehicles.[8] The A-3 was authorized in

September 1960, first tested on August 7, 1962, and operational in September 1964.[9]

During 1961 and 1962, while the A-3 was being developed, the capability of projected ABM systems changed considerably. A major study within the technical community, called Intercept-X, looked in great detail at the options with respect to ABM development and laid out the technical issues and uncertainties. It focused particularly on a new short-range, light-weight, high-acceleration interceptor and phased-array radar. Spurred on by the urgings of the technical community and an independent effort funded by ARPA, the Army instituted a phased-array radar development program in June 1961 in support of its Zeus BMD program.[10] The ability, promised by phased-array technology, to almost instantaneously redirect the radar beam greatly reduced the vulnerability of earlier ABM radars to saturation and confusion. The development of the new interceptor, called Sprint, was also initiated. Because Sprint could be fired after atmospheric drag had sorted light decoys from heavy vehicles it eliminated the early-commit requirement of Zeus and tremendously complicated the decoy problem.[11] By early 1963 the phased array radar and Sprint interceptor had become the basic components of the reoriented ABM development program called Nike-X.[12]

The nature of the anticipated Soviet threat also changed during this period. The Soviet high altitude nuclear tests of 1961 suggested that they might have developed a new type of high-yield warhead that could effectively destroy reentry vehicles before they reentered the atmosphere. Reports of construction around Leningrad suggested that they might be embarked on a major ABM defense program. It was of course assumed that the Soviets could also employ the technical advances recently envisioned in the United States. All this was exacerbated by statements of Soviet spokesmen claiming that they had solved the problems of defense against ballistic missiles.[a]

In the face of these two advances in ABM technology and the intelligence information about Soviet ABM development, a renewed effort was initiated by the Kennedy Administration to improve penetration techniques. The first Kennedy supplemental budget for FY 1962 included a large increase in funding for penetration work. This was later augmented by reprogramming other FY 1962 funds.[13] It was reported that the total increment that year was about $200 million. Several alternative penetration techniques were actively examined, including heavy decoys, chaff, reentry vehicle shielding, multiple azimuth attack, and multiple warheads.[14]

The work was conducted in two separate programs, one Air Force and one ARPA. In late 1961 the Ballistic Missile Reentry System (BMRS) Program was established within BSD and lead by Colonel Darwin Middlekauff, who had also been in charge of earlier reentry vehicle programs of BSD's

---

[a]See Appendix C for a discussion of intelligence information about Soviet ABM development and deployment.

predecessor organization, the Ballistic Missile Division of the Air Research and Development Command. Colonel Middlekauff later became the Deputy for Ballistic Missile Reentry Systems, a position he held until July 1965. In 1963 the Advanced Ballistic Reentry Systems (ABRES) program was created as a joint-service research, development, test, and evaluation program and assigned to the BSD Deputy for Ballistic Missile Reentry Systems. BMRS and ABRES had the task of investigating reentry phenomena and developing new concepts and hardware for reentry and penetration. They took the point of view of the offense. Project Defender, within ARPA, took the point of view of the defense. In September 1961, Project Defender was reorganized under Charles Herzfeld. Over the next few years, partially because of Herzfeld's insistence, a variety of decoy concepts were actually turned into hardware and flown with adequate instrumentation into the Amry's ABM test site at Kwajalein Atoll.

Primarily as a result of these programs a consensus gradually developed through the early and mid-1960s that multiple warheads were preferable to decoys. It was realized that reliance on decoys made the penetration capabilities of the offense very sensitive to the defense's discrimination capabilities and thereby introduced intrinsic unreliabilities. The possibility was taken seriously within DDR&E, for example, that a force relying on decoys could be degraded rapidly and secretly by unexpected advances in discrimination techniques by the other side. In fact, the Navy's efforts to design and build decoys for the A-2 and A-3, taking the Leningrad system as the design threat, were completely wasted when the Soviets scrapped this system in favor of a totally different and more capable one. The goal of achieving a decoy of only 10 percent of the weight of a reentry vehicle was also realized to be unattainable. As the weight of decoys compared to real reentry vehicles increased, cost-effectiveness alone soon dictated that multiple live reentry vehicles, not weight-consuming dummies, should be used.

The Ballistic Systems Division had been seeking funding for its multiple warhead schemes since about 1961. On July 31, 1962, Ballistic Systems Division Advisory Group gave its support to these efforts. The Group recommended development of multiples for Atlas, Titan II, and possibly Minuteman in order to improve their penetration capability.[15] In 1962 requests for proposals were issued for two versions of the Mark 12, a heavy reentry vehicle and a light reentry vehicle. The latter was intended for use in a multiple mode. After a long delay during which the heavy version was dropped and the specifications for the light version were altered, General Electric received the contract for the Mark 12 light in October 1963.[b] The same year a joint study by Aerospace Corporation and General Electric examined the possibility of putting multiple Mark 13 reentry vehicles on the Titan II, with or without accompanying penetration aids.[16] Neither the Mark 13 nor Mark 14 ever received major funding. Multiple

[b]See Chapter 1 for a more detailed discussion of this phase of the Mark 12 program.

warheads were also considered an option for the follow-on to the Polaris A-3 that the Special Projects Office had under active consideration by 1963. Initially none of these multiple warhead systems included the use of a maneuvering platform to provide independent targeting capability. Special Projects was considering mechanical separation similar to that used on the A-3. The Ballistic Systems Division examined spring loading, spinning the reentry vehicles off one at a time and the use of a small rocket on each reentry body.[17]

Lest the impression be created that the search for high-confidence penetration was the sole incentive for considering multiple warheads, reference must be made to other forces pushing in the same direction. Foremost among these was the interest of the technical community in building smaller warheads and reentry vehicles. Advances in reentry vehicle design had been an incremental process through the late 1950s and early 1960s. The initial problem was to build something that would survive reentry, without worrying about sophistication. The General Electric Mark 2 reentry vehicle, for example, used on the Thor intermediate range ballistic missiles, Atlas test vehicles, and early Atlas D models, had a copper heat sink and was large, heavy, and inaccurate. The second generation vehicles, the General Electric Mark 3 for later Atlas Ds, the Mark 4 for Atlas E and F models and Titan I, and the AVCO Mark 5 for Minuteman I employed improved ablative materials and more advanced weapon designs in order to reduce reentry vehicle weight, radar cross section and reentry time. As the feasibility of building small, accurate reentry vehicles became established, the designers were interested in moving in that direction. The technical objectives of the weapons community (cleaner, more efficient, and smaller warheads) also reinforced the impetus to use multiple warheads. The weaponeers tended to disparage the effectiveness of decoys and to insist that they could design weapons small enough for one missile to carry several. Early in 1964 the Atomic Energy Commission announced that small thermonuclear warheads were feasible.[18]

There was also some discussion in the early 1960s that multiple warheads might be a more efficient use of throw-weight than one large warhead. One General Electric Study, for example, was reported to indicate that "multiple reentry vehicles can achieve high probabilities of large-area kill, even with low survival probabilities for individual vehicles," that "multiple reentry vehicles with patterned aim points can give a point-target kill probability exceeding that for a single weapon of maximum payload weight," and that with multiple reentry vehicles there is "a much higher probability that at least one warhead will penetrate to the target" which was described as "an additional bonus."[19] This and similar studies must have addressed the design of the very large Titan II which could be used to place tens of weapons over tens of square miles. For smaller missiles, like Minuteman, multiples provide no advantage unless they are independently targetable. In all cases, however, since multiple warheads are much more expensive than one large warhead, they could not be cost-effective judged by the efficiency criterion only. The penetration rationale was more compelling.

The possible use of multiple warheads was closely connected to the very emotional issue of large versus small weapons. The Strategic Air Command, parts of the Air Staff, and the Chief of Staff, General Curtis LeMay, strongly resisted the initial studies of small multiple warheads. The Ballistic Systems Division, on the other hand, recognized the possible merits of multiples and shared the industrial community's interest in pursuing new areas of technology. Resistance to the use of small warheads did not exist as strongly within the Navy. Navy studies had shown that a large warhead, like that to be carried on the Jupiter missile, would overkill most targets and had argued in favor of a smaller warhead. Indeed the Polaris A-1 and A-2 carried weapons of less than one megaton, and the A-3 was being designed to carry three 200 kiloton warheads.

Appendix B:
The Technical Precursors
of the MIRV Bus

The development of a MIRV bus depends critically on five areas of technology: restartable rocket engines, vernier rockets, precise and reliable inertial guidance and control systems, high-accuracy reentry vehicles and small, efficient warheads. By about 1962 advances in all these areas were either in hand or foreseen, producing confidence in the technical community that a MIRV system was feasible.

In order to place each reentry vehicle on a different trajectory the main engine of the MIRV bus must be able to stop and restart. The technology of restartable rocket motors was initially developed for use in the military space program.[1] Bell Aerosystems developed such a motor for use in the second generation Lockheed Agena upper stage, which was used for years to carry a variety of photo-reconnaissance satellites. Aerojet-General Corporation also designed a restartable engine using hypergolic propellants (liquid propellants that ignite on contact) for the Able-Star second stage rocket.[2] Several of the advanced space-based ballistic missile defense systems would have also required restartable engines as would an orbiting bomb capability studied in 1960-61.[3] Although these latter systems never went beyond design studies, many of the military and industry personnel involved with them were later associated with some aspect of MIRV technology.

Vernier rockets are required to adjust precisely the trajectory of the MIRV bus just prior to dropping off each reentry vehicle. Difficult problems had to be solved before accurate and reliable vernier rockets were available. Although not all of these were fully resolved as late as 1965, approaches to their solution were foreseen earlier. Not only Air Force programs but also the space program of the National Aeronautics and Space Administration (NASA) contributed to the advance of vernier rocket technology.

Without precise and reliable guidance and control components delivery accuracy would not have been good enough to permit use of the relatively small warheads of the Minuteman and Poseidon MIRVs. Throughout the 1960s the services supported development programs for guidance systems and components at several of the major guidance contractors, particularly the Instrumentation Laboratory of the Massachusetts Institute of Technology (now the Charles Stark Draper Laboratory) and Autonetics Division of North American Aviation (now the Electronics Group of Rockwell International). Besides seeking accuracy improvements much of this work was directed toward hardening against nuclear effects and, particularly the Self-Aligning Boost and Reentry System (SABRE) at the Instrumentation Laboratory, withstanding high accelerations.[4] In addition effort was directed toward perfecting a guidance system, especially the computers and associated software, that could be used to place several reentry bodies on different trajectories. The Director of the Nose Cone Division (the predecessor of the ABRES program office) of the Ballistic Missile Division, was reported to have discussed the feasibility of such a guidance system with an M.I.T. guidance expert as early as 1960. The guidance requirements of NASA's space program also contributed to the overall improvement of inertial components during this period. By the early 1960s, guidance experts were fully convinced that the state of the art would permit development of a maneuvering bus to deliver small warheads accurately. This optimism was shared by Ballistic Systems Division, Aerospace Corporation, and Space Technology Laboratory engineers. In fact by the time the MIRV systems were deployed the most optimistic projections of that early period seem to have been fulfilled.

These guidance and propulsion developments permitted the approval in December 1962[5] of the Titan III transtage, a bus designed specifically for multiple satellite launchings.[a] Although the equivalent accuracy of the transtage was very far from that considered necessary for a useful weapon systems employing small warheads and although different teams within the Ballistic Systems Division and Aerospace Corporation worked on the Titan III than worked on Minuteman, there was almost certainly some transfer of technology. In 1968 the Director of Defense Research and Engineering, John S. Foster, Jr., responded to Senator Russell's doubts that the Poseidon MIRV would operate successfully by stating that the ability of the Titan III to change orbit, to shut down and restart its engine and to place satellites into different orbits demonstrated the feasibility of the MIRV concept.[7]

As important as inertial guidance systems for guaranteeing precision accuracy of small warheads was the design of the reentry vehicle itself.[8] Most important were slenderizing the vehicles to achieve high ballistic coefficients and permit rapid reentry, spin-stabilizing the vehicle as it fell through the atmosphere to avoid oscillations and uneven ablation that could degrade accuracy, and developing advanced ablative materials that would be relatively light but protect

---

aThe Agena and Star-Able had also been used for multiple satellite launchings, but neither of these resembled a true bus. In one case loaded springs were used and in the other each satellite had its own rocket motor. The required precision was not high.[6]

the vehicle from extreme heat during very rapid reentry. Much of the early development of these advanced designs was carried out under the direction of the Ballistic Systems Division's Nose Cone Division and later the Advanced Ballistics Reentry Systems (ABRES) program. By the time that the Mark 12 contract was awarded to General Electric in late 1963 the required technologies were foreseen if not in hand. The Mark 12, with its warhead, was designed to be about 350 pounds. By the time it was deployed this had increased to about 400 pounds.

The weapons laboratories had also been making strides in reducing the size and increasing the yield-to-weight ratio of nuclear weapons. By 1962 the Lawrence Radiation Laboratory at Livermore was designing a small warhead of about 50 kilotons[b] that together with its reentry vehicle would weigh about 100 pounds. This was the Mark 100, suggested by the weapons community for new Air Force and Navy missiles. It eventually became the Poseidon Mark 3, but weighed about 160 pounds by the time it was deployed.

---

[b] A kiloton is the explosive power equivalent to 1,000 tons of TNT.

Appendix C:
Intelligence Information
Concerning Soviet
Programs

The Soviet anti-ballistic missile (ABM) test site at Sary Shagan was identified during the late 1950s. Photographs taken by U-2 reconnaissance aircraft were very useful for determining the characteristics of the Soviet ABM radar. For example, a prototype of the Hen House radar was observed, and although it was seen to employ primitive phased-array technique it was also determined to be incapable of handling heavy traffic. Sary Shagan was out of range of the large radar deployed in Turkey that monitored Soviet ICBM tests from Kapustin Yar and therefore actual interceptor tests could not be detected.

Little seems to have been known prior to 1961 about the nature of Soviet ABM warheads and the capabilities of their interceptors. There were difficulties, for example, in distinguishing in photographs between surface-to-air missiles oriented toward defense against bombers and those intended for ballistic missile defense. The weight of evidence nevertheless suggested that the Soviets had a very active ABM development program underway by the early 1960s.[1] Richard S. Morse, Assistant Secretary of the Army (Research and Development), told a House committee in February 1961: "It is my opinion, based on my information, that the Russians have a large, a very large anti-missile effort and have had for some time."[2]

During 1961 both the information base and the uncertainties about Soviet ABM development increased. On September 1, the Soviets began a series of atmospheric nuclear tests widely claimed to have significantly advanced their ABM capability.[3] High-altitude tests were conducted above the ABM test site in order to study the performance of ABM radars in the environment of a nuclear explosion. Other detonations were evidently intended to test new or existing interceptor warheads.[4] Although the Soviets were widely reported to have tested a large X-ray, exo-atmospheric warhead,[5] there seems to have been no hard evidence to support this claim. Nonetheless, because the previous high-altitude tests conducted by the United States had not been designed to maximize X-ray emission,[6] very little was known about the potential of such an ABM warhead. While these ABM-related nuclear tests suggested a vigorous Soviet development program, they did not mean that a useful system was ready for deployment. On March 2, 1962, President Kennedy said that the Soviet tests "did not, in our judgment, reflect a developed system."[7]

Also during 1961, construction was observed[8] around Leningrad of what appeared to be an ABM complex.[9] Especially during the early stages of construction, the uncertainties regarding the nature and capabilities of this system were very large. In light of the Soviet high altitude tests in 1961 and particularly of the American high-altitude tests of mid-1962,[10] part of the intelligence community argued that this new system might be effective in an area-defense mode. Despite the fact that only about thirty interceptors were deployed around Leningrad, their placement along the corridor through which most American ICBMs would travel in an attack against European Russia, gave rise to some concern that, if the system grew, it might threaten the American deterrent.[11] Later, when the short range of the interceptor was realized, the system appeared much less significant. Still, some analysts argued that the interceptor might have very high acceleration like the Sprint, and therefore that the system could be an effective point of defense. If so, its deployment around all Soviet cities could seriously degrade the American offensive capability.[12] In the 1962-63 period, projections for the number of ABM interceptors that the Soviets might eventually deploy went as high as 8,000 to 10,000.[13]

Prior to 1961, when the Soviet Union was widely believed to have a lead over the United States in operational intercontinental ballistic missiles, Soviet declaratory policy on ABM stressed the infeasibility of preventing an attack with long-range nuclear missiles. For example, on October 5, 1960, Major General Nikolai Talensky, reported to be the foremost theoretician on the Soviet general staff, wrote that, "So far there is no practical way of repulsing a nuclear rocket attack."[14] During 1961, after the myth of the Soviet missile advantage had been dispelled and soon after the high altitude nuclear explosions, Soviet spokesmen became more positive about the possibility of developing an effective ABM system. On October 23, 1961, Soviet Defense Minister Marshal Rodion Y. Malinovsky told the Twenty-second Party Congress "I must report to you especially that the problem of destroying missiles in flight has been successfully solved."[15] This declaratory offensive continued through 1962 and 1963 while work proceeded on the Leningrad system. In his speech to a Moscow Peace Conference during the summer of 1962, Premier Khrushchev referred to anti-missile rockets as well as various offensive weaponry.[16] His most famous statement, that the Soviet Union had an anti-missile that could hit "a fly in outer space" was made to a group of American newspaper editors that July.[17] In February 1963 Marshal Sergei Biryuzov, Chief of the Strategic Rocket Forces, said that "the problem of destroying enemy rockets in flight has been successfully solved in our country."[18] Colonel General Tolubko echoed that statement by claiming that "the Soviet Union already has" anti-missile defense weapons.[19]

The Griffon interceptor was first displayed publicly during a Red Square Parade in November 1963. It was hailed by Marshal Biryuzov as capable of destroying "the enemy's rockets in the air" and other commentators indicated that this was the missile Khrushchev had said could hit a fly in space.[20] At the time, western analysts were reported to regard the Griffon as merely an enlarged version of earlier air defense missiles, as relatively slow, lacking high maneuverability and limited to between 10 and 20 miles altitude.[21] The general consensus about both the Griffon and the Leningrad system's radars seems to have been that they were primarily oriented toward interception of aircraft but might have a limited capability against cruise and short-range ballistic missiles such as Hounddog, Skybolt and perhaps the Polaris A-1.[22] In August 1963 Director of Defense Research and Engineering, Harold Brown, said, "Any deployed system which the Soviets are likely to have now, or in the near future does not appear to be as effective, almost certainly not more effective than Nike-Zeus."[23] The previous Director of Defense Research and Engineering, Herbert York, went further and stated that in his judgment, based on his knowledge of the intelligence estimates, changes being made in American missiles and problems that the United States had had with its own ABM, the Soviet system would not work.[24] Although this view was not shared by some members of Congress, particularly Senator Strom Thurmond, the Air Force seems to have agreed.[25] The Leningrad system never became operational. During 1964 the Soviets began to dismantle it.[26]

Construction of what appeared to be an ABM complex around Moscow was first observed in 1962.[27] The Try-Add target tracking and missile guidance radars were observed soon after. Although the Galosh interceptor may have been observed on the ground at Sary Shagan prior to its public display in a Moscow parade on November 7, 1964, its display inside a canister that obscured all features except its overall dimensions,[28] made determination of anything but its general characteristics difficult. The Galosh has been described as a solid-fuel, long-range interceptor probably carrying a high-yield warhead for exo-atmospheric destruction by high X-ray flux.[29] The range has been estimated at up to 400 miles,[30] suggesting that it is intended for area defense. About this time as well construction of the first operational Hen House radars was observed. Three of these were eventually deployed: near Irkutsk, near the Barents Sea, and in Latvia, not far from the Baltic Sea.[31] These radars provide both early warning of missile attack and some capability for missile tracking. Some time later, construction began on the large, advanced, phased-array Dog House acquisition radar deployed in the Moscow ABM complex.

About 1963 construction of another defensive system was observed in the northwest part of the Soviet Union. This system came to be called the Tallinn system after the Estonian capital close to which the first sites were observed. Eventually this system expanded into a line of installations stretching in a wide arc from Riga to far to the northeast of Archangelsk.[32] There was great uncertainty about the nature and purpose of this system. The radars were not phased-array, and their limited capability suggested that they were intended for defense against bombers, not ballistic missiles. The interceptor was reported to be an upgraded Griffon with a smaller warhead and shorter range than Galosh and, because of its aerodynamic surfaces, did not appear to be intended for exo-atmospheric operations.[33] However, the interceptors were clearly intended for high-altitude interception while the publicly stated tactic of American strategic bombers was to penetrate Soviet air space at low altitude. Moreover, unless it was intended to be a hedge against the unauthorized American Advanced Manned Strategic Aircraft, there seemed to be no bomber threat to the Soviet Union that would justify this extensive deployment. Also the placement of the sites across the corridor through which Minuteman missiles would travel on their way to attack European Soviet Union, and later across the corridor in the southwestern part of the country through which Polaris missiles fired from the eastern Mediterranean would travel, strongly suggested the system was intended for defense against missiles.[34]

For the reasons suggested, there was considerable uncertainty and debate within the intelligence and defense community about the capabilities of the Tallinn system. By early 1967 Central Intelligence Agency analysts were considering Tallinn to be an air defense system oriented against aircraft or winged missiles that fly in the atmosphere. Defense Intelligence Agency analysts, however, with extensive support in the military, were reported to believe that Tallinn had at least some ABM capability or would eventually be upgraded to provide it.[35] Secretary McNamara tried to take a middle position on the issue. In the FY 1968 Posture Statement he said that the new defense system was not intended primarily for antiballistic missile defense.[36] Nevertheless, the internal disagreements persisted.[37]

The technical arguments about Tallinn concerned its current capabilities to intercept ballistic missiles and the ease with which the system could be upgraded to make it really potent. However, behind these were more important uncertainties about Soviet intentions and commitments to widespread ABM deployment. If Tallinn were really intended to be or to become an ABM system, the Soviets had clearly made a commitment to missile defense comparable to their earlier commitment to bomber defense. However, if Tallinn were either not, or not primarily for missile defense, then the small Moscow deployment was the extent of their commitment to ABM. Both the technical and political uncertainties were very large. Since the cautious approach was to assume, for the sake of planning, that Tallinn had at least some ABM capability, the burden of proof lay primarily with the adherents to the contrary theory.

There was no disagreement in the intelligence community that the Moscow system was intended for ABM defense, although there seems to have been some argument about the system's capabilities. The Galosh interceptor, for example, was variously described as matching or exceeding the capabilities of Nike-Zeus[38] and as an effective area defense weapon covering an extremely broad area of industrial European Russia.[39] The precise nature of the interceptor's warhead and the capabilities of the anticipated kill mechanism also remained uncertain.[40] Although the U.S. high altitude tests in 1962 provided some information about explosions optimized for high X-ray flux, additional information had accumulated slowly over the next few years due to general skepticism about the utility of a long-range interceptor and concepts of area defense.[41] There was also disagreement about the capabilities of the acquisition and tracking radars. Those initially deployed were considered to be of marginal value. Like the radars associated with Nike-Zeus they could handle only one or two targets at the same time.[42] However, the Soviets were thought to have the technology to improve them.[43] Secretary McNamara tended to disparage the Soviet ABM efforts, claiming that although they were probably putting more emphasis on ABM than was the United States, their efforts would be unsuccessful.[44] Some influential senators, including Henry Jackson, did not agree with this relaxed attitude toward the evidence of Soviet deployment, particularly around Moscow.[45] By late 1966 construction on the Moscow system was proceeding rapidly. On November 10, McNamara announced that there was "considerable evidence that the Soviet Union was building and deploying an ABM and that we must assume that they will deploy an effective system."[46]

Through 1965 and 1966, while the deployment of the Moscow and Tallinn systems was continuing, the dominant theme in Soviet statements about ABM defenses was their feasibility. Retiring Chief of Staff Marshal Vasily D. Sokolovsky said on February 17, 1965, "We have successfully solved the complex problem of intercepting and destroying enemy rockets in flight."[47] The Galosh was again shown in the 1965 May Day parade and several days later a television movie shown in Moscow of Soviet missiles included pictures of ABM launch sites, computer centers, testing stations, and an interception of an ICBM.[48] On April 22, 1966 Defense Minister Malinovsky was quoted by the Hungarian press agency as having told soldiers of the Budapest garrison that the Soviet Union had brought into service a new long-range anti-missile missile.[49] Nonetheless, some dissenting voices were heard. In March 1965 G. Gerasimov wrote in *International Affairs* that the development of an ABM system capable of making victory possible would be a discovery "bordering on a miracle," and that there is "no absolute defense against missile salvo."[50] There is evidence of a widening disagreement within the Soviet military concerning the value and capabilities of the Moscow ABM system.[51] On February 20, 1967 General Pavel A. Kurochkin, head of the Frunze Military Academy, said that missiles fired at the Soviet Union would never reach their targets and that "detecting missiles in time and destroying them in flight is no problem."[52] This optimistic view was soon contradicted, however, by Defense Minister Andrei A. Grechko and Chief of Soviet Civil Defense Vasily I. Chuikov, who conceded that anti-missile defense systems could not prevent all enemy rockets from reaching their targets.[53]

By May 1967 it was reported that part of the Tallinn system was operational[54] and the uncertainties were becoming resolved. McNamara continued to discount the military contention that it was indeed an ABM system, but agreed that nevertheless the United States must assume that the Soviets would eventually build a nationwide system.[55] By the time he wrote his FY 1969 Posture Statement McNamara was able to claim:

> Now, I can tell you that the majority of our intelligence community no longer believes that this so-called 'Tallinn' system (which is being deployed across the northwestern approaches to the Soviet Union and in several other places) has any significant ABM capability. This system is apparently designed for use within the atmosphere, most likely against an aero-dynamic rather than a ballistic missile threat.[56]

Although virtual agreement had been reached concerning Tallinn as deployed, the controversy still did not go away. Rather it shifted to a concern over whether or how easily the system could be upgraded and given significant ABM capability. This Tallinn upgrade problem persisted through 1971 and, with decreasing credibility, until the signing of the SALT agreement specifically prohibited such upgrading or the testing of non-ABM systems in an ABM mode.

Construction continued "at a moderate pace"[57] at eight ABM sites around Moscow in 1967, but no effort was made to extend the system to other cities. In 1968 McNamara assessed the value of this system as follows: "It is the consensus of the intelligence community that this system could provide a limited defense of the Moscow area but that it could be seriously degraded by sophisticated penetration aids."[58] Only four sites, with a total of sixty-four missiles,[59] were completed. Secretary Clifford indicated in his FY 1970 Posture Statement "during the past year, the Soviets apparently curtailed construction of the Galosh ABM complexes they were deploying around Moscow."[60] This was reported to mean that construction was halted on the other four complexes during 1968.[61] The International Institute of Strategic Studies said about this slow-down:

> Deployment of the anti-ballistic missile (Galosh) was slowed down during the year, after reports of technical difficulties and rising costs, indicating that the dispute at the highest military level over the value of this system has been temporarily settled in favor of the doubters.[62]

Other analysts were reported to believe that a program to upgrade the system's radars was responsible for the slow-down.[63]

During 1969 a number of the Moscow ABM complexes "were reported to have reached operational status." Testing of "an improved Galosh missile" was also observed, but no firm estimate was available on the capabilities of this missile. "Research and development related to a new ABM system" was also reported "to be continuing."[64]

During the period between 1967 and 1970 Soviet statements on the subject of ABM were curtailed. Finally in February 1970 Defense Minister Andrei Grechko said:

> Great changes have taken place also in the country's air defense forces. We possess weapons capable of reliably hitting enemy aircraft and missiles irrespective of height or speed of their flight, at great distances from the defended targets.[65]

At the time some western observers were reported to consider this statement as part of an effort, by at least some in the Soviet military, to secure resources from the new five-year plan to be announced later that year in order to expand their ABM system. It could also have been an attempt to strengthen the Soviets' bargaining position at SALT.[66]

By March 1971 four Galosh sites were operational. Tests of the new interceptor, which was reported to have a controlled coast capability and a restartable engine, continued.[67] It was also reported that some new construction was undertaken in 1971. This included a new phased-array radar that would be a marked improvement on the older models deployed with Galosh, and installations that were expected to eventually receive the new, upgraded version of Galosh.[68]

The situation was partially stabilized with the signing in May 1972 of the SALT Treaty on the Limitation of Anti-Ballistic Missile Systems. The Soviets were permitted 100 interceptors around Moscow and 100 around one ICBM field east of the Urals. Qualitative improvements of the type reported to be under way in 1971 are still permitted, however. The Protocol to the ABM Treaty signed in Moscow in July 1974 limited the Soviet Union to only one ABM site of 100 interceptors. Unless the Moscow site were dismantled, therefore, the Protocol prohibits deployment of any additional interceptors except those used for development testing at Sary Shagan.

Appendix D:
Glossary of Acronyms
and Technical Terms

A-1, 2, 3. The numerical designation of the first, second, and third generation Polaris submarine-launched ballistic missiles.

ABM. Anti-ballistic Missile.

ABRES. Advanced Ballistic Reentry Systems.

ACDA. Arms Control and Disarmament Agency.

AEC. Atomic Energy Commission.

AFSC. Air Force Systems Command.

AMSA. Advanced Manned Strategic Aircraft; renamed B-1.

ARPA. Advanced Research Projects Agency.

Assured destruction. The strategic objective of deterring a deliberate nuclear attack upon the United States or its allies by maintaining at all times a clear and unmistakable ability to inflict an unacceptable degree of damage upon any aggressor, or combination of aggressors, even after absorbing a surprise first strike.

Athena. A rocket used for test purposes in the ABRES program.

Atlas. A first generation American liquid-fueled intercontinental ballistic missile.

B-1. Formerly called AMSA; a strategic intercontinental bomber currently being developed to replace the B-52.

B-3. The numerical designation of a Polaris submarine-launched ballistic missile that was never authorized.

B-52. A strategic intercontinental bomber currently in use.

B-70. A strategic intercontinental bomber that was never deployed.

Ballistic coefficient, β. $\beta = W/C_D A$, where W is the weight of a reentry body, A is its area and C_D is the drag coefficient determined by the body's shape. The higher the value of β, the faster and more precise is the reentry through the atmosphere.

BMD. Ballistic Missile Defense.

Booster. The part of a missile that is expended in launching a payload onto a specific trajectory.

BSD. Ballistic Systems Division of the Air Force Systems Command.

BSDAG. Ballistic Systems Division Advisory Group.

Bus. The maneuvering vehicle that carries and drops off reentry bodies in a MIRV system.

C-3. The numerical designation of the Poseidon submarine-launched ballistic missile.

CEP. Circular error probable. Ideally, the radius of a circle within which half of a large number of warheads would fall if all were fired at the same center.

Chaff. Small metal wires that are released in the path of incoming missiles in order to reflect the radar signals of and thereby confuse an opponent's anti-ballistic missile system.

CIA. Central Intelligence Agency.

CNO. Chief of Naval Operations.

Countercity. The strategic doctrine that prescribes attacking an enemy's urban population or such an attack.

Counterforce. The strategic doctrine that prescribes attacking an enemy's war-making capability, or such an attack.

Countervalue. The strategic doctrine that prescribes attacking an enemy's urban-industrial centers and other nonmilitary targets, or such an attack.

DAG. Division Advisory Group.

Damage limitation. The strategic objective of limiting damage to American population and industrial capacity in the event that deterrence fails and nuclear war occurs.

DDR&E. Director of Defense Research and Engineering and the office of same.

Decoy. Something carried and released by a ballistic missile in order to attract the fire of and thereby exhaust an opponent's anti-ballistic missile system.

DIA. Defense Intelligence Agency, Department of Defense.

Front end. That part of a missile that is carried by the booster and includes one or more reentry vehicles, perhaps a mechanism to deploy them, and possibly penetration aids.

FY. Fiscal year.

Galosh. A Soviet anti-ballistic missile deployed around Moscow.

Griffon. A Soviet surface-to-air missile that was claimed to be an anti-ballistic missile.

Hammerhead. A missile design in which the front end is wider than the upper stage of the booster.

Hypergolic propellants. Liquid rocket propellants that ignite spontaneously when brought into contact with each other.

ICBM. Intercontinental Ballistic Missile.

INR. Bureau of Intelligence and Research, Department of State.

IRBM. Intermediate Range Ballistic Missile.

JASON. A prestigious group of scientists who work parttime on military-related problems under the auspices of the Institute for Defense Analysis.
JCS. Joint Chiefs of Staff.
Kiloton. Explosive power equivalent to a thousand tons of TNT.
Leningrad System. A primitive Soviet missile defense system deployed around Leningrad in the early 1960s.
Mark 3. The reentry vehicle or reentry system deployed on the Poseidon missile.
Mark 11. The reentry vehicle deployed on the Minuteman II.
Mark 12. The reentry vehicle or reentry system deployed on Minuteman III.
Mark 13. A reentry vehicle conceived for multiple use on the Titan II but never developed.
Mark 14. A reentry vehicle conceived for multiple use on the Atlas and Titan I but never developed.
Mark 17. A large reentry vehicle intended for use on Poseidon and Minuteman III but never deployed.
Mark 18. A small reentry vehicle briefly under development by the Air Force for multiple use on Minuteman.
Mark 100. A small reentry vehicle and warhead conceived for multiple use on Polaris and Minuteman. It was a precursor of the Mark 3 and the Mark 18.
Megaton. Explosive power equivalent to a million tons of TNT.
Minuteman. An American solid-fuel intercontinental ballistic missile deployed successively in three versions, Minuteman I, II, and III.
MIRV. Multiple Independently-targetable Reentry Vehicle or a reentry system that includes multiple independently-targetable reentry vehicles.
MIT. Massachusetts Institute of Technology.
MMRBM. Mobile Medium Range Ballistic Missile.
Moscow System. The Soviet anti-ballistic missile system deployed around Moscow.
NIE. National Intelligence Estimate.
Nike-X. Second generation American anti-ballistic missile system, preliminary to Sentinel.
Nike-Zeus. First generation American anti-ballistic missile system, never deployed.
ONE. Office of National Estimates.
OSD. Office of the Secretary of Defense.
P-Ball. Precision Ballistic, a multiple warhead concept in which each reentry vehicle would carry its own guidance and propulsion.
PBCS. Post Boost Control System.
PBPS. Post Boost Propulsion System.
Penaids. See Penetration aids.
Penetration aids. Things carried and released by a ballistic missile in order to confuse or otherwise neutralize an opponent's anti-ballistic missile system

and thereby improve the ability of the missile's reentry vehicles to penetrate to their intended targets. Decoys and chaff are examples.

Pen-X. A major technical study of the mid-1960s which examined the offense-defense interaction and did design studies for MIRV.

Phased-array radar. A radar whose beam can be steered electronically rather than mechanically.

Polaris. An American solid-fuel submarine-launched ballistic missile deployed successively in three versions, Polaris A-1, A-2, and A-3.

Poseidon. An American solid-fuel submarine-launched ballistic missile deployed as a successor to Polaris.

PSAC. President's Science Advisory Committee.

R&D. Research and development.

RDT&E. Research, development, test, and evaluation.

Reentry vehicle. The vehicle that carries a missile's warhead and protects it during reentry through the atmosphere.

SA. Office of Systems Analysis.

SAB. Air Force Scientific Advisory Board.

SABMIS. Sea-Based Ballistic Missile Intercept Ship.

SAC. Air Force Strategic Air Command.

Safeguard. American anti-ballistic missile system, successor to Sentinel.

SALT. Strategic Arms Limitation Talks.

SAMSO. Air Force Space and Missile Systems Organization.

Sentinel. American anti-ballistic missile system, successor to Nike-X, predecessor to Safeguard.

SIG. Stellar Inertial Guidance.

SINS. Ship's Inertial Navigation System.

SP. Special Projects Office, United States Navy.

Spartan. American long range ballistic missile interceptor.

Sprint. American short range ballistic missile interceptor.

SS-9. Large Soviet storable-liquid fueled intercontinental ballistic missile.

SS-11. Soviet storable-liquid fueled intercontinental ballistic missile.

SS-13. Soviet solid fueled intercontinental ballistic missile.

STAFF. Stellar Acquisition Feasibility Flight program.

STL. Space Technology Laboratories Incorporated.

Strat-X. A large technical study in 1966 and 1967 that examined possible future American strategic weapons systems.

Tallinn System. A Soviet air defense system that was thought for some time to be the beginning of a large anti-ballistic missile system.

TFX. A fighter bomber originally intended for Navy and Air Force use, now the F-111.

Thor. An early American intermediate range ballistic missile.

Titan I. A first generation American liquid-fueled intercontinental ballistic missile.

Titan II. An American storable-liquid fueled intercontinental ballistic missile.

Titan III. A booster used for space launches.

Transtage. A maneuvering final stage of the Titan III used for multiple satellite launches.

Trident. A new American submarine-launched ballistic missile now under development and a new submarine built to carry it.

TRW. Thompson-Ramo-Wooldridge Corporation.

USIB. United States Intelligence Board.

Yield-to-weight-ratio. The quotient of the explosive power of a nuclear device divided by its weight.

Notes

Notes

Introduction

1. Testimony of Secretary of the Air Force Dr. John L. McLucas, United States Senate, Subcommittee of the Committee on Appropriations, *Department of Defense Appropriations for Fiscal Year 1975*, Part 4, 93rd Cong., 2nd sess., March 7, 1974, p. 63.
2. Testimony of Deputy of Chief of Naval Operations (Surface Warfare), Vice Admiral R.E. Adamson, Jr., *ibid.*, Part 3, pp. 815 and 817.
3. Robert A. Wright, "Prototype of B-1 Bomber, Plagued by Inflation and Facing 2 Years of Tests, is Rolled out for Display," *The New York Times*, October 27, 1974, p. 43.

Chapter One
Overview

1. For a detailed description of the Minuteman III bus see *Aerospace Daily* 148 (August 17, 1970): 3.
2. *The Military Balance 1972-73* (London: International Institute for Strategic Studies, 1971), p. 65.
3. Herbert York, "Multiple Warhead Missiles," *Scientific American* 229 (November 1973): 22.
4. *Polaris/Poseidon Chronology: Fleet Ballistic Missile Weapon System* (Washington: Strategic Systems Project Office, Department of the Navy, 1969) (hereafter cited as *Polaris/Poseidon Chronology*), pp. 5, 7, 9.
5. Barry Miller, "Studies of Penetration Aids Broadening," *Aviation Week and Space Technology* 80 (January 20, 1964): 72ff; and *Aviation Week and Space Technology* 79 (September 10, 1963): 23.
6. "Mark 12 Development Plan May Change," *Aviation Week and Space Technology* 77 (November 5, 1962): 29.
7. *Aviation Week and Space Technology* 79 (July 29, 1963): 24.

8. Irwin Stambler, "The Next ICBMs," *Space/Aeronautics* 45 (March 1966): 62; and *Defense Industry Bulletin* 1 (August 1965): 5.

9. Harvey M. Sapolsky, *The Polaris System Development: Bureaucratic and Programmatic Success in Government* (Cambridge: Harvard University Press, 1972), p. 22.

10. "The Text of President Johnson's Defense Message Presented to the 89th Congress," *The New York Times*, January 19, 1965, p. 16.

11. Statement of Secretary of Defense, Robert S. McNamara, United States House of Representatives, Committee on Armed Services, *Hearings on Military Posture and H.R. 4016 To Authorize Appropriations During Fiscal Year 1966 for Procurement of Aircraft, Missiles, and Naval Vessels, and Research, Development, Test, and Evaluation, for the Armed Forces, and For Other Purposes*, 89th Cong., 1st sess., February 2, 1965 (hereafter cited as "FY1966 Posture Statement"), p. 212.

12. *Ibid.*, p. 212.

13. *Ibid.*, p. 212.

14. *MIRV Chronology*, The Aerospace Corporation, March 14, 1972 (hereafter cited as "Aerospace MIRV Chronology"), p. 2. This is an unpublished document of the Aerospace Corporation that was provided to the author.

15. *Ibid.*, p. 2.

16. *Ibid.*, p. 2.

17. *Missiles and Rockets* 17 (August 9, 1965): 10.

18. *Ibid.*, 17 (October 25, 1965): 16.

19. Testimony of Robert A. Frosch, Assistant Secretary of the Navy for Research and Development, United States Senate, Subcommittee of the Committee on Appropriations, *Department of Defense Appropriations for Fiscal Year 1968*, Part 1, 90th Cong., 1st sess., January 25, 1967, p. 765.

20. Testimony of Secretary of the Navy, Paul H. Nitze, United States House of Representatives, Subcommittee of the Committee on Appropriations, *Department of Defense Appropriations for 1967*, Part I, 89th Cong., 2nd sess., July 18, 1966, p. 585.

21. Statement of Secretary of Defense, Robert McNamara, United States House of Representatives, Committee on Armed Services, *Hearings on Military Posture and H.R. 13456 to Authorize Appropriations During the Fiscal Year 1967 for Procurement of Aircraft, Missiles, Naval Vessels, and Tracked Combat Vehicles, and Research, Development, Test, and Evaluation for the Armed Forces, and to Maintain Parity Between Military and Civilian Pay, and for Other Purposes*, 89th Cong., 2nd sess., March 8, 1966, p. 7351.

22. *Ibid.*, p. 7350.

23. Testimony of General James Ferguson, Commander, Air Force Systems Command, United States Senate, Subcommittee of the Committee on Appropriations, *Department of Defense Appropriations for Fiscal Year 1971*, Part 4, 91st Cong., 2nd sess., May 6, 1970, p. 273.

24. *Aerospace Daily* 148 (August 27, 1970): 3.
25. *Aviation Week and Space Technology* 85 (August 29, 1966): 13.
26. *Polaris/Poseidon Chronology, op. cit.*, p. 12.
27. *Aviation Week and Space Technology* 82 (February 1, 1965): 13; 82 (March 8, 1965): 25; 82 (March 15, 1965): 145; 84 (April 18, 1966): 74; and *Defense Industry Bulletin* 2 (June 1966): 5.
28. Statement of Secretary of Defense, Robert S. McNamara, United States House of Representatives, Committee on Armed Services, *Hearings on Military Posture and A Bill (H.R. 9240) to Authorize Appropriations During the Fiscal Year 1968 For Procurement of Aircraft, Missiles, Naval Vessels, and Tracked Combat Vehicles, and Research Development, Test, and Evaluation for the Armed Forces, and for Other Purposes*, 90th Cong., 1st sess., March 2, 1967, (hereafter cited as FY 1968 Posture Statement), p. 408; and Richard L. Kugler, *The Politics of Restraint: Robert McNamara and the Strategic Nuclear Forces*, Ph.D. dissertation, Political Science Department, M.I.T., 1975 (to be completed).
29. FY 1968 Posture Statement, p. 408.
30. *Department of Defense Appropriations for Fiscal Year 1968, op. cit.*, Part 2, p. 499.
31. Statement of Secretary of the Navy, Paul H. Nitze, United States House of Representatives, Subcommittee of the Committee on Appropriations, *Department of Defense Appropriations for 1968*, Part 2, 90th Cong., 1st sess., January 23, 1967, p. 857.
32. Testimony of Rear Admiral E.E. Grimm, U.S. Navy, Office of the Navy Comptroller (Director of Budget and Reports), United States Senate, Subcommittee of the Committee on Appropriations, *Department of Defense Appropriations for Fiscal Year 1969*, Part 3, May 15, 1968, p. 1478.
33. Statement of Secretary of Defense, Melvin R. Laird, United States Senate, Subcommittee of the Committee on Appropriations, *Department of Defense Appropriations for Fiscal Year 1970*, Part 1, 91st Cong., 1st sess., June 10, 1969, p. 101.
34. "MMRBM-STINGS Program," *Missiles and Rockets* 13 (October 7, 1963): 43. David C. Breasted, "Navy Seeks Approval for Polaris Follow-on," *Missiles and Rockets* 13 (November 4, 1963): 18.
35. *The Wall Street Journal*, August 31, 1964, p. 18.
36. Statement of Secretary of Defense, Melvin R. Laird, *Department of Defense Appropriations for Fiscal Year 1970, op. cit.*, Part 1, June 10, 1969, p. 109.
37. Kugler, *op. cit.*
38. Statement of Former Secretary of Defense Robert McNamara, United States House of Representatives, Committee on Armed Services, *Hearings on Military Posture and An Act (S. 3293) to Authorize Appropriations During the Fiscal Year 1969 for Procurement of Aircraft, Missiles, Naval Vessels, and Tracked Combat Vehicles, Research, Development, Test, and Evaluation for the Armed Forces*

and to Prescribe the Authorized Personnel Strength of the Selected Reserve of Each Reserve Component of the Armed Forces, and for Other Purposes, 90th Cong., 2nd sess., April 30, 1968 (hereafter cited as FY 1969 Posture Statement), p. 8513.

39. Kugler, *op. cit.*

40. FY 1969 Posture Statement, *op. cit.*, p. 8513.

41. *Ibid.*, pp. 8513-14.

42. "Written Statement of Former Secretary of Defense Clark M. Clifford, Prepared January 15, 1969," United States House of Representatives, Committee on Armed Services, *Hearings on Military Posture and Legislation to Authorize Appropriations During the Fiscal Year 1970 for Procurement of Aircraft, Missiles, Naval Vessels and Tracked Combat Vehicles, Research, Development, Test, and Evaluation for the Armed Forces, and to Prescribe the Authorized Strength of the Reserve Forces, and for Other Purposes*, 91st Cong., 1st sess., January 27, 1969 (hereafter cited as "FY 1970 Posture Statement"), p. xxxii.

43. Testimony of Deputy Secretary of Defense, Paul H. Nitze, *Department of Defense Appropriations for Fiscal Year 1969, op. cit.*, Part 4, May 23, 1968, p. 2419.

44. *Polaris/Poseidon Chronology, op. cit.*, p. 13.

45. *Defense Industry Bulletin* 4 (September 1968): 5; and U.S. House of Representatives, Committee on Foreign Affairs, Subcommittee on National Security Policy and Scientific Developments, *Diplomatic and Strategic Impact of Multiple Warhead Missiles*, 91st Cong., 1st sess., July 8, 1969, p. 29.

46. *Department of Defense Appropriations for Fiscal Year 1971*, Part 1, *op. cit.*, February 2, 1970, p. 70.

47. *Polaris/Poseidon Chronology, op. cit.*, p. 14.

48. *Department of Defense Appropriations for Fiscal Year 1970, op. cit.*, Part 1, June 10, 1969, p. 19.

49. *Ibid.*, Part 1, p. 109.

50. *Ibid.*, Part 1, pp. 108-109.

51. Secretary of Defense, Melvin R. Laird, *National Security Strategy of Realistic Deterrence*, Annual Defense Department Report, February 15, 1972 (Washington, D.C.: Government Printing Office, 1972), p. 72.

52. U.S. Senate, Committee on Foreign Relations, Subcommittee on Arms Control, International Law and Organization, *Arms Control Implications of Current Defense Budget*, 92nd Cong., 1st sess., June 12, 1971, p. 23.

53. R.T. Pretty and D.H.R. Archer (eds.), *Janes Weapons Systems 1971-72* (New York: McGraw-Hill, 1970), p. 4.

54. *Poseidon and Polaris Fact Sheet*, News Bureau, Lockheed Missiles and Space Company, Sunnyvale, California, p. 2.

55. Testimony of John McLucas, Secretary of the Air Force, United States Senate, Subcommittee of the Committee on Appropriations, *Depart-*

ment of Defense Appropriations for Fiscal Year 1975, 93rd Cong., 2nd sess., Part 4, March 7, 1974, p. 63.

56. Testimony of Vice Admiral F.H. Price, Jr., *ibid.*, Part 3, April 24, 1974, p. 889.

57. Testimony of John McLucas, Secretary of the Air Force, *ibid.*, Part 4, March 7, 1974, p. 63; Secretary of Defense James R. Schlesinger, *Annual Defense Department Report FY 1975* (Washington, D.C.: Government Printing Office, 1974) (hereafter cited as FY 1975 Posture Statement), pp. 52-54; and Secretary of Defense James R. Schlesinger, *Annual Defense Department Report FY 1976 and FY 197T* (Washington, D.C.: Government Printing Office, 1975) (hereafter cited as FY 1976 Posture Statement), p. II-21.

58. FY 1976 Posture Statement, p. II-26.

59. *Ibid.*, p. II-30.

60. *Ibid.*, pp. II-30 and II-31.

61. FY 1975 Posture Statement, pp. 57-58.

62. *Ibid.*, p. 57.

63. FY 1976 Posture Statement, pp. II-21 to II-33.

Chapter Two
Innovation

1. U.S. Senate, Committee on Foreign Relations, Subcommittee on Arms Control, International Law and Organization, *ABM, MIRV, SALT and the Nuclear Arms Race*, 91st Cong., 2nd sess., March 16, 1970, p. 114. On the relationship between McNamara and the two presidents he served, see also Henry L. Trewitt, *McNamara* (New York: Harper and Row, 1971), especially Chapter 10; Lyndon B. Johnson, *The Vantage Point* (New York: Holt, Rinehart and Winston, 1971), p. 20; and William W. Kaufmann, *The McNamara Strategy* (New York: Harper and Row, 1964), p. 300.

2. Arthur Schlesinger, *A Thousand Days* (Boston: Houghton Mifflin, 1965), p. 319.

3. Eugene M. Zuckert, "The Service Secretary: Has He a Useful Role?" *Foreign Affairs* 44 (April 1966): 458 ff.

4. In clarifying this relationship the author acknowledges the assistance of the Chief Historian, Air Force Space and Missile Organization, in a private communication, January 9, 1975.

5. Personnel information from Paul Flam, *The Role of Aerospace and Mitre Corporations in Air Force R&D*, Master of Science Thesis, Sloan School of Management, Massachusetts Institute of Technology, 1965. For the role of STL Inc. before 1960 see U.S. House of Representatives, Subcommittee of the Committee on Government Operations, *Management of Missile Programs*, 86th Cong., 1st sess., February 2, 1959, especially the testimony of Simon Ramo. Harvey M. Sapolsky, *The Polaris System Development: Bureaucratic and Programmatic Success in Government* (Cambridge: Harvard Univer-

sity Press, 1972), p. 84ff, also provides a discussion of the role of STL Inc. and Aerospace Corp.

6. Testimony of General James Ferguson, U.S. Senate, Subcommittee of the Committee on Appropriations, *Department of Defense Appropriations for Fiscal Year 1971*, Part 4, 91st Cong., 2nd sess., May 6, 1970, p. 273.

7. See testimony of Secretary of the Air Force, James H. Douglas, *Management of Missile Programs, op. cit.*, pp. 6-7, 19.

8. Thomas A. Sturm, *The USAF Scientific Advisory Board: Its First Twenty Years, 1944-64*, (Washington: USAF Historical Division Liaison, 1967), pp. 104, 114.

9. *Ibid.*, Apendixes E and G.

10. The author is indebted to the Chief Historian, Air Force Space and Missile Organization, for information about this Panel. Private communication January 9, 1975.

11. For an account of the Great Circle Group and the Office of Strategic Offensive and Defensive Systems see Captain Dominic A. Paolucci, "The Development of Navy Strategic Offensive and Defensive Systems," *U.S. Naval Institute Proceedings* 96 (May 1970).

12. Vincent Davis, *The Politics of Innovation: Patterns in Navy Cases*, Monograph Series in World Affairs, Volume 4 (1966-67), University of Denver, p. 62.

13. See Sapolsky, *op. cit.*, Chapter 3, for a discussion of the organizational structure of the Navy.

14. For a discussion of these points see *Ibid.*, pp. 41-60.

15. *Ibid.*, pp. 74-75.

16. *Ibid.*, Chapter 5.

17. *Ibid.*, p. 89.

18. *Ibid.*, p. 145.

19. *Ibid.*, p. 144.

20. See Zuckert, *op. cit.*, and Alain Enthoven and K. Wayne Smith, *How Much Is Enough? Shaping the Defense Program, 1961-1969* (New York: Harper and Row, 1971), especially Chapters 2 and 3.

21. Testimony of DDR&E Dr. Harold Brown, *Systems Development and Management*, Part 2, Hearings before a Subcommittee of the Committee on Government Operation, House of Representatives, 87th Cong., 2nd sess., July 24, 1962, pp. 484-485.

22. Morton Halperin, "The Decision to Deploy the ABM: Bureaucratic and Domestic Politics in the Johnson Administration," *World Politics* 25 (October 1972): 70.

23. James Q. Wilson, "Innovation in Organization: Notes Toward a Theory," in James D. Thompson, *Approaches to Organizational Design* (Pittsburgh: University of Pittsburgh Press, 1966), p. 198.

24. Herbert F. York, "Multiple Warhead Missiles," *Scientific American* 229 (November 1973): 18-27.

25. The discussion was provoked by Jerome B. Wiesner, "Comprehensive Arms Limitation Systems," *Daedalus* 89 (Fall 1960): 915-950.

26. *Aviation Week and Space Technology* 77 (November 5, 1962): 29.
27. *Facts About Minuteman*, Autonetics Division, North American Rockwell, refers to this company-funded work.
28. MIRV Chronology, The Aerospace Corporation, March 14, 1972 (hereafter cited as Aerospace MIRV Chronology), p. 1. This is an unpublished document of the Aerospace Corporation that was provided to the author. The date given for this Task Group is 1963, but that is evidently incorrect.
29. Aerospace MIRV Chronology, p. 1.
30. Richard L. Durham, "Security Classification Policy and National Security: The Case of MIRV," Individual Research Paper of the Elective Studies Program, the National War College, 1970, p. 3.
31. Testimony of Secretary of Defense, Robert S. McNamara, U.S. Senate, Committee on Foreign Relations, *Nuclear Test Ban Treaty*, 88th Cong., 1st sess., August 13, 1963, pp. 102-103. For Dr. Brown's testimony see August 21, 1963, p. 529.
32. *Progress Report 1964 Aerospace Corporation*, pp. 9-10.
33. Aerospace MIRV Chronology, p. 2.
34. *Progress Report 1964 Aerospace Corporation*, p. 10.
35. *Ibid.*, p. 9.
36. Aerospace MIRV Chronology, *op. cit.*, p. 2.
37. *Ibid.*
38. *Aviation Week and Space Technology* 75 (September 4, 1961): 31; 77 (December 24, 1962): 13; 78 (March 11, 1963): 145; U.S. House of Representatives, Subcommittee of the Committee on Appropriations, *Department of Defense Appropriations for 1963*, Part 4, 87th Cong., 2nd sess., April 1, 1962, p. 148.
39. Sapolsky, *op. cit.*, p. 220.
40. Testimony of DDR&E Harold Brown, U.S. House of Representatives, Subcommittee of the Committee on Appropriations, *Department of Defense Appropriations for 1965*, Part 5, 88th Cong., 2nd sess., April 11, 1964, p. 148.
41. David C. Breasted, "Navy Seeks Approval for Polaris Follow-On," *Missiles and Rockets* 13 (November 4, 1963): 18.
42. See Paolucci, *op. cit.* and Sapolsky, *op. cit.*, pp. 17, 35 and Chapter 6 for discussions of these points.
43. *Aviation Week and Space Technology* 80 (June 29, 1964): 13.
44. Amrom H. Katz, "Thoughts on Reconnaissance," a paper presented to the Reconnaissance Symposium, November 24, 1948. Reprinted in Amrom H. Katz (ed.), *Selected Readings in Aerial Reconnaissance*, No. P-2762 (Santa Monica, Cal.: RAND Corporation, August 1963), p. 28.
45. James Q. Wilson, *op. cit.*
46. Jerald Hage and Michael Aiken, *Social Change in Complex Organizations* (New York: Random House, 1970).
47. Quoted in Curtis LeMay, *Mission with LeMay: My Story* (Garden City: Doubleday, 1965), p. 545.

194 Making the MIRV

48. *Aviation Week and Space Technology* 77 (November 5, 1962): 29, and 77 (November 26, 1962): 30.
49. For a discussion of the characteristics of military advocates of technical innovation see Davis, *op. cit.*, pp. 51-56. Since all of the cases Davis looked t involved overcoming internal opposition to innovation, he missed the point that an advocate is unnecessary when opposition is lacking.
50. Sturm, *op. cit.*, p. 176.
51. Durham, *op. cit.*, pp. 5-6.
52. Aerospace MIRV Chronology, *op. cit.*, p. 2.
53. *Ibid.*
54. Sturm, *op. cit.*, p. 174.
55. Aerospace MIRV Chronology, *op. cit.*, p. 2.
56. For example, one background paper by L.H. Gould and F.N. Spain of Aerospace Corp. was entitled "Design Analysis Study of Mark 12 MIRV: Inputs to First Cut Design for Wing 6 Minuteman II," dated November 1964.
57. *Aviation Week and Space Technology* 81 (July 6, 1964): 275.
58. *Aviation Week and Space Technology* 81 (September 14, 1964): 23.
59. *Aviation Week and Space Technology* 80 (June 15, 1964): 23.
60. *Defense Industry Bulletin* 1 (August 1965): 5.
61. Aerospace MIRV Chronology, *op. cit.*, p. 2.
62. Press Release from Southern California Public Relations Office, Philco-Ford Corporation, January 19, 1964.
63. *Ibid.*
64. Testimony of DDR&E Harold Brown, U.S. House of Representatives, Subcommittee of the Committee on Appropriations, *Department of Defense Appropriations for 1966*, Part 5, 89th Cong., 1st sess., March 3, 1965, p. 5.
65. Sapolsky, *op. cit.*, Chapter 7.
66. *Ibid.*, pp. 71-72.
67. "The Text of President Johnson's Defense Message Presented to the 89th Congress," *The New York Times*, January 19, 1965, p. 16.
68. Sapolsky, *op. cit.*, p. 220.
69. Statement of Secretary of Defense, Robert S. McNamara, U.S. House of Representatives, Committee on Armed Services, *Hearings on Military Posture and H.R. 13456 to Authorize Appropriations During the Fiscal Year 1966 for Procurement of Aircraft, Missiles, Naval Vessels, and Tracked Combat Vehicles, and Research, Development, Test, and Evaluation for the Armed Forces, and to Maintain Parity between Military and Civilian Pay, and for Other Purposes*, 89th Cong., 1st sess., February 2, 1965, p. 212.
70. Harvey M. Sapolsky, "Organizational Structure and Innovation," *The Journal of Business* 40 (October 1967): 497.
71. Wilson, *op. cit.*, p. 200.
72. Durham, *op. cit.*, pp. 4-5.
73. Nuclear Test Ban Treaty, *op. cit.*, pp. 99-101.

74. *Department of Defense Appropriations for 1966, op. cit.*, Part 3, April 9, 1965, Testimony of Secretary of the Navy, Paul H. Nitze, p. 662, and Testimony of Chief of Naval Operations, Admiral David L. McDonald, p. 675.
75. *Ibid.*, Part 1, p. 415.
76. York, *op. cit.*, p. 26.
77. Multiple Addressee Memorandum from Deputy Secretary of Defense, Cyrus R. Vance, October 17, 1966, on the subject, "Security of Strategic Concepts," given in Durham, *op. cit.*, p. 40.

Chapter Three
Bureaucracy, Strategy, and Politics

1. See Alain C. Enthoven and K. Wayne Smith, *How Much is Enough? Shaping the Defense Program 1961-1969* (New York: Harper and Row, 1971), Chapter 2, for a discussion of the attempts to make or justify decisions on the basis of national interest and cost-effectiveness in the McNamara Pentagon.
2. On this point see James Kurth, "A Widening Gyre: The Logic of American Weapons Procurement," *Public Policy* 19 (Summer 1971): 373.
3. See, for example, the testimony of Dr. John S. Foster, Jr., Director of Lawrence Livermore Laboratory, United States Senate, Committee on Foreign Relations, *Nuclear Test Ban Treaty*, 88th Cong., 1st sess., August 21, 1963, p. 614.
4. Testimony of General Maxwell D. Taylor, Chairman, Joint Chiefs of Staff, *Ibid.*, August 15, 1963, p. 274.
5. *Aviation Week and Space Technology* 81 (September 14, 1964): 23.
6. Testimony of Rear Admiral Ralph A. Ofstie, U.S. House of Representatives, Committee on Armed Services, *The National Defense Program—Unification and Strategy*, 81st Cong., 1st sess., October 18, 1949, p. 183.
7. The arguments of the Navy are developed in *Ibid.* during October, 1949. The Air Force's case for the B-36 had previously been presented to the House Armed Services Committee during the hearings entitled *Investigation of the B-36 Bomber Program* in August and early October, 1949. See also Paul Y. Hammond, "Super-carriers and B-36 Bombers: Appropriations, Strategy and Politics," in Harold Stein (ed.), *American Civil-Military Decisions: A Book of Case Studies* (University City: University of Alabama Press, 1963), pp. 465-567.
8. Allen Drury, "Burke Testifies of Need to Match Soviet Seapower," *The New York Times*, January 27, 1959, p. 1.
9. Harvey Sapolsky, *The Polaris System Development: Bureaucratic and Programmatic Success in Government* (Cambridge: Harvard University Press, 1972), pp. 37-40.
10. Enthoven and Smith, *op. cit.*, p. 174.
11. *Ibid.*, p. 175. Although other numbers are sometimes used to quantify the concept of assured destruction capability, they are not very different from those given.

12. Enthoven and Smith, *op. cit.*, p. 174.
13. See Rear Admiral George Miller, "Needed—A New Strategy for Preservation of the Republic," *Sea Power* 14 (December 1971): 5.
14. See Dominic Paolucci, "The Development of Navy Strategic Offensive and Defensive Systems," *U.S. Naval Institute Proceedings* 96 (May 1970).
15. Testimony of Rear Admiral Levering Smith, U.S. House of Representatives, Subcommittee of the Committee on Appropriations, *Department of Defense Appropriations for 1968*, Part 3, 90th Cong., 1st sess., April 6, 1967, p. 456.
16. Sapolsky, *op. cit.*, p. 22.
17. For a discussion of these bureaucratic fights see Michael H. Armacost, *The Politics of Weapons Innovation: The Thor-Jupiter Controversy* (New York: Columbia University Press, 1969), and Sapolsky, *op. cit.*, pp. 37-40.
18. For a discussion of the evolution of nuclear strategy in the Air Force during this period see Desmond J. Ball, *The Strategic Missile Program of the Kennedy Administration*, Ph.D. dissertation, Australian National University, 1972, pp. 46-51; and Richard Frykland, *100 Million Lives: Maximum Survival in a Nuclear War* (New York: Macmillan, 1962), Chapters 1-3.
19. Edward Randolph Jayne II, *The ABM Debate: Strategic Defense and National Security* (Cambridge: Center for International Studies, MIT, 1969), p. 229.
20. Quoted by Senator Fulbright in U.S. Senate, Committee on Foreign Relations, Subcommittee on Arms Control, International Law and Organization, *ABM, MIRV, SALT and the Nuclear Arms Race*, 91st Cong., 2nd sess., March 16, 1970, p. 96.
21. United States Senate, Committee on Armed Services, Preparedness Investigating Subcommittee, *Status of U.S. Strategic Power*, 90th Cong., 2nd sess., Part 1, April 23, 1968, p. 7.
22. *Ibid.*, Part 1, p. 7.
23. General Bernard A. Schriever, "Forecast," *Air University Review*, Volume 16 (March-April, 1965), p. 3.
24. Testimony of Secretary of the Air Force, Eugene Zuckert, U.S. Senate, Subcommittee of the Committee on Appropriations, *Department of Defense Appropriations for Fiscal Year 1966*, Part 1, 89th Cong., 1st sess., March 10, 1965, p. 954.
25. Testimony of Deputy Secretary of Defense Paul H. Nitze, U.S. Senate, Subcommittee of the Committee on Appropriations, *Department of Defense Appropriations for Fiscal Year 1969*, Part 4, 90th Cong., 2nd sess., July 13, 1968, p. 2418.
26. *Status of U.S. Strategic Power*, Part 1, *op. cit.*, p. 26.
27. *Ibid.*, Part 2, p. 283.
28. *Ibid.*, Part 2, p. 243.
29. *Ibid.*, Part 1, p. 36.
30. *Ibid.*, pp. 17 and 35.

31. General John D. Ryan, Address to the Air Force Association Annual Convention, September 22, 1970, quoted in a press release from the Office of Senator Edward Brooke, November 11, 1970.

32. *Aviation Week and Space Technology* 85 (September 26, 1966): 23; and 87 (October 23, 1967): 25.

33. Sapolsky, *op. cit.*, p. 30.

34. Private communication from the Media Services Office, Department of the Navy.

35. *Aviation Week and Space Technology* 86 (February 8, 1967): 26.

36. *Department of Defense Appropriations for Fiscal Year 1969, op. cit.*, Part 4, p. 2448.

37. *Ibid.*

38. *Ibid.*, Part 3, May 15, 1968, p. 1052.

39. *Missiles and Rockets*, 14 (January 13, 1964): 14; and Statement of Secretary of Defense Robert S. McNamara, U.S. House of Representatives, Committee on Armed Services, *Hearings on Military Posture and H.R. 4016, to Authorize Appropriations During Fiscal Year 1966 for Procurement of Aircraft, Missiles, and Naval Vessels, and Research, Development, Test, and Evaluation, for the Armed Forces, and for Other Purposes*, 89th Cong., 1st sess., February 2, 1965 (hereafter cited as FY 1966 Posture Statement), p. 173.

40. Robert S. McNamara, Address at the Commencement Exercises, University of Michigan, Ann Arbor, Michigan, June 16, 1962, quoted in William W. Kaufmann, *The McNamara Strategy* (New York: Harper and Row, 1964), p. 116.

41. For a discussion of the means by which McNamara became acquainted with and persuaded of this strategy see Ball, *op. cit.*, pp. 273-277 and Frykland, *op. cit.*, Chapter 3.

42. Air Force reaction to the counterforce doctrine is expressed in two editorials in *Air Force Magazine* shortly after the Ann Arbor speech. John F. Loosbrock, "Counterforce and Mr. McNamara," V. 45 (September 1962): 8; and John F. Loosbrock, "History and Mr. McNamara," V. 45 (October, 1962): 32.

43. Statement of Secretary of Defense Robert S. McNamara, U.S. House of Representatives, Committee on Armed Services, *Hearings on Military Posture and H.R. 2440, to Authorize Appropriations During Fiscal Year 1964 for Procurement, Research, Development, Test, and Evaluation of Aircraft, Missiles, and Naval Vessels for the Armed Forces, and For Other Purposes*, 88th Cong., 1st sess., January 30, 1963 (herafter cited as "FY 1964 Posture Statement"), pp. 309-310.

44. This and the following discussion of the damage limitation study relies on Ball, *op. cit.*, p. 290, and Jayne, *op. cit.*, pp. 226-240 and especially on Richard L. Kugler, *The Politics of Restraint: Robert McNamara and the Strategic Nuclear Forces*, Ph.D. dissertation, Political Science Department, Massachusetts Institute of Technology, 1975 (to be completed).

45. Statement of Secretary of Defense Robert McNamara, *Hearings on Military*

  Posture and H.R. 9637 to Authorize Appropriations During Fiscal Year 1965 for Procurement of Aircraft, Missiles, and Naval Vessels, and Research, Development, Test, and Evaluation, for the Armed Forces, and for Other Purposes before the Committee on Armed Services, House of Representatives, 88th Cong., 2nd sess., January 27, 1964 (hereafter cited as "FY 1965 Posture Statement"), p. 6919.

46. On this point see testimony of Dr. Alain Enthoven, *Status of U.S. Strategic Power*, Part 1, April 24, 1968, *op. cit.*, p. 138.

47. "The Text of President Johnson's Defense Message Presented to the 89th Congress," *The New York Times*, January 19, 1965, p. 16.

48. *Status of U.S. Strategic Power, op. cit.*, Part 1, p. 140.

49. On this point see testimony of Dr. Alain Enthoven, *ibid.*, Part 1, pp. 135-139.

50. This point has been made by DDR&E, Dr. John Foster, *Department of Defense Appropriations for Fiscal Year 1969, op. cit.*, Part 4, July 11, 1968, p. 2310; and by Deputy Secretary of Defense, David Packard, *Hearings on Military Posture and Legislation to Authorize Appropriations During the Fiscal Year 1970, op. cit.*, Part 1, p. 2022.

51. *Department of Defense Appropriations for Fiscal Year 1969, op. cit.*, Part 4, June 23, 1968, p. 2448.

52. See Foster's testimony in *Status of U.S. Strategic Power, op. cit.*, Part 1, p. 60-61; and Kugler, *op. cit.*

53. United States Senate, Subcommittee of the Committee on Appropriations, *Department of Defense Appropriations for Fiscal Year 1970*, Part 1, 91st Cong., 1st sess., August 10, 1969, pp. 109, 141.

54. Testimony of Dr. John S. Foster, Jr., United States House of Representatives, Committee on Foreign Affairs, Subcommittee on National Security Policy and Scientific Developments, *Diplomatic and Strategic Impact of Multiple Warhead Missiles*, 91st Cong., 1st sess., August 5, 1969, p. 261.

55. *Department of Defense Appropriations for Fiscal Year 1970*, Part 1, *op. cit.*, p. 109.

56. Testimony of Dr. Enthoven, *Status of U.S. Strategic Power, op. cit.*, Part 1, p. 106.

57. *Status of U.S. Strategic Power, op. cit.*, Part 1, p. 146.

58. Richard M. Nixon, *U.S. Foreign Policy for the 1970s: Building for Peace.* A Report to the Congress by the President of the United States (Washington: Government Printing Office, 1971), p. 170.

59. See Richard M. Nixon, *U.S. Foreign Policy for the 1970s: The Emerging Structure of Peace.* A Report to the Congress by the President of the United States, February 9, 1972, p. 158, and Richard M. Nixon, *U.S. Foreign Policy for the 1970s: Shaping a Durable Peace.* A Report by the President to the Congress, May 3, 1973, p. 182. See also William Beecher, "Major War Plans Are Being Revised by the White House," *The New York Times*, August 5, 1972, p. 1.

60. For a discussion of the changes introduced by Secretary Schlesinger see James R. Schlesinger, *Annual Defense Department Report, FY 1975* (Washington: Government Printing Office, 1974), pp. 35-43; and Secretary of Defense James R. Schlesinger, *Annual Defense Department Report, FY 1976 and FY 197T* (Washington: Government Printing Office, 1975), pp. I-13 to I-17, and pp. II-1 to II-11. An analysis of these changes may be found in Ted Greenwood and Michael L. Nacht, "The New Nuclear Debate: Sense or Nonsense?" *Foreign Affairs* 52 (July 1974): 761-780.

61. For a detailed discussion of the strategic missile programs of the Kennedy Administration see Ball, *op. cit.*

62. Testimony of Secretary of Defense, Melvin R. Laird, *Department of Defense Appropriations for Fiscal Year 1970, op. cit.*, Part 1, p. 585.

63. Enthoven and Smith, *op. cit.*, p. 259; and United States House of Representatives, Subcommittee of the Committee on Appropriations, *Department of Defense Appropriations for 1964*, Part 1, 88th Cong., 1st sess., February 6, 1973, p. 319.

64. FY 1966 Posture Statement, *op. cit.*, p. 211.

65. Arthur M. Schlesinger, Jr., *A Thousand Days: John F. Kennedy in the White House* (Boston: Houghton Mifflin, 1965), p. 500.

66. Statement of Secretary of Defense, Robert McNamara, United States House of Representatives, Committee on Armed Services, *Hearings on Military Posture and H.R. 9751 to Authorize Appropriations During Fiscal Year 1963 for Aircraft, Missiles, and Navy Vessels for the Armed Forces, and for Other Purposes*, 87th Cong., 2nd sess., January 24, 1962, p. 3162.

67. Samuel P. Huntington, *The Common Defense* (New York: Columbia University Press, 1966), Chapter IV.

68. John P. Crecine, "Defense Budgeting: Constraints and Organizational Adaptation," Discussion Paper Number 6, Institute of Public Policy Studies, University of Michigan (July, 1969). See also John P. Crecine and Gregory Fischer, "On Resource Allocation Processes in the U.S. Department of Defense," Discussion Paper Number 31, Institute of Public Policy Studies, University of Michigan (October, 1971).

69. James Trainor, "Advanced Minuteman Details Revealed," *Missiles and Rockets* 13 (October 7, 1963): 43; FY 1965 Posture Statement, *op. cit.*, p. 6923.

70. FY 1966 Posture Statement, *op. cit.*, p. 211.

71. See, for example, FY 1966 Posture Statement, *op. cit.*, pp. 211-212; and *Department of Defense Appropriations for 1966, op. cit.*, Part 1, pp. 385-386.

72. "The Text of President Johnson's Defense Message Presented to the 89th Congress," *The New York Times*, January 19, 1965, p. 16.

73. Wallace Turner, "Goldwater Sees Pentagon Deceit," *The New York Times*, April 21, 1964, p. 23; and Jack Raymond, "Goldwater Says Pentagon 'Fools' Public on Missiles," *The New York Times*, April 16, 1964, p. 1.

74. Hanson W. Baldwin, "Slow-Down in the Pentagon," *Foreign Affairs* 43 (January 1965): 262.
75. The following discussion of the relationship of MIRV to the bomber decisions of 1965 is based on Kugler, *op. cit.*
76. Statement of Secretary of Defense Robert McNamara, United States House of Representatives, Committee on Armed Services, *Hearings on Military Posture and H.R. 13456 to Authorize Appropriations During the Fiscal Year 1967 for Procurement of Aircraft, Missiles, Naval Vessels, and Tracked Combat Vehicles, and Research, Development, Test, and Evaluation for the Armed Forces, and to Maintain Parity between Military and Civilian Pay, and for Other Purposes*, 89th Cong., 2nd sess., (hereafter cited as "FY 1967 Posture Statement"), March 8, 1966, p. 7347.
77. FY 1967 Posture Statement, *op. cit.*, p. 7341.
78. *Ibid.*, p. 7343.
79. Henry L. Trewitt, *McNamara* (New York: Harper and Row, 1971), pp. 124-126.
80. Benjamin Welles, "Senate Panel Adds Antimissile Funds," *The New York Times*, April 22, 1966, p. 1; Benjamin Welles, "Senate Approves a Start on Nike X Missile Defense," *The New York Times*, April 29, 1966, p. 1; Marjorie Hunter, "House Panel Defies Johnson on Military Budget," *The New York Times*, May 4, 1966, p. 2; Edwin L. Dole, Jr., "House Unit Votes a Bigger Defense," *The New York Times*, June 25, 1966, p. 1; "$58-Billion Is Voted in House for Defense," *The New York Times*, July 21, 1966, p. 4; Benjamin Welles, "Senate Unit Asks Reserve Call-Up for Vietnam War," *The New York Times*, August 13, 1966, p. 2.
81. Morton Halperin, "The Decision to Deploy the ABM: Bureaucratic and Domestic Politics in the Johnson Administration," *World Politics* 25 (October 1972): 74-76, 82-86.
82. Jayne, *op. cit.*, p. 333-334.
83. "Transcript of Joint News Conference by President, McNamara and General Wheeler," *The New York Times*, November 11, 1966, p. 18.
84. See William Beecher, "Missile to Carry Warhead Cluster," *The New York Times*, January 20, 1967, p. 1; and Hanson Baldwin, "Soviet Anti-missile System Spurs New US System," *The New York Times*, February 5, 1967, p. 1.
85. FY 1966 Posture Statement, *op. cit.*, p. 495.
86. Trewitt, *op. cit.*, p. 127; Lloyd Norman, "Nike-X," *Army* 17 (March 1967): 28; Halperin, *op. cit.*, p. 89; and John Newhouse, *Cold Dawn: The Story of SALT* (New York: Holt, Rinehart and Winston, 1973), p. 86.
87. Robert S. McNamara, "The Dynamics of Nuclear Strategy," *Department of State Bulletin* 57 (October 9, 1967): 443-451; and Halperin, *op. cit.*, pp. 86-88.
88. "Defense Fantasy Now Come True: In an exclusive interview, Secretary McNamara explains in full the logic behind the ABM system," *Life* 63 (September 29, 1967): 28A-28C.
89. William Beecher, "Soviet Reported Stressing Multiple-Warhead Missile," *The New York Times*, September 10, 1967, p. 1.

90. On this point see Albert Wohlstetter, "Is there a Strategic Arms Race?" *Foreign Policy*, 15 (Summer 1974): 3.
91. FY 1968 Posture Statement, *op. cit.*, p. 392.
92. Statement of Former Secretary of Defense Robert S. McNamara, United States House of Representatives, Committee on Armed Services, *Hearings on Military Posture and an Act (S. 3293) to Authorize Appropriations During the Fiscal Year 1969 for Procurement of Aircraft, Missiles, Naval Vessels, and Tracked Combat Vehicles, Research, Development, Test and Evaluation for the Armed Forces and to Prescribe the Authorized Personnel Strength of the Selected Reserve of Each Reserve Component of the Armed Forces, and for Other Purposes*, 90th Cong., 2nd sess., April 30, 1968, p. 8504.
93. Written Statement of Former Secretary of Defense Clark M. Clifford, Prepared January 15, 1969, United States House of Representatives, Committee on Armed Services, *Hearings on Military Posture and Legislation to Authorize Appropriations During the Fiscal Year 1970 for Procurement of Aircraft, Missiles, Naval Vessels, and Tracked Combat Vehicles, Research, Development, Test, and Evaluation for the Armed Forces and to Prescribe the Authorized Strength of the Reserve Forces, and for Other Purposes*, 91st Cong., 1st sess., Appendix A, January 28, 1969, p. xxiii.
94. Statement of Admiral Thomas H. Moorer, Chairman, Joint Chiefs of Staff, United States Senate, Committee on Foreign Relations, *Strategic Arms Limitations Agreements*, 92nd Cong., 2nd sess., June 27, 1972, p. 70.
95. See, for example, the comment of Secretary of Defense Melvin R. Laird to Congressman Bennett in United States House of Representatives, Committee on Armed Services, *Supplementary Hearings on Defense Procurement Authorization Relating to SALT Agreement*, 92nd Cong., 2nd sess., June 6, 1972, p. 12098.19.
96. Testimony of Paul Nitze before the Subcommittee of the House Armed Services Committee, July 2, 1974, mimeograph copy, pp. 3-4.
97. Robert S. McNamara, "The Dynamics of Nuclear Strategy," *Department of State Bulletin* 57 (October 7, 1967): 450.
98. Ralph Lapp, *Arms Beyond Doubt: The Tyranny of Weapons Technology* (New York: Cowles, 1970), p. 177.
99. Kurth, *op. cit.*, p. 385.
100. Ronald Tammen, *MIRV and the Arms Race: An Interpretation of Defense Strategy* (New York: Praeger, 1973).
101. This description of President Johnson's perspective on MIRV relies on Morton Halperin's analysis of the ABM case. Halperin, *op. cit.*, pp. 74-76.

Chapter Four
Intelligence Information and Uncertainty

1. For a discussion of the American observation satellite programs and capabilities for monitoring Soviet missile tests and an assessment of the utility of these systems see the author's *Reconnaissance, Surveil-*

lance and Arms Control, Adelphi Paper number 88 (London: International Institute for Strategic Studies, 1972).

2. For a detailed description of the American intelligence community see Harry Howe Ransom, *The Intelligence Establishment* (Cambridge: Harvard University Press, 1970).

3. See Ransom, *op. cit.,* pp. 149-155.

4. Statement of Secretary of Defense Robert McNamara, United States House of Representatives, Committee on Armed Services, *Hearings on Military Posture and H.R. 9637 to Authorize Appropriations During Fiscal Year 1965 for Procurement of Aircraft, Missiles, and Naval Vessels, and Research, Development, Test, and Evaluation, for the Armed Forces, and for Other Purposes,* 88th Cong., 2nd sess., January 27, 1964, p. 6921.

5. Quoted by Senator McIntyre, *Congressional Record–Senate,* May 7, 1969, p. 18897.

6. United States Senate, Committee on Armed Services, Preparedness Investigating Subcommittee, *Status of U.S. Strategic Power,* Part 1, 90th Cong., 2nd sess., April 24, 1968, p. 49.

7. Statement of Dr. John S. Foster, Jr., United States House of Representatives, Committee on Armed Services, *Hearings on Military Posture and an Act (S. 3293) to Authorize Appropriations During the Fiscal Year 1969 for Procurement of Aircraft, Missiles, Naval Vessels, and Tracked Combat Vehicles, Research, Development, Test, and Evaluation for the Armed Forces and to Prescribe the Authorized Personnel Strength of the Selected Reserve of Each Reserve Component of the Armed Forces, and for Other Purposes,* 90th Cong., 2nd sess., p. 8662.

8. United States Senate, Committee on Armed Services, Preparedness Investigating Subcommitee, *Military Aspects and Implications of Nuclear Test Ban Proposal and Related Matters,* Part 2, 89th Cong., 1st sess., August 22, 1963, p. 860.

9. William Beecher, "Soviet Missile Deployment Puzzles Top U.S. Analysts," *The New York Times,* April 14, 1969, p. 1.

10. "President Nixon's News Conference April 18, 1969," *Department of State Bulletin* 60 (May 5, 1969): 380.

11. McNamara himself has claimed that the buildup was excessive. See his speech, "The Dynamics of Nuclear Strategy," an address before the annual convention of United Press International editors and publishers at San Francisco, California, September 18, 1967, reprinted in *Department of State Bulletin* 57 (October 9, 1967): 445-446.

12. On the difficulties of both developing and using intelligence estimates see Sherman Kent, "Estimates and Influence," *Foreign Service Journal* 46 (April 1969): 16.

13. Quoted in John W. Finney, "Sentinel Backed by Laird as Vital to Thwart Soviets," *The New York Times,* March 21, 1969, p. 1.

14. U.S. Senate, Committee on Foreign Relations, Subcommitee on International Organization and Disarmament Affairs, *Strategic and Foreign*

Policy Implications of ABM Systems, Part 1, 91st Cong., 1st sess., March 21, 1969, p. 196. See also John W. Finney, "Sentinel Backed by Laird as Vital to Thwart Soviets," *op. cit.*; and John W. Finney, "Fulbright Says Laird Uses Fear to Promote ABM," *The New York Times*, March 22, 1969, p. 1.

15. On this point see an exchange between Secretary of Defense Melvin Laird and Senator William Fulbright recorded in *Strategic and Foreign Policy Implications of ABM Systems*, Part 1, *op. cit.*, p. 203.

16. Beecher, "Soviet Missile Deployment Puzzles Top U.S. Analysts," *op. cit.*, reports on these differences. See also "Secretary Rogers' News Conference of April 7," *Department of State Bulletin* 60 (April 28, 1969): 363, for the Secretary's opinion on this subject.

17. Quoted in John W. Finney, "Pentagon Charged With Changing Data to Help Antimissile Plan," *The New York Times*, May 15, 1969, p. 6.

18. *Ibid.*

19. *Ibid.*

20. U.S. House of Representatives, Committee on Science and Astronautics, *Research and Development for Defense*, 87th Cong., 1st sess., February 17, 1961, pp. 70-71.

21. Edward Randolph Jayne II, *The ABM Debate: Strategic Defense and National Security* (Cambridge: Center for International Studies, MIT, 1969), pp. 185-188.

22. Major General I. Baryshev, "Nuclear Weapons and the PVO," *Krasnaia Zvezda*, November 13, 1963, quoted in Benjamin S. Lambeth, "The Sources of Soviet Military Doctrine," *Proceedings of the Conference on Comparative Defense Policy*, Department of Political Science, USAF Academy, Colorado, February 1973, p. 6.

23. William Beecher, "Soviet Reported Stressing Multiple-Warhead Missile," *The New York Times*, September 10, 1967, p. 1.

24. William Beecher, "Top Defense Strategists Review Missiles Policy with Senators," *The New York Times*, May 7, 1968, p. 1.

25. George C. Wilson, "Russians are Reported Testing Multi-Warhead," *The Washington Post*, September 4, 1968, p. A1.

26. "President Nixon's News Conference of June 19," *Department of State Bulletin* 56 (July 7, 1969): 5.

27. William Beecher, "Soviet Missile Sub on Atlantic Base," *The New York Times*, April 24, 1970, p. 1; and "MIRV and ABM: How Not to Make a Case," *The Washington Post*, May 1, 1970, p. A24.

28. William Beecher, "Soviet Reported to Achieve Gain in MIRV Program," *The New York Times*, June 9, 1969, p. 1.

29. "Secretary Rogers' News Conference of June 5," *Department of State Bulletin* 56 (June 23, 1969): 534.

30. U.S. House of Representatives, Committee on Foreign Affairs, Subcommittee on National Security Policy and Scientific Development, *Diplomatic and Strategic Impact of Multiple Warhead Missiles*, 91st Cong., 1st sess., August 5, 1969, pp. 244-245.

31. *Ibid.*, p. 246.

32. *Ibid.*, pp. 241-281.
33. *Status of U.S. Strategic Power*, Part 1, *op. cit.*, pp. 104-107.
34. Secretary of Defense, Melvin R. Laird, *Fiscal Year 1971 Defense Program and Budget* (Washington: Government Printing Office, 1970) (hereafter cited as FY 1971 Posture Statement), pp. 67-68.
35. Testimony of Dr. John S. Foster, Jr., United States House of Representatives, Committee on Armed Services, *Hearings on Military Posture and H.R. 8687 to Authorize Appropriations During the Fiscal Year 1972 for Procurement of Aircraft, Missiles, Naval Vessels, Tracked Combat Vehicles, Torpedoes, and Other Weapons, and Research, Development, Test, and Evaluation for the Armed Forces and to Prescribe the Authorized Personnel Strength for Each Active Duty Component and of the Selected Reserve of Each Component of the Armed Forces, and for Other Purposes*, 92nd Cong., 1st sess., April 18, 1971, p. 2948.
36. For statements that disagree with the Pentagon position on this issue see General Accounting Office, *Comparison of Military Research and Development Expenditures of the United States and the Soviet Union*, Staff Study for the Subcommittee on Research and Development, Committee on Armed Services, United States Senate, 92nd Cong., 1st sess., July 27, 1971; and *Is There an R&D Gap?*, Federation of American Scientists, printed in *Congressional Record—Senate*, May 10, 1971, pp. 56518-25.
37. FY 1971 Posture Statement, *op. cit.*, p. 159.
38. Secretary of Defense Melvin R. Laird, *Toward a National Security Strategy of Realistic Deterrence*, Statement on the Fiscal Year 1972-76 Defense Program and the 1972 Defense Budget before the House Armed Services Committee, March 9, 1971 (Washington, D.C.: Government Printing Office, 1971) (hereafter cited as "FY 1972 Posture Statement"), p. 163.
39. "Written Statement of Former Secretary of Defense Clark M. Clifford, Prepared January 15, 1969," United States House of Representatives, Committee on Armed Services, *Hearings on Military Posture and Legislation to Authorize Appropriations During the Fiscal Year 1970 for Procurement of Aircraft, Missiles, Naval Vessels, and Tracked Combat Vehicles, Research, Development, Test, and Evaluation for the Armed Forces and to Prescribe the Authorized Strength of the Reserve Forces, and for Other Purposes*, 91st Cong., 1st sess., Appendix A, January 28, 1969 (hereafter cited as FY 1970 Posture Statement), p. xxiv.
40. United States Senate, Committee on Armed Services, *Fiscal Year 1973 Authorization for Military Procurement, Research and Development, Construction Authorization for the Safeguard ABM and Active Duty and Selected Reserve Strength*, Part 2, 92nd Cong., 2nd sess., February 15, 1972, p. 474.
41. *Ibid.*, Part 3, p. 1812.
42. United States Senate, Committee on Armed Services, *Military Implications*

of the Treaty on the Limitations of Anti-Ballistic Missile Systems and the Interim Agreement on Limitations of Strategic Offensive Arms, 92nd Cong., 2nd sess., June 27, 1972, p. 149.

43. *Ibid.*, p. 149.
44. See Albert Wohlstetter, "Is There a Strategic Arms Race?" *Foreign Policy* 15 (Summer 1974): 3-20; and "Rivals, But No 'Race'," *Foreign Policy* 16 (Fall 1974): 48-81.
45. Ronald L. Tammen, *MIRV and the Arms Race: An Interpretation of Defense Strategy* (New York: Praeger, 1973), p. 139.
46. *Aviation Week and Space Technology* 77 (December 17, 1962): 25.
47. On this point see the testimony of Dr. John S. Foster, Jr., *Diplomatic and Strategic Impact of Multiple Warhead Missiles, op. cit.*, p. 243.
48. This indeed was the official explanation. See the Statement of Secretary of Defense Robert S. McNamara, United States House of Representatives, Committee on Armed Services, *Hearings on Military Posture and H.R. 13456 to Authorize Appropriations During the Fiscal Year 1967 for Procurement of Aircraft, Missiles, Naval Vessels, and Tracked Combat Vehicles, and Research, Development, Test, and Evaluation for the Armed Forces, and to Maintain Parity Between Military and Civilian Pay, and for Other Purposes*, 89th Cong., 2nd sess., March 8, 1966, p. 7346. For the impact of the Tallinn system on the Poseidon deployment decision see testimony of Dr. John S. Foster, Jr., *Status of U.S. Strategic Power*, Part 1, *op. cit.*, p. 52.
49. Testimony of Secretary of Defense, Robert S. McNamara, United States House of Representatives, Committee on Armed Services, *Hearings on Military Posture and a Bill (H.R. 9240) to Authorize Appropriations During the Fiscal Year 1968 for Procurement of Aircraft, Missiles, Naval Vessels, and Tracked Combat Vehicles, and Research, Development, Test, and Evaluation for the Armed Forces, and for Other Purposes*, 90th Cong., 1st sess., March 2, 1967 (hereafter cited as FY 1968 Posture Statement), p. 408.
50. John W. Finney, "SS-9 Helps Administration Score Points in Missile Debate," *The New York Times*, March 24, 1969, p. 30, suggests 1966 was the date of first deployment of the SS-9.
51. FY 1968 Posture Statement, p. 394.
52. The memorandum is quoted in Richard L. Durham, "Security Classification Policy and National Security: The Case of MIRV," Individual Research Paper of the Elective Studies Program, The National War College, Washington, March 1970, p. 40.
53. Status of U.S. Strategic Power, *op. cit.*, Part 1, p. 143.
54. Statement of Former Secretary of Defense Robert S. McNamara, *Hearings on Military Posture and an Act (S. 3293) to Authorize Appropriations during Fiscal Year 1969, etc., op. cit.* (hereafter cited as FY 1969 Posture Statement), April 30, 1968, p. 8506.
55. *Ibid.*
56. FY 1970 Posture Statement, *op. cit.*, p. xxiii.
57. *Strategic Survey 1968* (London: Institute for Strategic Studies, 1969), p. 24.

58. FY 1969 Posture Statement, *op. cit.*, pp. 8507-8508.
59. Dr. John S. Foster, Jr. gave these reasons for continuing the Poseidon program. See *Status of U.S. Strategic Power*, Part 1, *op. cit.*, p. 52.
60. *Aviation Week and Space Technology* 86 (December 12, 1966): 23.
61. William Beecher, "Pentagon Awaits Guide on Missiles," *The New York Times*, July 17, 1967, p. 1.
62. FY 1968 Posture Statement, *op. cit.*, pp. 394-395.
63. FY 1969 Posture Statement, *op. cit.*, p. 8508.
64. "Plan for Rock Silos for ICBM's Dropped," *The New York Times*, August 26, 1970, p. 31; Michael Getler, "U.S. Drops 'Hard-Rock' ICBM Plan," *Washington Post*, August 25, 1970, p. A1.
65. William Beecher, "500 Missile Silos Being Reinforced by the Air Force," *The New York Times*, December 6, 1970, p. 1.
66. For a discussion of the Safeguard defense of the Minuteman force, see the author's *The Utility of Safeguard for the Defense of Minuteman* (Cambridge, Ma.: Center for International Studies, MIT, 1972).
67. Admiral Thomas H. Moorer, Chairman of the Joint Chiefs of Staff, *United States Military Posture for FY 1974*, (Washington: Government Printing Office, 1973), pp. 12-13.
68. Richard Nixon, *United States Foreign Policy for the 1970's: Shaping a Durable Peace*, May 3, 1973, p. 177; and FY 1972 Posture Statement, *op. cit.*, pp. 66-67.
69. *Status of U.S. Strategic Power*, Part 1, *op. cit.*, pp. 110-111.

Chapter Five
Controversy

1. On the relationship of the city-avoidance strategy to arms control see the address by Deputy Assistant Secretary of Defense (International Security Affairs) for Arms Control, John T. McNaughton, before the International Arms Control Symposium, University of Michigan, Ann Arbor, Michigan, December 11, 1962, quoted in William W. Kaufmann, *The McNamara Strategy* (New York: Harper and Row, 1964), pp. 145-146.
2. "Message from President Johnson to Eighteen Nation Disarmament Committee, January 21, 1964," United States Arms Control and Disarmament Agency, *Documents on Disarmament 1964* (Washington: Government Printing Office, October 1965), p. 8.
3. "Statement by the Acting United States Representative [Fisher] to the Eighteen Nation Disarmament Committee: Freeze on Strategic Delivery Systems, April 16, 1964," *Ibid.*, pp. 157-162.
4. James Trainor, "DOD Has New Warhead Plan," *Missiles and Rockets* 14 (April 27, 1964): 15.
5. From the sanitized and declassified version of J.P. Ruina, "A Comment on Future Weapons Systems (U), (Letter to Charles Herzfeld, ARPA, and George Rathjens, ACDA)," September 3, 1964, JASON Division, Institute for Defense Analysis, Washington, D.C.

6. On this change in emphasis see John Newhouse, *Cold Dawn: The Story of SALT* (New York: Holt, Rinehart and Winston, 1973), p. 70.
7. On the relationship between ACDA and the Department of Defense see Duncan L. Clarke, "The Role and Influence of the U.S. Arms Control and Disarmament Agency in National Security Policy Formulation," unpublished paper prepared for Conference on Executive-Legislative Interactions in U.S. Foreign Policy, sponsored by the School of International Service, The American University, May 4-6, 1972, pp. 19-22; and Duncan L. Clarke, "Congress, Interest Groups, and the U.S. Arms Control and Disarmament Agency," unpublished paper prepared for the International Studies Association Convention, New York, March 14, 1973, pp. 4-7.
8. Herbert Scoville, "The Politics of the ABM Debate: The View from the Arms Control and Disarmament Agency," paper prepared for the American Political Science Association Panel on the Politics of the ABM Debate, September 1970, *passim.*
9. Duncan L. Clark, "Congress, Interest Groups, and the U.S. Arms Control and Disarmament Agency," *op. cit.*, pp. 5-6.
10. John W. Finney, "MIRV, Being Tested by Both Sides, Is a Key Issue at Arms Talks," *The New York Times*, November 17, 1969, p. 12.
11. Statement of Secretary of Defense Robert S. McNamara, United States House of Representatives, Committee on Armed Services, *Hearings on Military Posture and a Bill (H.R. 9240) to Authorize Appropriations During the Fiscal Year 1968 for Procurement of Aircraft, Missiles, Naval Vessels, and Tracked Combat Vehicles, and Research, Development, Test, and Evaluation for the Armed Forces, and for Other Purposes,* 90th Cong., 1st sess., March 2, 1967, p. 395.
12. See Richard L. Kugler, "The Politics of Restraint: Robert McNamara and the Strategic Nuclear Forces, 1963-68," Ph.D. dissertation, Political Science Department, Massachusetts Institute of Technology, 1975.
13. Two documents from the middle 1960s, one a committee report and the other an article by a former senior defense official illustrate this point. See "Report of the Committee on International Arms Control and Disarmament of the National Citizens' Commission on International Cooperation," United States Arms Control and Disarmament Agency, *Documents on Disarmament 1965* (Washington: Government Printing Office, December 1966), p. 565; and Roswell Gilpatric, "Are We on the Brink of Another Arms Race?" *The New York Times Magazine*, January 15, 1967, p. 32.
14. United States Senate, Committee on Foreign Relations, Subcommittee on Disarmament, *United States Armament and Disarmament Problems*, 90th Cong., 1st sess., February 6, 1967, p. 7.
15. *Ibid.*, p. 88.
16. William Beecher, "Pentagon Readies Arms to Penetrate Soviet's Suspected New Defense," *The Wall Street Journal*, February 21, 1966, p. 1; William Beecher, "Air Force Plans on Giant Missile to Thwart Radar," *The New York Times*, June 20, 1966, p. 1; Hanson Baldwin,

"A New Round Begins in the Battle of Sword vs. Shield," *The New York Times*, November 27, 1966, Section IV, p. 3; William Beecher, "Missile to Carry Warhead Cluster," *The New York Times*, January 20, 1967, p. 1.

17. The *Washington Post* article is referred to in Chalmers Roberts, *The Nuclear Years: The Arms Race and Arms Control 1945-70* (New York: Praeger, 1970), p. 85. *The New York Times* picked it up immediately, see Hanson Baldwin, "Soviet Anti-missile System Spurs New U.S. Systems," February 5, 1967, p. 1.

18. *Aviation Week and Space Technology* 81 (July 27, 1964): 13.

19. "Defense Fantasy Now Come True: In an exclusive interview, Secretary McNamara explains in full the logic behind the ABM system," *Life* 63 (September 29, 1967): 28A-28C.

20. Robert Kleiman, "MIRV and the Offensive Missile Race," *The New York Times*, October 9, 1967, p. 36.

21. "Delay the MIRV Tests," *The New York Times*, August 5, 1968, p. 38; and "Decision on MIRV," *The New York Times*, August 10, 1968, p. 26.

22. Newhouse, *op. cit.*, pp. 99-101.

23. See Thomas W. Wolfe, *Soviet Power and Europe, 1945-1970* (Baltimore: Johns Hopkins Press, 1970), pp. 437-441.

24. Morton Halperin, "The Decision to Deploy the ABM: Bureaucratic and Domestic Politics in the Johnson Administration," *World Politics* 25 (October 1972): 82-84.

25. For an account of the American efforts to convince the Soviets to begin talks, see Johnson, *The Vantage Point* (New York: Holt, Rinehart and Winston, 1971), pp. 480-485; Newhouse, *op. cit.*, pp. 94-95; and "Defense Fantasy Now Come True," *op. cit.*

26. Johnson, *op. cit.*, p. 485.

27. On these points see "After the Pentagon Papers: Talk with Kistiakowsky, Wiesner," *Science* 173 (November 26, 1971): 923-928.

28. *Congressional Record—Senate*, August 22, 1967, pp. 23451-53 and 23460-504.

29. *Ibid.*, June 18, 1968, pp. 17629, 18410-11 and October 2, 1968, pp. 29164-87.

30. On the role of the scientists, see Anne Hessing Cahn, *Eggheads and Warheads: Scientists and the ABM* (Cambridge: Center for International Studies, MIT, 1971).

31. United States Senate, Subcommittee of the Committee on Appropriations, *Department of Defense Appropriations for Fiscal Year 1969*, 90th Cong., 2nd sess., May 8, 1968, Part 3, pp. 1413-18, 1444-48; and May 23, 1968, Part 4, pp. 2109-17, 2477-80.

32. Harvey M. Sapolsky, *The Polaris System Development: Bureaucratic and Programmatic Success in Government* (Cambridge: Harvard University Press, 1972), p. 225.

33. United States Senate, Subcommittee of the Committee on Appropriations, *Department of Defense Appropriations for Fiscal Year 1971*, Part 2, 91st Cong., 2nd sess., April 16, 1970, p. 70.

34. John W. Finney, "MIRV Being Tested by Both Sides, Is a Key Issue at Arms Talks," *op. cit.*

35. Newhouse, *op. cit.*, p. 122.

36. Tammen's contention that Secretary Rusk shared the view that the MIRV tests should be postponed is evidently incorrect. See Tammen, *MIRV and the Arms Race: An Interpretation of Defense Strategy* (New York: Praeger, 1973), p. 115.

37. Peter Grose, "Clifford Exempts Missile Defense From Budget Cuts," *The New York Times*, September 6, 1968, p. 1.

38. *Ibid.*

39. E.W. Kenworthy, "Yarborough Supports McCarthy Bid," *The New York Times*, August 10, 1968, p. 14. The relevant excerpt from the McCarthy position paper is reprinted in the *Congressional Record—Senate*, April 1, 1969, p. 8277.

40. Wilford, "Two New Missiles to Get Test Today," *op. cit.*

41. On this point, see Newhouse, *op. cit.*, p. 108.

42. See, for example, the "Statement on the Sentinel Anti-Ballistic-Missile Defense System," by Hans Bethe, Bernard T. Feld, David R. Inglis, Ralph E. Lapp, and Harold C. Urey, printed in *Congressional Record—Senate*, June 24, 1968, p. 18405.

43. John Noble Wilford, "Multiples Pass Test in Flight," *The New York Times*, August 17, 1968, p. 1.

44. Wilford, "Two New Missiles to Get Test Today," *op. cit.*; and Wilford, "Multiples Pass Test in Flight," *op. cit.*

45. Johnson, *op. cit.*, pp. 488-490 and Newhouse, *op. cit.*, pp. 136-137.

46. George C. Wilson, "Multi-Warhead Missile Tests in Russia Cited," *The Washington Post*, September 4, 1968, p. A1.

47. Newhouse, *op. cit.*, p. 182.

48. *Ibid.*, p. 141.

49. *Ibid.*, pp. 149 and 159.

50. On this philosophy of linkage, see "The White House, Congressional Briefing by Dr. Henry A. Kissinger, Assistant to the President for National Security Affairs—The State Dining Room," United States Senate Committee on Armed Services, *Military Implications of the Treaty on the Limitations of Anti-Ballistic Missile Systems and the Interim Agreement on the Limitation of Strategic Offensive Arms*, 92nd Cong., 2nd sess., June 20, 1972, p. 117.

51. Newhouse, *op. cit.*, p. 159.

52. *Ibid.*, p. 149.

53. *Ibid.*, p. 160; Hedrick Smith, "Nixon's Advisors Divided on Whether to Propose MIRV Test Ban to Soviets," *The New York Times*, August 20, 1969, p. 13; and John W. Finney, "Compromise Plan Is Adopted by U.S. for Arms Parley," *The New York Times*, November 11, 1969, p. 1; Robert Kleiman, "Nixon Confronts a Momentous Decision on the Hydra-Headed MIRV," *The New York Times*, August 17, 1969, IV, p. 2.

54. Chalmers Roberts, "Democrats Back Arms Freeze," *The Washington Post*,

April 8, 1970, p. A12, and Hedrick Smith, "Panel Urges Concession to Win MIRV Ban," *The New York Times*, January 29, 1971.

55. John W. Finney, "Missile Testing Divides U.S. Aides," *The New York Times*, May 22, 1969, p. 11.
56. Newhouse, *op. cit.*, p. 161; Hedrick Smith, "Nixon's Advisors Divided on Whether to Propose MIRV Test Ban to Soviets," *op. cit.*
57. Kleiman, "Nixon Confronts a Momentous Decision on the Hydra-Headed MIRV," *op. cit.*
58. Newhouse, *op. cit.*, p. 161.
59. *Ibid.*, pp. 159-162.
60. Some observers stress that this structural equality made an actual difference in ACDA's influence in decision making. See Herbert Scoville, *op. cit.*; and Duncan L. Clarke, "The Role and Influence of the U.S. Arms Control and Disarmament Agency in National Security Policy Formulation," *op. cit.*, and "Congress, Interest Groups and the U.S. Arms Control and Disarmament Agency," *op. cit.*, pp. 12-14.
61. "President Nixon's News Conference of June 19," *Department of State Bulletin* 56 (July 7, 1969): 2.
62. United States House of Representatives, Committee on Foreign Affairs, Subcommittee on National Security Policy and Scientific Developments, *Diplomatic and Strategic Impact of Multiple Warhead Missiles*, 91st Cong., 1st sess., August 5, 1969, pp. 284-286.
63. *Ibid.*, p. 285.
64. "President Nixon's News Conference of June 19," *op. cit.*, p. 2.
65. Newhouse, *op. cit.*, p. 170.
66. Finney, "MIRV, Being Tested by Both Sides, Is a Key Issue at Arms Talks," *op. cit.*
67. Newhouse, *op. cit.*, p. 171.
68. *Ibid.*, p. 173.
69. *Ibid.*, p. 179.
70. Hedrick Smith, "Panel Urges Concession to win MIRV Ban," *op. cit.*
71. *Ibid.*, and Newhouse, *op. cit.*, p. 180.
72. "The White House, Question and Answer Session After A Briefing by Dr. Henry Kissinger, Assistant to the President for National Security Affairs—State Dining Room," *Military Implications of the Treaty on the Limitations of Anti-Ballistic Missile Systems and the Interim Agreement on Limitation of Strategic Offensive Arms, op. cit.*, pp. 136-139.
73. Newhouse's discussion on pp. 160-161 seems to support this view.
74. *Ibid.*, p. 181.
75. "The White House, Congressional Briefing by Dr. Henry Kissinger," *Military Implications of the Treaty on the Limitations of Anti-Ballistic Missile Systems and the Interim Agreement on Limitation of Strategic Offensive Arms, op. cit.*, p. 117.
76. William Beecher, "Soviet Diplomats Said to Hint Interest in MIRV Curbs," *The New York Times*, March 12, 1970, p. 14.
77. "Moscow Says Deployment of MIRV in June Could Threaten Arms Talks," *The New York Times*, March 15, 1970, p. 22.

78. "MIRV Double Talk," *The New York Times*, March 30, 1970, p. 42.
79. United States Senate, Committee on Foreign Relations, Subcommittee on Arms Control, International Law and Organization, *Arms Control Implications of Current Defense Budget*, 92nd Cong., 1st sess., June 16, 1971, p. 25.
80. "A Trawler Misses Hitting U.S. Vessel," *The New York Times*, August 4, 1970, p. 1; and "Second Poseidon Is Fired, Without Russian Spectators," *The New York Times*, August 18, 1970, p. 1.
81. Chalmers Roberts, "Democrats Back Arms Freeze," *op. cit.*
82. See U.S. Senate, Committee on Foreign Relations, Subcommittee on Arms Control, International Law and Organization, *ABM, MIRV, SALT, and the Nuclear Arms Race*, 91st Cong., 1st sess., and House of Representatives, Committee on Foreign Affairs, Subcommittee on National Security Policy and Scientific Developments, *Diplomatic and Strategic Impact of Multiple Warhead Missiles*, 91st Cong., 1st sess., July and August 1969.
83. See Jonathon Medalia, *The U.S. Senate and Strategic Arms Limitation Policymaking, 1963-1972*, Ph.D. dissertation, Political Science Department, Stanford University, 1975, Chapter 4, for a discussion of the role of the United States Senate in the MIRV debate.
84. *Ibid.*, Chapter 7.
85. See, for example, the "Statement of Philip J. Farley, Alternate U.S. Representative for the Strategic Arms Limitation Talks with the Soviet Union, and Nominee of the President for the Position of Deputy Director, Arms Control and Disarmament Agency," *Diplomatic and Strategic Impact of Multiple Warhead Missiles, op. cit.*, July 24, 1969, pp. 197-210.
86. ACDA's efforts to maintain its credibility by refraining from participating in public criticism of Administration positions is discussed, in the ABM case, by Scoville, *op. cit.*
87. Medalia, *op. cit.*, Chapter 4.
88. *Congressional Record—Senate*, July 14, 1971, p. 24992.
89. Interested readers are referred to Medalia, *op. cit.*, and Ronald Tammen, *op. cit.*, Chapter 6.
90. U.S. Senate, Committee on Armed Services, Report No. 91-1016 *Authorizing Appropriations for Fiscal Year 1971 for Military Procurement, Research and Development, for the Construction of Facilities for the Safeguard Anti-ballistic Missile System, Reserve Component Strength, and for Other Purposes*, 91st Cong., 2nd sess., July 1970, p. 82.

Chapter Six
Propositions and Implications

1. James R. Kurth, "A Widening Gyre: The Logic of American Weapons Procurement," *Public Policy* 19 (Summer 1971): 373-404.
2. Ronald Tammen, *MIRV and the Arms Race: An Interpretation of Defense Strategy* (New York: Praeger, 1973), Chapter 7.

3. Kurth, *op. cit.*, p. 385.
4. *Ibid.*
5. Herbert York, "Multiple-Warhead Missiles," *Scientific American* 229 (November 1973): 18-25.
6. Ralph Lapp, *Arms Beyond Doubt: The Tyranny of Weapons Technology* (New York: Cowles, 1970), p. 177.
7. Harvey M. Sapolsky, *The Polaris System Development: Bureaucratic and Programmatic Success in Government* (Cambridge: Harvard University Press, 1972), pp. 236-237.
8. Richard R. Nelson, Merton J. Peck, and Edward D. Kalachek, *Technology, Economic Growth and Public Policy* (Washington: Brookings, 1967), p. 96.
9. Statement of Dr. John S. Foster, Jr., U.S. House of Representatives, Committee on Armed Services, *Hearings on Military Posture and an Act (S. 3293) to Authorize Appropriations During the Fiscal Year 1969 for Procurement of Aircraft, Missiles, Naval Vessels, and Tracked Combat Vehicles, Research, Development, Test and Evaluation for the Armed Services and to Prescribe the Authorized Personnel Strength of Selected Reserve of Each Reserve Component of the Armed Forces, and for Other Purposes*, 90th Cong., 2nd sess., 1968, p. 8662.
10. Testimony of Dr. John S. Foster, Jr., U.S. Senate, Committee on Armed Services, Preparedness Investigating Subcommittee, *Status of U.S. Strategic Power*, Part I, 90th Cong., 2nd sess., April 24, 1968, p. 50.
11. On this point, see Edward B. Roberts, "How the U.S. Buys Research," in David Allison (ed.), *The R&D Game* (Cambridge: MIT Press, 1969), pp. 280-296.
12. On the problems of defense management and the Packard reforms see Robert J. Art, "Why We Overspend and Underaccomplish," *Foreign Policy*, 6 (Spring 1972): 95-117.
13. On this point see Martin McGuire, *Secrecy and the Arms Race* (Cambridge: Harvard University Press, 1965).
14. Statement of Secretary of Defense Robert S. McNamara, U.S. House of Representatives, Committee on Armed Services, *Hearings on Military Posture and H.R. 2440 to Authorize Appropriations During Fiscal Year 1965 for Procurement of Aircraft, Missiles, and Naval Vessels, and Research, Development, Test, and Evaluation, for the Armed Forces, and for Other Purposes*, 88th Cong., 2nd sess., January 27, 1964, p. 6921.

Appendix A
Early Considerations of Multiple Warheads

1. Fred A. Payne, "A Discussion of Nike-Zeus Decision," speech delivered to a meeting at the Brookings Institution, Washington, D.C., October 1, 1964, p. 5. Quoted in Edward Randolph Jayne II, *The ABM Debate: Strategic Defense and National Security* (Cambridge: Center for International Studies, MIT, 1969), p. 42.

2. Herbert York, "Multiple Warhead Missiles," *Scientific American* 229 (November 1973): 21.
3. United States House of Representatives, Subcommittee of the Committee on Government Operations, *Organization and Management of Missile Programs*, 86th Cong., 1st sess., February 3, 1959, p. 43.
4. Payne, *op. cit.*, p. 7. Quoted in Jayne, *op. cit.*, p. 135.
5. Jayne, *op. cit.*, p. 145.
6. William J. Coughlin, "Project SLAM Awaits Go-Ahead," *Missiles and Rockets* 6 (March 28, 1960): 14-15.
7. For a discussion of this point see Daniel J. Fink, "Strategic Warfare," *Science and Technology*, 82 (October 1968): 58.
8. York, *op. cit.*, pp. 22-23.
9. *Polaris/Poseidon Chronology: Fleet Ballistic Missile Weapon System*, Strategic Systems Project Office, Navy Department, Washington, D.C., 1969, pp. 5, 7, 9.
10. Jayne, *op. cit.*, p. 137.
11. Payne, *op. cit.*, p. 9. Quoted in Jayne, *op. cit.*, p. 147.
12. For a discussion of this transition see Jayne, *op. cit.*, pp. 175-178.
13. Statement of Secretary of Defense Robert S. McNamara, House of Representatives, Committee on Armed Services, *Hearings on Military Posture and H.R. 9751 to Authorize Appropriations During Fiscal Year 1963 for Aircraft, Missiles, and Naval Vessels for the Armed Forces, and for Other Purposes*, 87th Cong., 2nd sess., January 24, 1962, p. 3176.
14. Fink, *op. cit.*, p. 59.
15. *MIRV Chronology*, The Aerospace Corporation, March 14, 1972, (hereafter cited as "Aerospace MIRV Chronology") p. 1. This is an unpublished document of the Aerospace Corporation that was provided to the author.
16. Aerospace MIRV Chronology, *op. cit.*, p. 1.
17. The use of small rockets was considered for the Titan II Mark 13 according to the Aerospace MIRV Chronology, *op. cit.*, p. 1.
18. Aerospace MIRV Chronology, *op. cit.*, p. 2; and John W. Finney, "Power Increased in Nuclear Arms," *The New York Times*, January 31, 1964, p. 1.
19. "Multiple Re-entry Vehicles Urged," *Missiles and Rockets* 13 (October 21, 1963): 37.

Appendix B
The Technical Precursors of the MIRV Bus

1. For greater detail concerning the Agena upper stage, the Able-Star, and other technical precursors to MIRV see Herbert F. York, "Multiple-Warhead Missiles," *Scientific American* 229 (November 1973): 18-25.
2. *Aviation Week and Space Technology* 72 (April 18, 1960): 29.
3. On space-based ballistic missile defense systems see *Aviation Week and Space Technology* 73 (September 19, 1960): 23; 73 (October 31,

214 Making the MIRV

1960): 33; 74 (January 16, 1961): 26; 74 (April 10, 1961): 34; 74 (April 24, 1961): 23; 74 (May 1, 1961): 23; 75 (August 21, 1961): 23; 75 (October 16, 1961): 23; and York, *op. cit.*, pp. 6-8. The orbiting bomb study is mentioned in *MIRV Chronology*, The Aerospace Corporation, March 14, 1972, p. 1. This is an unpublished document of the Aerospace Corporation that was provided to the author.

4. Barry Miller, "U.S. Penetration Capability Erodes," *Aviation Week and Space Technology* 87 (October 23, 1967): 94.
5. *Aerospace Corporation 1969 Annual Report*, p. 6.
6. *Aviation Week and Space Technology* 72 (June 27, 1960): 26; and York, *op. cit.*
7. U.S. Senate, Subcommittee of the Committee on Appropriations, *Department of Defense Appropriations for Fiscal Year 1969*, Part 4, 90th Cong., 2nd sess., July 8, 1968, p. 2110.
8. J.S. Butz, Jr., "Growth Potential Defined for Heat Sink, Ablative Shields," *Aviation Week* 71 (September 7, 1959): 68-81; and "Penetration Aids," *Space/Aeronautics* 47 (February 1964): 47-59.

Appendix C
Intelligence Information Concerning
Soviet ABM Programs

1. *Aviation Week and Space Technology* 75 (July 24, 1961): 25; and Tad Szulc, "Soviet Test Laid to Defense Goals," *The New York Times*, September 6, 1961, p. 3.
2. United States House of Representatives, Committee on Science and Astronautics, *Research and Development for Defense*, 87th Cong., 1st sess., February 17, 1961, pp. 70-71.
3. See for example Tad Szulc, "Soviet Test Laid to Defense Goal," *op. cit.*; "Russians' Blast Held 'Blackmail,' " *The New York Times*, October 31, 1961, p. 15; "Biggest Arms Race—The One Russia May be Winning," *U.S. News and World Report*, September 25, 1961, p. 46; and "Teller on Soviet Weapons Tests," *The New York Times*, October 31, 1961, p. 15.
4. See Lloyd Norman, "Nike-X," *Army* 17 (March 1967): 28.
5. "U.S. Project Underway," *The New York Times*, October 24, 1961, p. 3.
6. Edward Randolph Jayne II, *The ABM Debate: Strategic Defense and National Security* (Cambridge: Center for International Studies, MIT, 1969), p. 79.
7. "Text of Kennedy's address on U.S. Plans to Resume Nuclear Testing in April," *The New York Times*, March 3, 1962, p. 2.
8. After 1961 reconnaissance satellites became the primary means of gathering information about Soviet ABM systems. For a history of the United States' reconnaissance satellite programs and an assessment of their utility see the author's "Reconnaissance and Arms Control," *Scientific American* 228 (February 1973): 14-25.

9. Jayne, *op. cit.,* p. 185.
10. Jayne says, "Initial interpretations of these exo-atmospheric blasts appeared to support the idea that ABM intercept at such heights allowed a great increase in kill radius." (Jayne, *op cit.*, p. 166). See also "The H-Bomb vs. Missiles," *Business Week*, July 14, 1962, pp. 106-110.
11. Robert S. Allen and Paul Scott, "Red Anti-Missile Lead May Force Production of Nike-Zeus," *Shreveport [Louisiana] Times*, April 27, 1963, quoted in Jayne, *op. cit.*, p. 187. Jayne says, "This news source appears to have excellent direct connections with key southern senators, and it is therefore deemed to be highly reliable on this particular matter."
12. *Aviation Week and Space Technology* 77 (December 17, 1962): 25.
13. Paul H. Nitze, *Foreign Policy* 16 (Fall 1974): 82.
14. "Russian Warns on Atomic War," *The New York Times*, October 6, 1960, p. 17; and Osgood Caruthers, "Soviet Minimizes Advantages of a Surprise Nuclear Attack," *The New York Times*, October 13, 1960, p. 15.
15. Theodore Shabad, "Russian Reports Solving Rocket Defense Problem," *The New York Times*, October 24, 1961, p. 1; and "Soviet Union Claims 100-Megaton Warhead, Emphasize Anti-Missile," *Aviation Week and Space Technology* 75 (November 27, 1961): 23.
16. "Excerpts from Premier Khrushchev's Address at Peace Conference in Moscow," *The New York Times*, July 11, 1962, p. 4.
17. Theodore Shabad, "Khrushchev Says Missile Can 'Hit a Fly in Space'," *The New York Times*, July 17, 1962, p. 1.
18. "Rockets from Satellites," *The New York Times*, February 23, 1963, p. 2.
19. *Aviation Week and Space Technology* 78 (February 25, 1963): 25.
20. Henry Tanner, "Soviet Parades 'Anti-missile Missiles' on the 46th Anniversary of Revolution," *The New York Times*, November 8, 1963, p. 1.
21. *Ibid.*; and "Soviets Unveil Air Defense Missile in SA-2, SA-3 Family," *Aviation Week and Space Technology* 79 (November 18, 1963): 29.
22. John W.R. Taylor (ed.), *Jane's All the World's Aircraft 1966-67* (New York: McGraw-Hill, 1966), p. 468; Jayne, *op. cit.*, pp. 185-189; and Norman, *op. cit.*, p. 8.
23. United States Senate, Committee on Foreign Relations, *Nuclear Test Ban Treaty*, 88th Cong., 1st sess., August 21, 1963, p. 531.
24. *Ibid.*, pp. 777-779.
25. Testimony of General Curtis LeMay, Chief of Staff, United States Air Force, United States Senate, Committee on Armed Services, Preparedness Investigating Subcommittee, *Military Aspects of Nuclear Test Ban Proposals and Related Matters*, 88th Cong., 1st sess., August 14, 1963, p. 760.
26. Testimony of General Earle G. Wheeler, Chairman of the Joint Chiefs of Staff, United States Senate, Committee on Armed Services, Preparedness Investigating Subcommittee, *Status of U.S. Strategic Power*, Part I, 90th Cong., 2nd sess., April 23, 1968, p. 16; William

Beecher, "Missile Defenses Slowed by Soviet," *The New York Times*, February 13, 1969, p. 1.

27. Testimony of Admiral Thomas H. Moorer, Chairman of the Joint Chiefs of Staff, United States Senate, Committee on Armed Services, *Fiscal Year 1974 Authorization for Military Procurement, Research and Development, Construction Authorization for the Safeguard ABM, and Active Duty and Selected Reserve Strengths,* Part 1, 93rd Cong., 1st sess., March 29, 1973, p. 240.

28. "Soviet Missile Parade Features Anti-ICBM, Wheeled Carriers," *Aviation Week and Space Technology* 81 (November 16, 1964): 26.

29. Richard J. Whalen, "The Shifting Equation of Nuclear Defense," *Fortune* 75 (June 1, 1967): 176; and "Soviets Brandish Medium, Long Range Missiles," *Aviation Week and Space Technology* 82 (May 24, 1965): 22.

30. Norman, *op. cit.*, p. 30.

31. R.T. Pretty and D.H.R. Archer (eds.), *Jane's Weapons Systems 1972-73* (New York: McGraw-Hill, 1972), p. 519.

32. Whalen, *op. cit.*, p. 84.

33. Hanson Baldwin, "Soviet Antimissile System Spurs New U.S. Weapons," *The New York Times*, February 5, 1967, p. 1.

34. Baldwin, "Soviet Antimissile System Spurs New U.S. Weapons," *op. cit.*; William Beecher, "Soviet Reported Building a Vast Anti-Missile System," *The New York Times*, December 8, 1966, p. 1.

35. Baldwin, "Soviet Antimissile System Spurs New U.S. Weapons," *op. cit.*; Beecher, "Soviet Reported Building a Vast Anti-Missile System," *op. cit.*; and Whalen, *op. cit.*, p. 176.

36. Statement of Secretary of Defense Robert S. McNamara, United States House of Representatives, Committee on Armed Services, *Hearings on Military Posture and A Bill (H.R. 9240) to Authorize Appropriations During the Fiscal Year 1968 for Procurement of Aircraft, Missiles, Naval Vessels, and Tracked Combat Vehicles, and Research, Development, Test, and Evaluation for the Armed Forces, and for other Purposes,* 90th Cong., 1st sess., March 2, 1967, p. 392.

37. William Beecher, "Clarification by Pentagon," *The New York Times*, February 23, 1967, p. 10.

38. William Beecher, "Soviet's Antimissile Steps Spur Study of U.S. Needs," *The New York Times*, December 8, 1966, p. 1.

39. William Beecher, "Pentagon Readies Arms to Penetrate Soviet's Suspected New Defense," *The Wall Street Journal*, February 21, 1966, p. 1; and "Soviets May Unveil Advances in ICBMs," *Aviation Week and Space Technology* 86 (March 6, 1967): 108.

40. Baldwin, "Soviet Anti-Missile Spurs New U.S. Weapons," *op. cit.*

41. Jayne, *op. cit.*, pp. 279-280.

42. William Beecher, "Laird Says Soviet Renews ABM Work," *The New York Times*, April 28, 1971, p. 1.

43. "Soviet ABM Cost Pegged at $25 Billion," *Aviation Week and Space Technology* 87 (October 23, 1967): 78.

44. George C. Wilson, "Senate May Force New Anti-Missile Policy," *Aviation Week and Space Technology* 84 (May 2, 1966): 28.
45. "Combat Shortage Denied by Vance," *The New York Times*, April 25, 1966, p. 3.
46. Robert B. Semple, "McNamara Hints Soviet Deploys Anti-Missile Net," *The New York Times*, November 11, 1966, p. 1.
47. Theodore Shabad, "Sokolovsky Says Soviet Matches U.S. Fleet of Atomic Submarines," *The New York Times*, February 18, 1965, p. 6.
48. "Soviet Film Shows Missiles in Action," *The New York Times*, May 11, 1965, p. 3.
49. "Malinovsky Lauds New Missile Might," *The New York Times*, April 23, 1966, p. 13.
50. G. Gerasimov, "The First Strike Theory," *International Affairs* 3 (March 1955): 35-39, quoted in Edgar M. Bottome, *The Balance of Terror* (Boston: Beacon Press, 1971), p. 124 from William Zimmerman, *Soviet Perspectives on International Relations 1956-1967* (Princeton: Princeton University Press, 1969), pp. 229-230.
51. On this point see Thomas W. Wolfe, *Soviet Power and Europe, 1945-1970* (Baltimore: Johns Hopkins Press, 1970), pp. 439-440.
52. "Russians Say Antimissile System Will Protect Them From Attack," *The New York Times*, February 21, 1967, p. 5.
53. Raymond H. Anderson, "Russians Concede Missile Net Flaw," *The New York Times*, February 23, 1967, p. 1.
54. Hanson W. Baldwin, "Military Concern on Lack of Missile Defense Growing," *The New York Times*, May 21, 1967, p. 1.
55. "U.S. Bars Attack on MIG Bases Now," *The New York Times*, April 21, 1967, p. 7.
56. Statement of former Secretary of Defense, Robert S. McNamara, United States House of Representatives, Committee on Armed Services, *Hearings on Military Posture and An Act (S. 3293) to Authorize Appropriations During the Fiscal Year 1969 for Procurement of Aircraft, Missiles, Naval Vessels, and Tracked Combat Vehicles, Research, Development, Test and Evaluation for the Armed Forces and to Prescribe the Authorized Personnel Strength of the Selected Reserve of Each Reserve Component of the Armed Forces, and for Other Purposes*, 90th Cong., 2nd sess., March 30, 1968, p. 8506.
57. *Ibid.*
58. *Ibid.*
59. "Written Statement of Former Secretary of Defense Clark M. Clifford, Prepared January 15, 1969," United States House of Representatives, Committee on Armed Services, *Hearings on Military Posture and Legislation to Authorize Appropriations during the Fiscal Year 1970 for Procurement of Aircraft, Missiles, Naval Vessels, and Tracked Combat Vehicles, Research, Development, Test and Evaluation for the Armed Forces, and for Other Purposes*, 91st Cong., 1st sess., January 28, 1969, Appendix A, p. xxiii.
60. Testimony of Admiral Thomas H. Moorer, Chairman of the Joint Chiefs of

Staff, *Fiscal Year 1974 Authorization for Military Procurement, Research and Development, Construction Authorization for the Safeguard ABM, and Active Duty and Selected Reserve Strengths, op. cit.*, Part 1, p. 240.

61. Beecher, "Laird Says Soviet Renews ABM Work," *op. cit.*

62. *Strategic Survey, 1968* (London: Institute of Strategic Studies, 1969), p. 24.

63. Beecher, "Missile Defenses Slowed by Soviet," *op. cit.*

64. Secretary of Defense Melvin R. Laird, House of Representatives, Subcommittee of the Committee on Appropriations, *Fiscal Year 1971 Defense Program and Budget*, 91st Cong., 2nd sess., February 25, 1970, p. 106.

65. Bernard Gwertzman, "Soviet Says its ABM can 'Reliably Hit' Attacking Missiles," *The New York Times*, February 24, 1970, p. 1.

66. *Ibid.*

67. Secretary of Defense, Melvin R. Laird, *Toward A National Security Strategy of Realistic Deterrence*, Statement on the Fiscal Year 1972-76, Defense Program and the 1972 Defense Budget, (Washington: Government Printing Office, 1971), p. 47, 169.

68. Beecher, "Laird Says Soviet Renews ABM Work," *op. cit.*

Bibliography

Bibliography

BOOKS

Allen, Jonathan (ed.). *March 4: Scientists, Students and Society*. Cambridge: M.I.T. Press, 1970.

Armacost, Michael. *The Politics of Weapons Innovation: The Thor-Jupiter Controversy*. New York: Columbia University Press, 1969.

Art, Robert J. *The TFX Decision: McNamara and the Military*. Boston: Little, Brown, 1968.

Bottome, Edgar M. *The Balance of Terror*. Boston: Beacon Press, 1971.

Brodie, Bernard. *Strategy in the Missile Age*. Princeton: Princeton University Press, 1959.

Cahn, Anne Hessing, *Eggheads and Warheads: Scientists and the ABM*. Cambridge: Center for International Studies, 1971.

Davis, Vincent. *The Admirals Lobby*. Chapel Hill: University of North Carolina Press, 1967.

Davis, Vincent. *The Politics of Innovation: Patterns in Navy Cases*. Monograph Series in World Affairs, University of Denver, 1966-67.

Enthoven, Alain and K. Wayne Smith. *How Much Is Enough? Shaping the Defense Program, 1961-1969*. New York: Harper and Row, 1971.

Hage, Jerald and Michael Aiken. *Social Change in Complex Organizations*. New York: Random House, 1970.

Hilsman, Roger. *Strategic Intelligence and National Decision*. Glencoe: Free Press, 1956.

Hitch, Charles J. and Roland N. McKean. *The Economics of Defense in the Nuclear Age*. Cambridge: Harvard University Press, 1960.

Huntington, Samuel P. *The Common Defense*. New York: Columbia University Press, 1966.

Institute for Strategic Studies. *Strategic Survey, 1968*. London: Institute for Strategic Studies, 1969.

Institute for Strategic Studies. *The Military Balance 1962-63*. London: Institute for Strategic Studies, 1962.

International Institute for Strategic Studies, *Military Balance 1972-73*. London: International Institute for Strategic Studies, 1971.

Jayne, Edward Randolph II. *The ABM Debate: Strategic Defense and National Security*. Cambridge: Center for International Studies, 1969.

Johnson, Lyndon B. *The Vantage Point*. New York: Holt, Rinehart and Winston, 1971.

Kahn, Herman. *On Thermonuclear War*. Princeton: Princeton University Press, 1960.

Kaufmann, William W. *The McNamara Strategy*. New York: Harper and Row, 1964.

Kirkpatrick, Lyman B., Jr. *The U.S. Intelligence Community: Foreign Policy and Domestic Activities*. New York: Hill and Wang, 1973.

Kissinger, Henry. *Nuclear Weapons and Foreign Policy*. New York: Harper and Brothers, 1957.

Kissinger, Henry. *The Troubled Partnership: A Re-Appraisal of the Atlantic Alliance*. New York: McGraw-Hill, 1965.

Lapp, Ralph. *Arms Beyond Doubt. The Tyranny of Weapons Technology*. New York: Cowles, 1970.

Lapp, Ralph. *The Weapons Culture*. New York: Norton, 1968.

LeMay, Curtis E. *Mission With LeMay: My Story*. Garden City: Doubleday, 1965.

McGuire, Martin. *Secrecy and the Arms Race*. Cambridge: Harvard University Press, 1965.

Nelkin, Dorothy. *The University and Military Research: Moral Politics at M.I.T.* Ithaca: Cornell University Press, 1972.

Nelson, Richard R., Merton J. Peck, and Edward D. Kalacheck. *Technology, Economic Growth and Public Policy*. Washington: Brookings, 1967.

Newhouse, John. *Cold Dawn: The Story of SALT*. New York: Holt, Rinehart and Winston, 1973.

Peck, Merton J. and Frederic M. Scherer. *The Weapons Acquisition Process: An Economic Analysis*. Boston: Graduate School of Business Administration, Harvard University, 1962.

Pretty, R.T. and D.H.R. Archer (eds.). *Jane's Weapons Systems 1971-72*. New York: McGraw-Hill, 1970.

Pretty, R.T. and D.H.R. Archer (eds.). *Jane's Weapons Systems 1972-73*. New York: McGraw-Hill, 1972.

Quade, E.J. and W.I. Boucher. *Systems Analysis and Foreign Policy Planning: Applications in Defense*. New York: Elsevier, 1968.

Ransom, Harry Howe. *Central Intelligence and National Security*. Cambridge: Harvard University Press, 1958.

Ransom, Harry Howe. *The Intelligence Establishment*. Cambridge: Harvard University Press, 1970.

Roberts, Chalmers. *The Nuclear Years: The Arms Race and Arms Control 1945-70*. New York: Praeger, 1970.

Sapolsky, Harvey. *The Polaris System Development: Bureaucratic and Programmatic Success in Government*. Cambridge: Harvard University Press, 1972.

Schelling, Thomas C. *Arms and Influence*. New Haven: Yale University Press, 1966.
Schelling, Thomas C. *The Strategy of Conflict*. Cambridge: Harvard University Press, 1960.
Schilling, Warner, Paul Hammond, and Glenn H. Snyder. *Strategy, Politics and Defense Budgets*. New York: Columbia University Press, 1962.
Schlesinger, Arthur. *A Thousand Days*. Boston: Houghton Mifflin, 1965.
Sturm, Thomas A. *The USAF Scientific Advisory Board: Its First Twenty Years 1944-64*. Washington: USAF Historical Division Liaison Office, 1967.
Tammen, Ronald L. *MIRV and the Arms Race: An Interpretation of Defense Strategy*. New York: Praeger, 1973.
Taylor, John W.R. (ed.). *Jane's All the World's Aircraft 1966-67*. New York: McGraw-Hill, 1966.
Trewitt, Henry L. *McNamara*. New York: Harper and Row, 1971.
Wolfe, Thomas W. *Soviet Power and Europe, 1945-1970*. Baltimore: Johns Hopkins Press, 1970.
York, Herbert. *Race to Oblivion*. New York: Simon and Schuster, 1970.

PAPERS AND ARTICLES*

"After the Pentagon Papers: Talk with Kistiakowsky, Wiesner." *Science* 174 (November 26, 1971): 923-928.
Arbatov, G.A. "A New Round of the Arms Race—Is It Inevitable?" *Proceedings of the Nineteenth Pugwash Conference on Science and World Affairs*, Sochi, October 22-27, 1969.
Art, Robert J. "Why We Overspend and Underaccomplish." *Foreign Policy*, 6 (Spring 1972): 95-117.
Baldwin, Hanson. "Slow-Down in the Pentagon." *Foreign Affairs* 43, 2 (January 1965): 262-280.
"Biggest Arms Race—The One Russia May Be Winning." *U.S. News and World Report* 51 (September 25, 1961): 46-48.
Breasted, David C. "Navy Seeks Approval for Polaris Follow-on." *Missiles and Rockets* 13 (November 4, 1963): 18.
Butz, J.S., Jr. "Growth Potential Defined for Heat Sink, Ablation Shields." *Aviation Week* 71 (September 7, 1959): 68-81.
Cooper, Chester L. "The CIA and Decision-Making." *Foreign Affairs* 50 (January 1972): 223-236.
Crecine, John P. "Defense Budgeting: Constraints and Organizational Adaptation." Discussion Paper No. 6, Institute of Public Policy Studies, University of Michigan (July, 1969).
Crecine, John P. and Gregory Fischer. "On Resource Allocation Processes in the U.S. Department of Defense." Discussion Paper Number 31, Insti-

*Not included here are the many entries in the *Congressional Record* and the *Department of State Bulletin*, newspaper articles and unauthored entries in various periodicals that were used in this study. The reader is referred to *Aerospace Daily, Aviation Week and Space Technology, The Boston Globe, Defense Industry Bulletin, Missiles and Rockets, The New York Times, The Wall Street Journal*, and *The Washington Post*.

tute of Public Policy Studies, University of Michigan (October, 1971).

"Defense Fantasy Come True: In an Exclusive Interview Secretary McNamara Explains in Full the Logic Behind the ABM System." *Life* 63, (September 29, 1967): 28 A-C.

Federation of American Scientists. *Is There an R&D Gap?* Washington: Federation of American Scientists, 1971.

Fink, Daniel J. "Strategic Warfare." *Science and Technology*, 82 (October 1968): 54-68.

Gilpatrick, Roswell, "Are We on the Brink of Another Arms Race?" *New York Times Magazine*, January 15, 1967.

Graham, Daniel O. "Estimating the Threat: A Soldier's Job." *Army* 35 (April 1973).

Greenwood, Ted. "Reconnaissance and Arms Control." *Scientific American* 228 (February 1973): 14-25.

Greenwood, Ted. *Reconnaissance, Surveillance and Arms Control.* Adelphi Paper 88. London: International Institute for Strategic Studies, 1972.

Greenwood, Ted. *The Utility of Safeguard for the Defense of Minuteman.* Cambridge: Center for International Studies, 1972.

Greenwood, Ted and Michael L. Nacht. "The New Nuclear Debate: Sense or Nonsense?" *Foreign Affairs* 52 (July 1974): 761-780.

Halperin, Morton. "The Decision to Deploy the ABM: Bureaucratic and Domestic Politics in the Johnson Administration." *World Politics* 25 (October 1972): 68-83.

Hammond, Paul Y. "Supercarriers and B-36 Bombers: Appropriations, Strategy and Politics." In Herbert Stein (ed.), *American Civil-Military Decisions: A Book of Case Studies.* University City: University of Alabama Press, 1963.

"The H-Bomb Vs. Missiles." *Business Week*, July 14, 1962, pp. 106-110.

Katz, Amrom H. "Thoughts on Reconnaissance." In Amrom H. Katz (ed.), *Selected Readings in Aerial Reconnaissance*, P-2762. Santa Monica: The RAND Corporation, 1963.

Kent, Glenn. *On the Interaction of Opposing Forces Under Possible Arms Control Agreements.* Cambridge: Center for International Affairs, 1963. Occasional Paper No. 5.

Kent, Sherman. "Estimates and Influence." *Foreign Service Journal* 46 (April 1969): 14-23.

Kurth, James. "A Widening Gyre: The Logic of American Weapons Procurement." *Public Policy* 19 (Summer 1971): 373-404.

Lambeth, Benjamin S. "The Sources of Soviet Military Doctrine." *Proceedings of the Conference on Comparative Defense Policy*, Department of Political Science, USAF Academy, Colorado, February 1973.

Loosbrock, John F. "History and Mr. McNamara." *Air Force Magazine/Space Digest* 45 (October 1962): 32-33.

Loosbrock, John F. "Counterforce and Mr. McNamara." *Air Force Magazine/ Space Digest* (September 1962).

McNamara, Robert S. "The Dynamics of Nuclear Strategy." *Department of State Bulletin* 57 (October 9, 1967): 450-467.

Miller, Barry. "Studies of Penetration Aids Broadening." *Aviation Week and Space Technology* 80 (January 20, 1964): 73-93.

Miller, Barry. "U.S. Penetration Capability Erodes." *Aviation Week and Space Technology* 87 (October 23, 1967): 90-109.

Miller, George. "Needed—A New Strategy for Preservation of the Republic." *Sea Power* 14 (December 1971): 5-11.

Norman, Lloyd. "Nike-X." *Army* 17 (March 1967): 25-33.

Orr, Samuel C. "Defense Report/National Security Council Network Gives White House Tight Reign Over SALT Strategy." *National Journal* 3 (April 24, 1971): 877-886.

Orr, Samuel C. "Defense Report/Slow Pace of SALT Negotiations Prompts Proposals for Change in U.S. Position." *National Journal* 3 (May 1, 1971): 947-950.

Paolucci, Captain Dominic A. "The Development of Navy Strategic Offensive and Defensive Systems." *U.S. Naval Institute Proceedings* 96 (May 1970).

"Penetration Aids." *Space/Aeronautics* 41 (February 1964): 47-59.

Rathjens, George W. and George B. Kistiakowsky. "Strategic Arms Limitation." *Proceedings of the Nineteenth Pugwash Conference on Science and World Affairs*, Sochi, October 22-27, 1969.

Roberts, Edward B. "How the U.S. Buys Research." In David Allison (ed), *The R&D Game*. Cambridge: MIT Press, 1969.

Sapolsky, Harvey M. "Organizational Structure and Innovation." *Journal of Business* 40 (October 1967): 497-510.

Sartori, Leo. "The Myth of MIRV." *Saturday Review* 52 (August 30, 1969): 10-15 and 32.

Schilling, Warner R. "The H-Bomb Decision: How to Decide Without Actually Choosing." *Political Science Quarterly* 76 (March 1961): 24-46.

Schriever, Bernard A. "Forecast." *Air University Review* 16 (March-April 1965): 2-12.

Stambler, Irwin. "The Next ICBMs." *Space/Aeronautics* 45 (March 1966): 56-65.

Trainor, James. "Advanced Minuteman Details Revealed." *Missiles and Rockets* 11 (October 15, 1962): 12.

Trainor, James. "DOD Has New Warhead Plan." *Missiles and Rockets* 14 (April 27, 1964): 15.

Ulsamer, Edgar. "ABRES . . . The Cutting Edge of the U.S. Deterrent." *Air Force Magazine/Aerospace International* 54 (December 1971): 39-43.

Union of Concerned Scientists. *ABM ABC*. Cambridge: Union of Concerned Scientists, 1969.

Union of Concerned Scientists. *MIRV*. Cambridge: Union of Concerned Scientists, 1969.

Whalen, Richard J. "The Shifting Equation of Nuclear Defense." *Fortune* 75 (June 1, 1967): 85-89, 175-183.

Wiesner, Jerome B. "Comprehensive Arms Limitation Systems." *Daedalus* 89 (Fall 1960): 915-950.

Wilson, James Q. "Innovation in Organizations: Notes Toward a Theory." In

James W. Thompson, *Approaches to Organizational Design*. Pittsburgh: University of Pittsburgh Press, 1966.

York, Herbert F. "Multiple-Warhead Missiles." *Scientific American* 229 (November 1973): 18-27.

Zuckert, Eugene M. "The Service Secretary: Has He a Useful Role?" *Foreign Affairs* 44 (April 1966): 458-479.

PUBLIC DOCUMENTS

Defense Intelligence Agency, Directorate for Intelligence. *Mathematical Background and Programming Aids for the Physical Vulnerability System for Nuclear Weapons*. Washington: Defense Intelligence Agency, 1974.

Defense Intelligence Agency. *Physical Vulnerability Handbook—Nuclear Weapons (U)*. Washington: Defense Intelligence Agency, 1974.

General Accounting Office. *Comparison of Military Research and Development Expenditures of the United States and the Soviet Union*. General Accounting Office Staff Study for the Subcommittee on Research and Development of the Committee on Armed Services, United States Senate, July 27, 1971.

Laird, Melvin R. *Fiscal Year 1971 Defense Program and Budget*. A Statement Before the House Subcommittee on Department of Defense Appropriations, February 25, 1970. Washington: Government Printing Office, 1970.

Laird, Melvin R. *National Security Strategy of Realistic Deterrence: FY 1973 Defense Budget and FY 1973-1977 Program*. A Statement Before the Senate Committee on Armed Services, February 15, 1972. Washington: Government Printing Office, 1972.

Laird, Melvin R. *Toward a National Security Strategy of Realistic Deterrence: Fiscal Year 1972-76 Defense Program and the 1972 Defense Budget*. A Statement Before the House Armed Services Committee, March 9, 1971. Washington: Government Printing Office, 1971.

Moorer, Thomas H. *United States Military Posture for 1974*. A Statement Before the Senate Armed Services Committee, March 29, 1973. Washington: Government Printing Office, 1973.

Nixon, Richard M. *U.S. Foreign Policy for the 1970s: Building the Peace*. A Report to Congress by the President of the United States, February 25, 1971. Washington: Government Printing Office, 1971.

Nixon, Richard M. *U.S. Foreign Policy for the 1970s: The Emerging Structure of Peace*. A Report to the Congress by the President of the United States, February 9, 1972. Washington: Government Printing Office, 1972.

Nixon, Richard M. *United States Foreign Policy for the 1970s: Shaping a Durable Peace*. A Report to the Congress by the President of the United States, May 3, 1973. Washington: Government Printing Office, 1973.

Richardson, Elliot L. *Annual Defense Department Report FY 1974: FY 1974*

Defense Budget and FY 1974-1978 Program. A Statement Before the Senate Committee on Armed Services, March 28, 1973. Washington: Government Printing Office, 1973.

Schlesinger, James R. *Annual Defense Department Report, FY 1975.* Washington: Government Printing Office, 1974.

Schlesinger, James R. *Annual Defense Department Report, FY 1976 and FY 197T.* Washington: Government Printing Office, 1975.

Strategic Systems Project Office, Navy Department. *Polaris/Poseidon Chronology: Fleet Ballistic Missile Weapon System.* Washington: Government Printing Office, 1969.

United States Arms Control and Disarmament Agency. *Documents on Disarmament 1964.* Washington: Government Printing Office, 1965.

United States Arms Control and Disarmament Agency. *Documents on Disarmament 1965.* Washington: Government Printing Office, 1966.

United States Congress, Subcommittee on Military Applications of the Joint Committee on Atomic Energy. *Scope, Magnitude, and Implications of the United States Anti-ballistic Missile Program*, 90th Cong., 1st sess., November 6-7, 1967.

United States House of Representatives, Committee on Armed Services. *Hearings on Military Posture and H.R. 9751 to Authorize Appropriations During Fiscal Year 1963 for Aircraft, Missiles, and Naval Vessels for the Armed Forces, and for Other Purposes*, 87th Cong., 2nd sess., January, February 1962.

United States House of Representatives, Committee on Armed Services. *Hearings on Military Posture and H.R. 2440, to Authorize Appropriations During Fiscal Year 1964 for Procurement, Research, Development, Test, and Evaluation of Aircraft, Missiles, and Naval Vessels for the Armed Forces, and for Other Purposes*, 88th Cong., 1st sess., January, February, and March, 1963.

United States House of Representatives, Committee on Armed Services. *Hearings on Military Posture and H.R. 9637 to Authorize Appropriations During Fiscal Year 1965 for Procurement of Aircraft, Missiles, and Naval Vessels, and Research, Development, Test, and Evaluation, for the Armed Forces, and for Other Purposes*, 88th Cong., 2nd sess., January, February 1964.

United States House of Representatives, Committee on Armed Services. *Hearings on Military Posture and H.R. 4016 to Authorize Appropriations During Fiscal Year 1966 for Procurement of Aircraft, Missiles, and Naval Vessels, and Research, Development, Test, and Evaluation for the Armed Forces, and for Other Purposes*, 89th Cong., 1st sess., February, March 1965.

United States House of Representatives, Committee on Armed Services. *Hearings on Military Posture and H.R. 13456 to Authorize Appropriations During the Fiscal Year 1967 for Procurement of Aircraft, Missiles, Naval Vessels, and Tracked Combat Vehicles, and Research, Development, Test,and Evaluation for the Armed Forces, and to Maintain Parity Between Military and Civilian Pay, and for Other Purposes*, 89th Cong., 2nd sess., March, April 1966.

United States House of Representatives, Committee on Armed Services. *Hearings on Military Posture and a Bill (H.R. 9240) to Authorize Appropriations During the Fiscal Year 1968 for Procurement of Aircraft, Missiles, Naval Vessels, and Tracked Combat Vehicles, and Research, Development, Test, and Evaluation for the Armed Forces, and for Other Purposes*, 90th Cong., 1st sess., March, April, and May 1967.

United States House of Representatives, Committee on Armed Services. *Hearings on Military Posture and an Act (S. 3293) to Authorize Appropriations During the Fiscal Year 1969 for Procurement of Aircraft, Missiles, Naval Vessels, and Tracked Combat Vehicles, Research, Development, Test, and Evaluation for the Armed Forces and to Prescribe the Authorized Personnel Strength of the Selected Reserve of Each Reserve Component of the Armed Forces, and for Other Purposes*, 90th Cong., 2nd sess., April-May 1968.

United States House of Representatives, Committee on Armed Services. *Hearings on Military Posture and Legislation to Authorize Appropriations During the Fiscal Year 1970 for Procurement of Aircraft, Missiles, Naval Vessels and Tracked Combat Vehicles, Research, Development, Test, and Evaluation for the Armed Forces, and to Prescribe the Authorized Strength of the Reserve Forces, and for Other Purposes*, 91st Cong., 1st sess., January, February, and March 1969.

United States House of Representatives, Committee on Armed Services. *Hearings on Military Posture and H.R. 8687 to Authorize Appropriations During the Fiscal Year 1972 for Procurement of Aircraft, Missiles, Naval Vessels, Tracked Combat Vehicles, Torpedoes, and Other Weapons, and Research, Development, Test, and Evaluation for the Armed Forces and to Prescribe the Authorized Personnel Strength for Each Active Duty Component and of the Selected Reserve of Each Reserve Component of the Armed Forces, and for Other Purposes*, 92nd Cong., 1st sess., March, April, and May 1971.

United States House of Representatives, Committee on Armed Services. *Investigation of the B-36 Bomber Program*, 81st Cong., 1st sess., August-October 1949.

United States House of Representatives, Committee on Armed Services. *The National Defense Program—Unification and Strategy*, 81st Cong., 1st sess., October 1949.

United States House of Representatives, Committee on Armed Services. *Supplementary Hearings on Defense Procurement Authorization Relating to SALT Agreement*, 92nd Cong., 2nd sess., June 6, 13, 1972.

United States House of Representatives, Committee on Science and Astronautics. *Research and Development for Defense*, 87th Cong., 1st sess., February 1961.

United States House of Representatives, Subcommittee of the Committee on Appropriations. *Department of Defense Appropriations for 1963*, 87th Cong., 2nd sess., January-March 1962.

United States House of Representatives, Subcommittee of the Committee on Appropriations. *Department of Defense Appropriations for 1965*, 88th Cong., 2nd sess., January-April 1964.

United States House of Representatives, Subcommittee of the Committee on Appropriations. *Department of Defense Appropriations for 1966*, 89th Cong., 1st sess., February-May 1965.

United States House of Representatives, Subcommittee of the Committee on Appropriations. *Department of Defense Appropriations for 1967*, 89th Cong., 2nd sess., February-June 1966.

United States House of Representatives, Subcommittee of the Committee on Appropriations. *Department of Defense Appropriations for 1968*, 90th Cong., 1st sess., January-May 1967.

United States House of Representatives, Subcommittee of the Committee on Government Operations. *Management of Missile Programs*, 86th Cong., 1st sess., February 2, 1959.

United States House of Representatives, Subcommittee of the Committee on Government Operations. *Organization and Management of Missile Programs*, 86th Cong., 2nd sess., July 1959.

United States House of Representatives, Subcommittee of the Committee on Government Operations. *Systems Development and Management*, 87th Cong., 2nd sess., June-August 1962.

United States House of Representatives, Subcommittee on National Security Policy and Scientific Developments of the Committee on Foreign Affairs. *Diplomatic and Strategic Impact of Multiple Warhead Missiles*, 91st Cong., 1st sess., July and August 1969.

United States Senate, Committee on Armed Services. *Fiscal Year 1974 Authorization for Military Procurement, Research and Development, Construction Authorization for the Safeguard ABM, and Active Duty and Selected Reserve Strengths*, 93rd Cong., 1st sess., February-August 1973.

United States Senate, Committee on Armed Services. *Military Implications of the Treaty on the Limitations of Anti-Ballistic Missile Systems and the Interim Agreement on Limitation of Strategic Offensive Arms*, 92nd Cong., 2nd sess., June-July 1972.

United States Senate, Committee on Armed Services. *Report No. 91-1016 Authorizing Appropriations for Fiscal Year 1971 for Military Procurement, Research and Development, for the Construction of Facilities for the Safeguard Anti-ballistic Missile System, Reserve Component Strength and for Other Purposes*, 91st Cong., 2nd sess., March-June 1970.

United States Senate, Committee on Armed Services, Preparedness Investigating Subcommittee. *Military Aspects and Implications of Nuclear Test Ban Proposals and Related Matters*, 89th Cong., 1st sess., May-August 1963.

United States Senate, Committee on Armed Services, Preparedness Investigating Subcommittee. *Status of U.S. Strategic Power*, 90th Cong., 2nd sess., April, May 1968.

United States Senate, Committee on Foreign Relations. *Nuclear Test Ban Treaty*, 88th Cong., 1st sess., August 1963.

United States Senate, Committee on Foreign Relations, Subcommittee on Arms Control, International Law and Organization. *ABM, MIRV, SALT and the Nuclear Arms Race*, 91st Cong., 2nd sess., March-June 1970.

United States Senate, Committee on Foreign Relations, Subcommittee on Arms Control, International Law and Organization. *Arms Control Implications of Current Defense Budget*, 92nd Cong., 1st sess., June-July 1971.

United States Senate, Committee on Foreign Relations, Subcommittee on Disarmament. *United States Armament and Disarmament Problems*, 90th Cong., 1st sess., February and March 1967.

United States Senate, Committee on Foreign Relations, Subcommittee on International Organization and Disarmament Affairs. *Strategic and Foreign Policy Implications of ABM Systems*, 91st Cong., 1st sess., May 1969.

United States Senate, Subcommittee of the Committee on Appropriations. *Department of Defense Appropriations for Fiscal Year 1966*, 89th Cong., 1st sess., February, March and July 1965.

United States Senate, Subcomittee of the Committee on Appropriations. *Department of Defense Appropriations for Fiscal Year 1968*, 90th Cong., 1st sess., January-July 1967.

United States Senate, Subcommittee of the Committee on Appropriations. *Department of Defense Appropriations for Fiscal Year 1969*, 90th Cong., 2nd sess., January-July 1968.

United States Senate, Subcommittee of the Committee on Appropriations. *Department of Defense Appropriations for Fiscal Year 1970*, 91st Cong., 1st sess., June-December 1969.

United States Senate, Subcommittee of the Committee on Appropriations. *Department of Defense Appropriations for Fiscal Year 1971*, 91st Cong., 2nd sess., February-November 1970.

United States Senate, Subcommittee of the Committee on Appropriations. *Department of Defense Appropriations for Fiscal Year 1973*, 92nd Cong., 2nd sess., February-June 1972.

INDUSTRIAL PUBLICATIONS

Aerospace Corporation. *1969 Annual Report*.
Aerospace Corporation. *Progress Report 1965 Aerospace Corporation*.
Aerospace Corporation. *Progress Report 1964 Aerospace Corporation*.
Autonetics Division, North American Rockwell. *Facts About Minuteman*.
Lockheed Missiles and Space Company News Bureau. *Poseidon and Polaris Fact Sheet*.
Philco-Ford Corporation. Press Release from Southern California Public Relations Office, January 19, 1964.

UNPUBLISHED DOCUMENTS

Aerospace Corporation. *MIRV Chronology*, unpublished paper dated March 14, 1972.
Allison, Graham T. "Questions About the Arms Race: Who's Racing Whom? A Bureaucratic Perspective." Presented at the Conference on Arms

Competition and Strategic Doctrine, California Arms Control and Foreign Policy Seminar, June 1974.

Ball, Desmond J. *The Strategic Missile Program of the Kennedy Administration.* Ph.D. dissertation, Australian National University, 1972.

Clark, Duncan C. "The Role and Influence of the U.S. Arms Control and Influence of the U.S. Arms Control and Disarmament Agency in National Security Policy Formulation." Unpublished paper prepared for Conference on Executive-Legislative Interactions in U.S. Foreign Policy, sponsored by the School of International Service, The American University, May 4-6, 1972.

Clarke, Duncan L. "Congress, Interest Groups and the U.S. Arms Control and Disarmament Agency." Unpublished paper prepared for the International Studies Association Convention, New York, March 14, 1973.

Durham, Richard L. "Security Classification Policy and National Security: The Case of MIRV." Unpublished Individual Research Paper of the Elective Studies Program, the National War College, 1970.

Flam, Paul. *The Role of Aerospace and Mitre Corporations in Air Force R&D.* Unpublished Master of Science thesis, Sloan School of Management, Massachusetts Institute of Technology, 1965.

Kugler, Richard L. *The Politics of Restraint: Robert McNamara and the Strategic Nuclear Forces, 1963-68.* Ph.D. dissertation, Political Science Department, Massachusetts Institute of Technology, 1975.

Kugler, Richard L. "U.S. Government Process for National Intelligence Estimates: Implications for Rationality in Defense and Foreign Policy Making." Unpublished paper dated December 1972, Massachusetts Institute of Technology.

McGovern, George. *An Alternative Defense and Economic Posture.*

Medalia, Jonathan. *The U.S. Senate and Strategic Arms Limitation Policy-making, 1963-1972.* Ph.D. dissertation, Political Science Department, Stanford University, 1975.

Nitze, Paul. Testimony before a Subcommittee of the House Armed Services Committee, July 2, 1974, mimeographed copy.

Press release from the Office of Senator Edward Brooke, March 25, 1970.

Press release from the Office of Senator Edward Brooke, November 11, 1970.

Ruina, J.P. "A Comment on Future Weapons Systems (U), (Letter to Charles Herzfeld, ARPA, and George Rathjens, ACDA)," September 3, 1964, Jason Division, Institute for Defense Analysis, sanitized and declassified version.

Index

ABM, 4; arms control in Congress, 121; Intercept X, 162; Soviet, 76; Soviet arsenal, 104, 172; Tallinn, 174
ABRES, 10, 163; FY 1971 reduction, 137; Project 75, 33; Reentry Committee, 41
accuracy: American superiority, 96; and arms control, 138; criteria, 38; and Poseidon cancellation, 150; as a priority, 2; and reduction in yield, 43; Soviets, 113; SP position, 56; technological goal, 72; as a trade-off, 51
ACDA, 107–109; initiative, 113; MIRV opposition, 130, 131; position, 123; power, 150
advocacy: and bureaucracy, 14; contractors, 20; MIRV and Soviet missile build-up, 103; in Wilson, 27
Aerojet General Corp., 167
Aeronautic, 30; bus contract, 43
Aerospace Corp., 20, 168; and JASON, 110; MIRV feasibility, 47; MIRV development, 29; representation, 22; role of, 147
Air Force, 14; argument/need for MIRV/ Mark 12, 61; component improvement, 35; counterforce issue, 55; manipulation by McNamara, 142; Mark 18, 63; MIRV consensus, 146; MIRV innovation, 16; retaliation, 58; on strategic warfare, 46
Allison, R.B., 123, 135
ANCO: bus market, 43
appropriations: authorization, 35; to circumvent will of Congress, 138; cuts and timing, 137; role of Congress, 150; Russell cut, 122
arms control: concept of limitation, 123; in Davis, 109; foresight, 138; on-site inspection, 111; and Senate Foreign Relations Committee, 120; special interest groups, 150; strategic and uncertainty, 155; testing delay, 126
arms race: and Ruina, 111; nature of, 103, 104; and weapons acquisition, 141

assured destruction: McNamara FY 1968 Posture Statement, 78; Poseidon MIRV, 105
Atlas, 19; --/Titan I, 4
Autonetics, 6, 168; guidance components, 35; Latter and bus development, 32; Minuteman bus, 30, 30; and MIRV bus, 8; MIRV feasibility, 47; MIRV invention, 28
autonomy: and political motivation, 79
AVCO, 9

Baldwin, Hanson W., 75
Bell Aerospace, 6, 167
Biryozov, Marshal Sergei, 172, 173
Bradley, William, 159; Committee, 98
Brooke, Edward, 114; position on MIRV and SALT, 129
Brown, Harold, 18, 22, 75, 173; 1964 recommendation, 99; DDR&E, 45; decisionmaking role, 80; deployment, 48; Latter report, 40; Mark 12, 62; MIRV innovation, 32; on Poseidon, 70
BSD: history of, 4; involvement in development, 57; Minuteman program, 19; procedures, 21
Bundy, McGeorge, 16
bureaucracy: program advocacy, 57; role of MIRV for McNamara, 73; strategic argumentation, 52

Charles Stark Draper Laboratory, 60, 168
Chuikov, Vasily I., 176
CIA: on Tallinn, 174
Clifford, Clark, 78, 124; arsenal rationale, 90; on Galosh, 176
commitment: interpretation of Soviet build-up, 103; history of, 43
communication: interservice, 27
competition: arms race, 111; concept of self competition, 88; and contracts, 152; interservice, 14, 56, 85; and Soviets, 77; and SP management, 24

Congress' advocacy, 120; approval, 107; appropriations strategy, 120; cooption by military, 141; and MIRV, 15; necessary persistence, 138; opposition to testing, 126; SALT program presentation, 79; and weapons acquisition decisions, 149

consensus: building support for MIRV in Air Force, 60; life cycle, 146; Navy, 37; Navy/Air Force, 46; support, 56

controversy: cancellation of Poseidon stellar inertial guidance, 136; development, 116; lack of effect, 138, 139; MIRV debate, 94; Safeguard vote, 122; structure, 108

Cooper, John Sherman, 122, 126

cost-effectiveness: and accuracy, 69; argument for development, 52; Mark 17, 71; and MIRV, 2; and weapon life cycle, 148

counterforce: Foster position, 94; and interest in Poseidon, 101; and interservice competition, 55; Mark 3 system and Poseidon, 57; Mark 12 MIRV, 80; strategy, 38; as strategic rationale, 53

Crecine, J.P., 74

damage limitations, 55; concept of, 68, 69; and concept of assured destruction, 66; strategy, 89

Davis, W. Austin, 21, 23, 32, 109

DDR&E: arms control and negotiation, 123, 124; authority, 21; Brown and Foster role, 80; cost-effectiveness, 69; industry personnel, 26; influence, 154; and innovation, 14; and MIRV accuracy predictions, 113; and MIRV innovation, 47; and Poseidon development program, 8; power and restraint, 151; role of, 5, 147; Soviet AB activity, 97; and stellar inertial guidance, 65

Dean, Allen, 28, 30

decisionmaking: complexity, 80; complexity and inevitability, 105; criteria, 65; evolution of DDR&E authority, 48; funding strategy, 75; ideology of excess force, 68; and ineffective controversy, 139; Kennedy and Johnson administration pattern, 15; methodology of, 143; MIRV options, 133; Polaris/Poseidon, 23; power of special interest groups, 150; role of individuals, 52; strategic rationale, 54

Defense Dept.: ACDA, 112; damage limitation, 68; hierarchy, 25; MIRV as hedge, 117; and MIRV innovation, 16; power of Secretary, 145

delivery, 38

deployment, 70; attitude toward, 48; schedule, 146

deterrent: concept of, 58

development: control and scrutiny, 157

diplomacy: arms control, 107; efforts, 79

Draper, Charles S., 21

Enthoven, Alain, 69, 101

escalation: concept of assured destruction, 66; defense strategy, 72

feasibility: demonstrations, 41

Ferguson, James, 40, 41; Mark 12 vs Mark 17, 62

Ferri, Antonio, 21

Fink, Daniel, 130

first strike: concept of, 57–59, 67; and Minuteman MIRV, 105; Soviety deployment, 89

Fisher, Adrian, 108

Flax, Alexander, 18

forecasts, 86; models, 112

Foster, John S., Jr., 21, 71, 168; accuracy and counterforce, 70; and DDR&E, 26; decisionmaking role, 80; innovation, 147; and "margin of strategic safety," 149; and "matching argument," 93; and MIRV ban strategy, 130; on overinvestment, 87; position on counterforce, 94

Foster, William, 112

Fraser, Donald, 135

Freeman, Dyson, 110

Fulbright, Senator, 91

FY *1962:* penetration funding, 162; *1963,* 73; *1965,* 73; *1965:* McNamara on damage limitation strategy, 68; *1966:* assured destruction, 66; McNamara Posture Statement, 74; Poseidon funding, 44; *1967:* AMSA, 75; *1968:* and Minuteman, 9; *1969:* and Minuteman III, 9; and Russell weapon cut, 122; *1970:* Poseidon conversions, 10; and stellar inertial program, 71; *1971:* ABRES, 137; *1974:* Minuteman III, 10; *1975:* and Poseidon conversion, 10; *1976:* Minuteman III, 10; *1979:* Trident I, 11

Galantin, I.J., 34

Galosh, 172–177

Gell-Mann, Murray, 110

General Electric: bus market, 43; Mark 12, 10, 30, 163; reentry state-of-the-art, 35; role, 5

Gerasimov, G., 175

Goldwater, Barry, 75

Gore, Albert, 91, 115, 121

Graham, William, 22

Giechko, Andrei, 175, 177

Griffon, 98

Griggs, David T., 21

Hage, J. and Aiken, M., 36

Halperon, Morton, 26, 124

Hart, Philip, 122, 126

Haussmann, Carl, 22, 45

Hercules Powder Co., 8

Herzfeld, Charles, 110, 162

Hickenlooper, Bourke, 121

Hitch, Charles, 113

Holaday, William M., 159

Hoopes, Townsend, 126

Hornig, Donald, 114, 119

Humphrey, Hubert, 135

Ignatius, Paul, 64

implementation: concession and compromise, 56
innovation: criticism, 75; cycles of, 46; in Kurth, 80; Mark 18, 63; and political support, 144; procedure review, 153; and restraint, 151; and strategic nuclear forces, 13; subsystems and contracts, 24; in Wilson, 27
Instrumentation Lab., 35
intelligence: concept of assured destruction, 66; concept of excess force, 68; exaggerated claims for SS-9, 136; field possibility, 84; inherent uncertainties, 142; MIRV and interpretation of Soviet build-up, 103; misreading of Tallinn, 104; projections, 148; Soviet capabilities, 171; Soviet deployment, 100; Soviet ICBM deployment, 86

Jackson, Henry, 120, 175
JASON, 110
Johnson, L.B.: ABM deployment, 77; damage limitation and expense, 69; freeze proposal, 108, 109; Poseidon, 44; and Poseidon development program, 6; and responsibility allocation, 16

Katz, Amron, 36
Kaysen, Carl, 16
Kearfott Division, 9; stellar inertial guidance concept, 35
Kendall, James T., 58
Kennedy, J.F.: decisionmaking and intelligence information, 90; on Soviet tests, 172
Kenny, Mr. Spurgeon, 119, 126
Kent, Glenn, 28, 39, 60, 99; damage limitation, 68; and Krause on MIRV innovation, 30
Krushchev, Premier, 97, 172
Kissinger, H., 129; and MIRV testing, 133
Kleiman, Robert, 115, 126
Krause, Ernst, 28
Kurochkin, Pavel A., 175
Kurth, James R., 80, 141

Laird, Melvin R., 71; Soviet first strike capability, 90; on SS-9, 136
Lapp, Ralph, 79, 143
Latter, Albert, 21, 28; innovation, 31; 1964 report, 40
Latter, Richard, 21, 28; innovation, 31
Lawrence Livermore Laboratory, 22, 169
Lees, Lester, 22
LeLevier, Robert, 110
LeMay, Curtis, 18, 37
Limited Test Ban Treaty, 48
Lincoln Lab, 22
Livermore Laboratory, 7, 40; Haussmann, 45; Mark 18, 63; MIRV consensus, 47; penetraton and counterforce, 53
Lockheed Missiles and Space Co., 10, 24; MIRV invention, 33; Wilson, 45

McCarthy, Eugene, 118
McConnell, John, 18, 37

McDonald, Admiral, 44; on deployment, 48
McMillan, Brockway, 18
McMillan, William G., 21, 37
McNamara, Robert, 16; arms limitation, 118; assured destruction, 66, 67; cost-effectiveness, 52; decisionmaking patterns, 25; intelligence and lead time, 155; MIRV/Life interview, 77; on Nike-Zeus, 160; Polaris and Navy, 34; on projections, 86; and Soviet "threat," 101; strategic perspectives, 65; on Tallinn, 174; on Tallinn in 1969, 176; view of MIRV, 48; and whiz kids, 44
Malinovsky, Marshal Roniony, 172, 175
management: and decisionmaking center, 48; impact and service difference, 36; on-site inspection, 111; review, 153; SP programs, 23; techniques, 15
Mark 12, 4, 8, 60; MIRV and countervalue attacks, 50; preferences for, 61; specification adaptation, 98; Task Group, 53
Mark 17, 71; cancellation, 62
Medalia, Jonathan, 135
media: Kleiman, 128; Life, 77: MIRV issue, 115, 134; New York Times, 76
Merkle, Ted, 160
Middlekauff, Darwin, 162
military-industrial complex: contractors and advocacy, 20; cooption of Congress, 141
Miller, George, 22, 55
Minuteman, 4; ABRES, 33; arsenal size, 73; controversy, 94; counterforce, 58; General Wheeler, 63; Latter report, 40; second strike counterforce, 68; silos, 31; -- II: status review, 42; --- III: appropriations, 10; tests, 132
MIRV: Air Force position, 42; assist to Johnson and McNamara, 75; capability, 1; controversy, 116; counterforce asset, 59; development cycle, 6, 108; improbability of a ban, 128; interservice politics, 142; invention, 28; political utility, 73; as reaction to Soviet missile build up, 103; Rogers, 93; Ruina, 110; selling of, 54; service input, 36; and strategic preferences, 148; strategic rationale, 53; testing, 125
Moorer, Admiral, 79; on Soviet SS-9, 96
Morse, Richard S., 91, 171

national security, 51
NATO, 67
Navy, 14; anxiety over Poseidon, 44; attitude on Polaris/Poseidon, 46; interservice attitudes, 23; MIRV consensus, 146; MIRV and penetration problem, 64; on Polaris, 34
Newhouse, J., 130, 133
Nelson, R., Peck, M., and Kalachek, E., 146
Nike-Zeus, 4, 160; in Brown, 89; deployment, 92; phased-array techniques, 22, 98
Nitze, Paul H., 22, 44; re American position, 79; on deployment, 48; Mark 16/Poseidon, 71
Nixon, Richard M.: counterforce and Mark

12 MIRV, 63; definition of "sufficiency" for weapons, 72; "leak" strategy, 93; Minuteman III, 10; MIRV moratorium, 131; Safeguard, 129; on Soviet intentions, 89
NonProliferation Treaty, 118

options: and countermeasures, 149; strategic preferences, 67
Osborn, James B., 23
Packard, David, 153
Panofsky, Wolfgang, 97
Payne, Fred, 1964 recommendation, 99
penaids, 3
penetration: Kent study, 44; massive investment, 87; priority, 161; and selling of MIRV, 54; as a tradeoff, 51
Pentagon: decisionmaking cycles, 48; internal politics, 73
Pen-X study, 40; initiation, 99
Polaris: as hedge, 117; redesign, 34; strategic rationale, 54
policy advocacy: ACDA, 112; and agency self-interest, 144; Air Force/Navy, 46; Brooke Senate Resolution, 135; concept of assured destruction, 66; and Soviet threat, 149; and special interest groups, 150; and strategy, 57; and strategic justifications, 51
politics: in decisionmaking, 81; interservice in bureaucracies, 141; MIRV and Sentinel, 127; and MIRV success, 138
Poseidon: in Enthoven, 101; FY 1967 budget, 100; Great Circle Group, 64; Nitze role, 23; and SINS, 8; and USS James Madison, 134
PBCS, 2
private firms: capabilities, 47
production: cycle and innovation, 13
Project 75: 32, 33
Project Blue Dart, 41
Project Forecast, 32

Rand: consultant interpretation, 53; innovation, 31
Rathjens, George, 109; Ruina, 110
reentry: Air Force modifications, 57; and Air Force target list, 75; concept of, 29; as a priority, 2; system selection, 7; vehicle development and institutions, 19
resource allocation, 39
restraint: counterforce ideology, 59
review procedure, 65; MIRV and interpretation of Soviet build-up, 103
Rivers, Mendel, 120
Rockefeller, Nelson, 126
Rocketdyne, 30
Rogers, William, 93
Rostow, Walt, 119
Rowen, Henry, 28
Ruina, Jack, 110; on Nike-Zeus, 160
Rusk, Dean, 124
Russell, Richard, 92, 120
Ryan, General: Minuteman III, 63

Safeguard: and Minuteman, 94
SALT, 78; and ACDA, 112; Galosh, 176, 177; intergovernment bargaining, 124; MIRV discussion, 119; MIRV opposition, 107; planning, 123; and testing schedule, 134
Sandia Corporation, 22
Sapolsky, H.M., 24, 43, 122
Sary Shagan, 98, 171
Schlesinger, Arthur, 73
Schlesinger, James,: targeting options, 72
Schreiver, Bernard A., 32, 60
second strike: Minuteman, 102; retaliation concept, 58; strategic preferences, 67
Selin, Ivan, 71, 125
Semenov,Vladimir Semonovich, 135
Skybolt, 9
Smith, Gerard C., 135
Smith, Levering, 45, 56, 148
Sokolovsky, Vasily D., 175
Soviets: ABM 76; ABM activity and U.S. projections, 97; ABM system, 44; ABM system and MIRV hedge, 50; eventual arenasal, 73; ICBM deployment, 78, 129; intelligence estimates of capability, 85; Latter response to threats, 31; leadership competition, 3; MIRV as response to threat, 59; penetration of, 63; retaliation, 58; SS–9 warhead, 132; and strategic rationale, 53; Tallinn deployment, 100; targetable warhead threat, 92; and US concept of excess force, 68; U.S. interpretation of build-up, 104; weapon deployment, 40, 66; weapon development, 175
SP: management, 36; MIRV advocacy, 34
Stenniss, John, 120
STL, 19, 20, 168; MIRV feasibility, 47; role of, 147
Strategic Air Command: Mark 17, 71; resistance, 42
strategy, 27; on basis of Soviet threat, 92; to circumvent will of Congress, 138; and counterforce, 59; in decisionmaking, 81; Halperin-Selin on tests, 126; and policy advocacy, 65; preferences, 148; rationale, 52
survival: pressures and new technology, 53
Symington, Stuart, 121

Talensky, Nikolai, 172
Tallinn: and DDR&E, 124; first detection, 99; installation, 173; line, 86; misinterpretation, 104; upgrading, 176
Tammen, Ronald, 81, 142; and Soviet weapon impact, 97
technical community: diffusion, 28; innovation atmosphere, 36; as decisionmakers, 13; effectiveness with MIRV, 138; impetus to penetration techniques, 97; MIRV innovation, 49; role, 4
technological determinism: concept of, 104; and ineffective controversy, 138; potency, 141; power, 145

Teller, Edward, 21
technology: commitment, 14; in decision-
  making, 81; at·Instrumentation Laboratory,
  60; leadership, 95; life cycle and engineer-
  ing development, 145; Lockheed and
  maneuvering bus, 98; MIRV bus, 167;
  MIRV overview, 3; on-site inspection, 111;
  and organizational structure, 19; R&D, 87;
  and restraint, 151; SALT research and
  development, 79; in Wilson, 27
testing, 125; first Poseidon, 8; MIRVs, 93;
  Nixon on MIRV moratorium, 131;
  Poseidon and Minuteman III, 10; Sary
  Shagan, 177
Thiokol Chemical Corp, 8, 35
Thompson Ramo Wooldridge, 19
Thor, 19
Thurmond, Strom, 92, 173
Titan I, 19: -- II, 4, ABRES, 33
Tolubko, Colonel General, 172
Trident I, 11
Trudeau, Arthur G., 91
Truson, Konstantine, 135

Vance, Cyrus, 50; ACDA, 112; MIRVs
  security regulation, 101
Vietnam, 16, 114
Vinson, Carl, 120

weapons: acquisition and concept of
  restraint, 151; multiple warheads, 162–
  165; program oversight, 26; size, 38;
  Soviet development, 175
Weisner, Jerome, 16
Wertheim, Robert, 45
Wheeler, Earle G., 59, 62, 115; targeting
  policy, 70
Wilson, James Q., 27, 36; innovation, 46
Wilson, Lloyd, 45
Wohlstetter, Albert, 28

York, Herbert, 26, 49, 143, 173; innovation,
  147

Zuckert, Eugene, 18; on accuracy, 61

About the Author

Ted Greenwood is an Assistant Professor of Political Science at the Massachusetts Institute of Technology and a Research Associate of the Program for Science and International Affairs, Harvard University. He received a B.Sc. in mathematics and physics from the University of Toronto in 1967, an S.M. in physics from M.I.T. in 1970 and a Ph.D. in political science from M.I.T. in 1973.